ACT Practice Tests, Edition 1.0

Resources & Downloads:

IVYGLOBAL.COM/STUDY

ACT Practice Tests, Edition 1.0

This publication was written and edited by the team at Ivy Global.

Editor-in-Chief: Nathan Létourneau

Editors: Sacha Azor, Corwin Henville, Clark Kim, Sarah Pike, Kristin Rose, and Nathan TeBokkel

Contributors: Thea Bélanger-Polak, Stephanie Bucklin, Alexandra Candib, Isabel Carlin, Aleah Gornbein, Ali Haydaroglu, Elizabeth Hilts, Lei Huang, Heeju Kim, Zoë Martin, Amelia McLeod, Mark Mendola, Geoffrey Morrison, Rachel Schloss, Yolanda Song, Meena Sundararaj, Isabel Villeneuve, and Charlie Wolock

About the Publisher

Ivy Global is a pioneering education company that delivers a wide range of educational services.

Email: publishing@ivyglobal.com
Website: www.ivyglobal.com

Introduction

Introduction

Welcome, students, parents, and teachers! This book is intended to help students prepare for the ACT, a test created and administered by ACT, Inc.

Many colleges and universities in the United States require the ACT as part of the application process. It's our goal to help you do your best on the ACT by offering you 4 full-length practice tests with full online answer explanations and detailed scoring.

Visit our website for additional resources, including review of foundational concepts, extra practice, answer explanations, and interactive scoring and personal reports. You'll also find information about upcoming tests, tutoring services, prep classes, and other tips to help you succeed. Happy studying!

 For additional resources, please visit **ivyglobal.com/study**.

What is the ACT?

Introduction

The ACT is a standardized examination designed to measure students' abilities in four areas: English, Math, Reading, and Science. There is also an optional Writing component. Many American colleges and universities require ACT scores for admission and consider these scores an important factor in assessing applications.

Why do colleges care about the ACT? Since grading standards vary from one high school to another, it can be hard for colleges to know whether two applicants with the same grades are performing at the same level. Therefore, having everyone take the same standardized test gives colleges another metric for comparing students' abilities.

Of course, ACT scores aren't the only things that colleges consider when assessing applicants. Your high school grades, course selection, extracurricular activities, recommendation letters, and application essays are all factors that colleges will use to decide whether you are a good fit for their school. However, in today's highly competitive admissions process, a solid ACT score may provide you with the extra edge needed to be successful.

The ACT in Detail

Understanding the format and scoring of the new ACT will help you pick appropriate strategies and know what to expect on test day.

The Format

The ACT is 2 hours and 55 minutes long (plus 40 minutes for the optional essay). It is composed of the following sections:

- English Test (45 minutes, 75 questions)
- Math Test (60 minutes, 60 questions)
- Reading Test (35 minutes, 40 questions)
- Science Test (35 minutes, 40 questions)
- Optional Writing Test/Essay section (40 minutes)

The ACT also includes two breaks, one approximately 10 minutes long between the Math and Reading Tests, and one approximately 5 minutes long between the Science Test and the optional Writing Test.

The Scoring System

The ACT uses scaled test scores. First, the ACT calculates how many questions you correctly answered in each section; this is your **raw score**. **Scaled scores** are calculated by taking your raw test scores and adjusting them to a score from 1 to 36 according to a chart that the ACT develops. These charts are exam-specific, and so may vary slightly from one exam to the next. There are four scaled scores, one for each test: the English Test, the Math Test, the Reading Test, and the Science Test. Together, the average of these four scaled scores generates the ACT **composite score**, which is also scored from 1 to 36.

If you take the Writing Test, you will receive an additional scored average, from 2 to 12. This optional component is scored separately and does not affect your scores in other areas, or your overall ACT composite score.

The ACT also provides you with **subscores**, which are subject- or area-specific results. These do not affect your scaled test scores, but rather provide institutions with more detailed information about your exam results. Subscores for three of the four main tests (the Science Test does not have subscores) are each calculated from 1 to 18. The English test is subdivided into Usage/Mechanics and Rhetorical Skills. The Math Test is subdivided into Pre-Algebra/Elementary Algebra, Algebra/Coordinate Geometry, and

Plane Geometry/Trigonometry. The Reading Test is subdivided into Social Studies/Sciences and Arts/Literature.

The optional Writing Test is scored on a scale from 1 to 36. The Writing Test also reports four subscores: Ideas and Analysis, Development and Support, Organization, and Language Use and Conventions. Each area score is reported on a scale from 2 to 12. The average of these four scores, from 2 to 12, is reported to you when you get your results.

The ACT includes two additional scores. The first is the Science, Technology, Engineering, and Mathematics or STEM score. The second is for English Language Arts or ELA, and is only included if the optional Writing Test is taken. These scores are each calculated from 1 to 36. The following table summarizes the scoring for the ACT:

ACT Scoring	
Raw Test Scores	• English Test (75) • Math Test (60) • Reading Test (40) • Science Test (40) • Optional Writing Test (36), changing to (48) after September 2016
Scaled Scores (1 to 36)	• English Test • Math Test • Reading Test • Science Test • Optional Writing Test (not included in the ACT exam final subscore)
Optional Writing Test (2 to 12)	• The rounded average of the four Writing Test subscores
Composite ACT Score (1 to 36)	• The average of the English, Math, Reading, and Science scaled scores

Practice Test 1

The ACT

This practice test contains tests in English, Math, Reading, and Science. These tests measure skills and abilities related to high school course work and college preparedness. **You can use a calculator on the math test only.**

The questions in each test are numbered, and the suggested answers for each question are lettered. On the answer sheet, the rows are numbered to match the questions, and the circles in each row are lettered to correspond to the suggested answers.

For each question, choose the best answer and fill in the corresponding circle on your answer document. Use a soft lead pencil and make your marks heavy and black. **Do not use a ballpoint pen.**

Fill in only one answer to each question. If you change your mind about an answer, completely erase your first mark before filling in your new answer. For each question, make certain that you mark in the row of ovals with the same number as the question.

Only responses marked on your answer sheet will be scored. Your score on each test will be based only on the number of questions you answer correctly during the time allowed for that test. You will NOT be penalized for guessing. **Even if you are unsure about an answer, you should make a guess.**

You may work on each test ONLY when your proctor tells you to do so. If you complete a test before the end of your allotted time, use the extra minutes to check your work on that section only. Do NOT use the time to work on another section. Doing this will disqualify your scores.

Put down your pencil immediately when time is called at the end of each test. You are not allowed to continue answering questions after the allotted time has run out. This includes marking answers on your answer sheet that you previously noted in your test booklet.

You are not allowed to fold or tear the pages of your test booklet.

Do Not Open This Booklet Until You Are Told to Do So.

NAME: _____

DATE: _____

TEST 1

1 Ⓐ Ⓑ Ⓒ Ⓓ	14 Ⓕ Ⓖ Ⓗ Ⓙ	27 Ⓐ Ⓑ Ⓒ Ⓓ	40 Ⓕ Ⓖ Ⓗ Ⓙ	53 Ⓐ Ⓑ Ⓒ Ⓓ	66 Ⓕ Ⓖ Ⓗ Ⓙ
2 Ⓕ Ⓖ Ⓗ Ⓙ	15 Ⓐ Ⓑ Ⓒ Ⓓ	28 Ⓕ Ⓖ Ⓗ Ⓙ	41 Ⓐ Ⓑ Ⓒ Ⓓ	54 Ⓕ Ⓖ Ⓗ Ⓙ	67 Ⓐ Ⓑ Ⓒ Ⓓ
3 Ⓐ Ⓑ Ⓒ Ⓓ	16 Ⓕ Ⓖ Ⓗ Ⓙ	29 Ⓐ Ⓑ Ⓒ Ⓓ	42 Ⓕ Ⓖ Ⓗ Ⓙ	55 Ⓐ Ⓑ Ⓒ Ⓓ	68 Ⓕ Ⓖ Ⓗ Ⓙ
4 Ⓕ Ⓖ Ⓗ Ⓙ	17 Ⓐ Ⓑ Ⓒ Ⓓ	30 Ⓕ Ⓖ Ⓗ Ⓙ	43 Ⓐ Ⓑ Ⓒ Ⓓ	56 Ⓕ Ⓖ Ⓗ Ⓙ	69 Ⓐ Ⓑ Ⓒ Ⓓ
5 Ⓐ Ⓑ Ⓒ Ⓓ	18 Ⓕ Ⓖ Ⓗ Ⓙ	31 Ⓐ Ⓑ Ⓒ Ⓓ	44 Ⓕ Ⓖ Ⓗ Ⓙ	57 Ⓐ Ⓑ Ⓒ Ⓓ	70 Ⓕ Ⓖ Ⓗ Ⓙ
6 Ⓕ Ⓖ Ⓗ Ⓙ	19 Ⓐ Ⓑ Ⓒ Ⓓ	32 Ⓕ Ⓖ Ⓗ Ⓙ	45 Ⓐ Ⓑ Ⓒ Ⓓ	58 Ⓕ Ⓖ Ⓗ Ⓙ	71 Ⓐ Ⓑ Ⓒ Ⓓ
7 Ⓐ Ⓑ Ⓒ Ⓓ	20 Ⓕ Ⓖ Ⓗ Ⓙ	33 Ⓐ Ⓑ Ⓒ Ⓓ	46 Ⓕ Ⓖ Ⓗ Ⓙ	59 Ⓐ Ⓑ Ⓒ Ⓓ	72 Ⓕ Ⓖ Ⓗ Ⓙ
8 Ⓕ Ⓖ Ⓗ Ⓙ	21 Ⓐ Ⓑ Ⓒ Ⓓ	34 Ⓕ Ⓖ Ⓗ Ⓙ	47 Ⓐ Ⓑ Ⓒ Ⓓ	60 Ⓕ Ⓖ Ⓗ Ⓙ	73 Ⓐ Ⓑ Ⓒ Ⓓ
9 Ⓐ Ⓑ Ⓒ Ⓓ	22 Ⓕ Ⓖ Ⓗ Ⓙ	35 Ⓐ Ⓑ Ⓒ Ⓓ	48 Ⓕ Ⓖ Ⓗ Ⓙ	61 Ⓐ Ⓑ Ⓒ Ⓓ	74 Ⓕ Ⓖ Ⓗ Ⓙ
10 Ⓕ Ⓖ Ⓗ Ⓙ	23 Ⓐ Ⓑ Ⓒ Ⓓ	36 Ⓕ Ⓖ Ⓗ Ⓙ	49 Ⓐ Ⓑ Ⓒ Ⓓ	62 Ⓕ Ⓖ Ⓗ Ⓙ	75 Ⓐ Ⓑ Ⓒ Ⓓ
11 Ⓐ Ⓑ Ⓒ Ⓓ	24 Ⓕ Ⓖ Ⓗ Ⓙ	37 Ⓐ Ⓑ Ⓒ Ⓓ	50 Ⓕ Ⓖ Ⓗ Ⓙ	63 Ⓐ Ⓑ Ⓒ Ⓓ	
12 Ⓕ Ⓖ Ⓗ Ⓙ	25 Ⓐ Ⓑ Ⓒ Ⓓ	38 Ⓕ Ⓖ Ⓗ Ⓙ	51 Ⓐ Ⓑ Ⓒ Ⓓ	64 Ⓕ Ⓖ Ⓗ Ⓙ	
13 Ⓐ Ⓑ Ⓒ Ⓓ	26 Ⓕ Ⓖ Ⓗ Ⓙ	39 Ⓐ Ⓑ Ⓒ Ⓓ	52 Ⓕ Ⓖ Ⓗ Ⓙ	65 Ⓐ Ⓑ Ⓒ Ⓓ	

TEST 2

1 Ⓐ Ⓑ Ⓒ Ⓓ Ⓔ	11 Ⓐ Ⓑ Ⓒ Ⓓ Ⓔ	21 Ⓐ Ⓑ Ⓒ Ⓓ Ⓔ	31 Ⓐ Ⓑ Ⓒ Ⓓ Ⓔ	41 Ⓐ Ⓑ Ⓒ Ⓓ Ⓔ	51 Ⓐ Ⓑ Ⓒ Ⓓ Ⓔ
2 Ⓕ Ⓖ Ⓗ Ⓙ Ⓚ	12 Ⓕ Ⓖ Ⓗ Ⓙ Ⓚ	22 Ⓕ Ⓖ Ⓗ Ⓙ Ⓚ	32 Ⓕ Ⓖ Ⓗ Ⓙ Ⓚ	42 Ⓕ Ⓖ Ⓗ Ⓙ Ⓚ	52 Ⓕ Ⓖ Ⓗ Ⓙ Ⓚ
3 Ⓐ Ⓑ Ⓒ Ⓓ Ⓔ	13 Ⓐ Ⓑ Ⓒ Ⓓ Ⓔ	23 Ⓐ Ⓑ Ⓒ Ⓓ Ⓔ	33 Ⓐ Ⓑ Ⓒ Ⓓ Ⓔ	43 Ⓐ Ⓑ Ⓒ Ⓓ Ⓔ	53 Ⓐ Ⓑ Ⓒ Ⓓ Ⓔ
4 Ⓕ Ⓖ Ⓗ Ⓙ Ⓚ	14 Ⓕ Ⓖ Ⓗ Ⓙ Ⓚ	24 Ⓕ Ⓖ Ⓗ Ⓙ Ⓚ	34 Ⓕ Ⓖ Ⓗ Ⓙ Ⓚ	44 Ⓕ Ⓖ Ⓗ Ⓙ Ⓚ	54 Ⓕ Ⓖ Ⓗ Ⓙ Ⓚ
5 Ⓐ Ⓑ Ⓒ Ⓓ Ⓔ	15 Ⓐ Ⓑ Ⓒ Ⓓ Ⓔ	25 Ⓐ Ⓑ Ⓒ Ⓓ Ⓔ	35 Ⓐ Ⓑ Ⓒ Ⓓ Ⓔ	45 Ⓐ Ⓑ Ⓒ Ⓓ Ⓔ	55 Ⓐ Ⓑ Ⓒ Ⓓ Ⓔ
6 Ⓕ Ⓖ Ⓗ Ⓙ Ⓚ	16 Ⓕ Ⓖ Ⓗ Ⓙ Ⓚ	26 Ⓕ Ⓖ Ⓗ Ⓙ Ⓚ	36 Ⓕ Ⓖ Ⓗ Ⓙ Ⓚ	46 Ⓕ Ⓖ Ⓗ Ⓙ Ⓚ	56 Ⓕ Ⓖ Ⓗ Ⓙ Ⓚ
7 Ⓐ Ⓑ Ⓒ Ⓓ Ⓔ	17 Ⓐ Ⓑ Ⓒ Ⓓ Ⓔ	27 Ⓐ Ⓑ Ⓒ Ⓓ Ⓔ	37 Ⓐ Ⓑ Ⓒ Ⓓ Ⓔ	47 Ⓐ Ⓑ Ⓒ Ⓓ Ⓔ	57 Ⓐ Ⓑ Ⓒ Ⓓ Ⓔ
8 Ⓕ Ⓖ Ⓗ Ⓙ Ⓚ	18 Ⓕ Ⓖ Ⓗ Ⓙ Ⓚ	28 Ⓕ Ⓖ Ⓗ Ⓙ Ⓚ	38 Ⓕ Ⓖ Ⓗ Ⓙ Ⓚ	48 Ⓕ Ⓖ Ⓗ Ⓙ Ⓚ	58 Ⓕ Ⓖ Ⓗ Ⓙ Ⓚ
9 Ⓐ Ⓑ Ⓒ Ⓓ Ⓔ	19 Ⓐ Ⓑ Ⓒ Ⓓ Ⓔ	29 Ⓐ Ⓑ Ⓒ Ⓓ Ⓔ	39 Ⓐ Ⓑ Ⓒ Ⓓ Ⓔ	49 Ⓐ Ⓑ Ⓒ Ⓓ Ⓔ	59 Ⓐ Ⓑ Ⓒ Ⓓ Ⓔ
10 Ⓕ Ⓖ Ⓗ Ⓙ Ⓚ	20 Ⓕ Ⓖ Ⓗ Ⓙ Ⓚ	30 Ⓕ Ⓖ Ⓗ Ⓙ Ⓚ	40 Ⓕ Ⓖ Ⓗ Ⓙ Ⓚ	50 Ⓕ Ⓖ Ⓗ Ⓙ Ⓚ	60 Ⓕ Ⓖ Ⓗ Ⓙ Ⓚ

TEST 3

1 Ⓐ Ⓑ Ⓒ Ⓓ	8 Ⓕ Ⓖ Ⓗ Ⓙ	15 Ⓐ Ⓑ Ⓒ Ⓓ	22 Ⓕ Ⓖ Ⓗ Ⓙ	29 Ⓐ Ⓑ Ⓒ Ⓓ	36 Ⓕ Ⓖ Ⓗ Ⓙ
2 Ⓕ Ⓖ Ⓗ Ⓙ	9 Ⓐ Ⓑ Ⓒ Ⓓ	16 Ⓕ Ⓖ Ⓗ Ⓙ	23 Ⓐ Ⓑ Ⓒ Ⓓ	30 Ⓕ Ⓖ Ⓗ Ⓙ	37 Ⓐ Ⓑ Ⓒ Ⓓ
3 Ⓐ Ⓑ Ⓒ Ⓓ	10 Ⓕ Ⓖ Ⓗ Ⓙ	17 Ⓐ Ⓑ Ⓒ Ⓓ	24 Ⓕ Ⓖ Ⓗ Ⓙ	31 Ⓐ Ⓑ Ⓒ Ⓓ	38 Ⓕ Ⓖ Ⓗ Ⓙ
4 Ⓕ Ⓖ Ⓗ Ⓙ	11 Ⓐ Ⓑ Ⓒ Ⓓ	18 Ⓕ Ⓖ Ⓗ Ⓙ	25 Ⓐ Ⓑ Ⓒ Ⓓ	32 Ⓕ Ⓖ Ⓗ Ⓙ	39 Ⓐ Ⓑ Ⓒ Ⓓ
5 Ⓐ Ⓑ Ⓒ Ⓓ	12 Ⓕ Ⓖ Ⓗ Ⓙ	19 Ⓐ Ⓑ Ⓒ Ⓓ	26 Ⓕ Ⓖ Ⓗ Ⓙ	33 Ⓐ Ⓑ Ⓒ Ⓓ	40 Ⓕ Ⓖ Ⓗ Ⓙ
6 Ⓕ Ⓖ Ⓗ Ⓙ	13 Ⓐ Ⓑ Ⓒ Ⓓ	20 Ⓕ Ⓖ Ⓗ Ⓙ	27 Ⓐ Ⓑ Ⓒ Ⓓ	34 Ⓕ Ⓖ Ⓗ Ⓙ	
7 Ⓐ Ⓑ Ⓒ Ⓓ	14 Ⓕ Ⓖ Ⓗ Ⓙ	21 Ⓐ Ⓑ Ⓒ Ⓓ	28 Ⓕ Ⓖ Ⓗ Ⓙ	35 Ⓐ Ⓑ Ⓒ Ⓓ	

TEST 4

1 Ⓐ Ⓑ Ⓒ Ⓓ	8 Ⓕ Ⓖ Ⓗ Ⓙ	15 Ⓐ Ⓑ Ⓒ Ⓓ	22 Ⓕ Ⓖ Ⓗ Ⓙ	29 Ⓐ Ⓑ Ⓒ Ⓓ	36 Ⓕ Ⓖ Ⓗ Ⓙ
2 Ⓕ Ⓖ Ⓗ Ⓙ	9 Ⓐ Ⓑ Ⓒ Ⓓ	16 Ⓕ Ⓖ Ⓗ Ⓙ	23 Ⓐ Ⓑ Ⓒ Ⓓ	30 Ⓕ Ⓖ Ⓗ Ⓙ	37 Ⓐ Ⓑ Ⓒ Ⓓ
3 Ⓐ Ⓑ Ⓒ Ⓓ	10 Ⓕ Ⓖ Ⓗ Ⓙ	17 Ⓐ Ⓑ Ⓒ Ⓓ	24 Ⓕ Ⓖ Ⓗ Ⓙ	31 Ⓐ Ⓑ Ⓒ Ⓓ	38 Ⓕ Ⓖ Ⓗ Ⓙ
4 Ⓕ Ⓖ Ⓗ Ⓙ	11 Ⓐ Ⓑ Ⓒ Ⓓ	18 Ⓕ Ⓖ Ⓗ Ⓙ	25 Ⓐ Ⓑ Ⓒ Ⓓ	32 Ⓕ Ⓖ Ⓗ Ⓙ	39 Ⓐ Ⓑ Ⓒ Ⓓ
5 Ⓐ Ⓑ Ⓒ Ⓓ	12 Ⓕ Ⓖ Ⓗ Ⓙ	19 Ⓐ Ⓑ Ⓒ Ⓓ	26 Ⓕ Ⓖ Ⓗ Ⓙ	33 Ⓐ Ⓑ Ⓒ Ⓓ	40 Ⓕ Ⓖ Ⓗ Ⓙ
6 Ⓕ Ⓖ Ⓗ Ⓙ	13 Ⓐ Ⓑ Ⓒ Ⓓ	20 Ⓕ Ⓖ Ⓗ Ⓙ	27 Ⓐ Ⓑ Ⓒ Ⓓ	34 Ⓕ Ⓖ Ⓗ Ⓙ	
7 Ⓐ Ⓑ Ⓒ Ⓓ	14 Ⓕ Ⓖ Ⓗ Ⓙ	21 Ⓐ Ⓑ Ⓒ Ⓓ	28 Ⓕ Ⓖ Ⓗ Ⓙ	35 Ⓐ Ⓑ Ⓒ Ⓓ	

Use a soft lead No. 2 pencil only. Do NOT use a mechanical pencil, ink, ballpoint, or felt-tip pens.

Begin WRITING TEST here.

If you need more space, please continue on the next page.

WRITING TEST

_____

_____

_____

_____

_____

_____

_____

_____

_____

_____

_____

_____

_____

_____

_____

_____

_____

_____

_____

_____

_____

_____

_____

_____

_____

_____

_____

_____

If you need more space, please continue on the back of this page.

2

WRITING TEST

If you need more space, please continue on the next page.

WRITING TEST

_____

_____

_____

_____

_____

_____

_____

_____

_____

_____

_____

_____

_____

_____

_____

_____

_____

_____

_____

_____

_____

_____

_____

_____

_____

_____

_____

_____

_____

_____

STOP!

4

English Test
45 Minutes—75 Questions

DIRECTIONS: In the five passages that follow, certain words and phrases are underlined and numbered. In the right-hand column, you will find alternatives for the underlined part. In most cases, you are to choose the one that best expresses the idea, makes the statement appropriate for standard written English, or is worded most consistently with the style and tone of the passage as a whole. If you think the original version is best, choose "NO CHANGE." In some cases, you will find in the right-hand column a question about the underlined part. You are to choose the best answer to the question.

You will also find questions about a section of the passage, or about the passage as a whole. These questions do not refer to an underlined portion of the passage, but rather are identified by a number or numbers in a box.

For each question, choose the alternative you consider best and fill in the corresponding circle on your answer document. Read each passage through once before you begin to answer the questions that accompany it. For many of the questions, you must read several sentences beyond the question to determine the answer. Be sure that you have read far enough ahead each time you choose an alternative.

Passage I

Idia: The First Queen Mother of Benin

[1]

When the king of Benin, oba Ozolua, died in the late fifteenth century, the kingdom was thrown into a state of chaos as his two sons battled for the monarchy. One son, Esigie, controlled the kingdom's political and cultural center, Benin City while his brother, Ahruaran ruled in the equally important city of Udo.

[2]

In addition to dividing the country, the war led to the conquest of Benin's northern territories by the neighboring Igala peoples. Faced with the destruction of the country, Esigie made an unprecedented move, he turned to his mother, Idia, to help him gain control by using her mystical powers and providing political counsel.

1. **A.** NO CHANGE
    B. century, as the kingdom
    C. century, when the kingdom
    D. century. The kingdom

2. **F.** NO CHANGE
    G. Benin City, while his brother, Ahruaran
    H. Benin City while his brother, Ahruaran,
    J. Benin City, while his brother, Ahruaran,

3. **A.** NO CHANGE
    B. unprecedented move he turned
    C. unprecedented move; he turned
    D. unprecedented move and he turned

GO ON TO THE NEXT PAGE.

[3]

Esigie faced his brother and the Igala, as well as the
<u>4</u>
daunting task of reuniting the kingdom and restoring Benin
<u>4</u>
as a regional power. Much of his success was attributed to
<u>4</u>
the counsel and mystical support of his mother, leading to a

significant change in the status of Idia, <u>who was the first</u>
<u>5</u>
<u>king's mother to become the first Queen Mother of Benin.</u>
<u>5</u>

[4]

Prior to Idia's elevation to Queen Mother, mothers of

the oba's first-born sons lived according to very strict rules.

They were not allowed to have additional children,

instead devoting <u>herself</u> to the wellbeing of the future rulers
<u>6</u>
and, by extension, the wellbeing of the kingdom. Once their

sons <u>took rulership upon the throne,</u> it was customary to
<u>7</u>
behead the mothers to prevent them from using their

mystical powers <u>to magically harm the country.</u> Esigie,
<u>8</u>

however, asked that his people reward his mother by not

<u>only allowing her to live but also honoring</u> her with the title
<u>9</u>

4. Which choice most effectively guides the reader from the preceding paragraph into this new paragraph?

   F. NO CHANGE
   G. With Idia's guidance and help, Esigie was able to defeat his brother and the Igala, reuniting Benin and securing its role as a regional power.
   H. Esigie's reliance on his mother's council stood out in a culture in which women typically played more passive roles.
   J. Idia was reluctant, but eventually she decided to help her son.

5. A. NO CHANGE
   B. the first Queen Mother of Benin, Queen Mother Idia.
   C. who became the first Queen Mother of Benin.
   D. who became the first Queen Mother of Benin as a result of the counsel and support she provided.

6. F. NO CHANGE
   G. hers
   H. themselves
   J. oneself

7. A. NO CHANGE
   B. undertook
   C. assumed
   D. sat down at

8. F. NO CHANGE
   G. to cause harm to the country by supernatural means.
   H. to harm the country.
   J. OMIT the underlined portion.

9. A. NO CHANGE
   B. allowed her to live but also by honored
   C. allowing her to live but also honored
   D. allowed her to live but also by honoring

GO ON TO THE NEXT PAGE.

of iyoba, or Queen Mother. <u>Bestowing upon her certain</u>
₁₀
<u>political powers.</u> The people agreed, but only on the
₁₀

condition that Esegie and Idia would never again <u>has direct</u>
₁₁
contact.

[5]

Soon after, Idia was installed in her own palace

outside the capital city. <u>It's hard to believe, but she never</u>
₁₂
<u>saw her son again!</u> However, from that time forward, iyobas
₁₂

remained powerful members of society and <u>their sons', the</u>
₁₃
<u>obas,</u> wore carved ivory pendant masks representing the
₁₃
iyoba during ceremonies designed to rid the kingdom of

malevolent spiritual forces.

10. **F.** NO CHANGE
   G. Queen Mother and bestowing upon her certain political powers.
   H. Queen Mother, and bestowing upon her certain political powers.
   J. Queen Mother bestowing upon her certain political powers.

11. **A.** NO CHANGE
   B. have
   C. had have
   D. has had

12. Which choice best maintains the tone of the passage?
   F. NO CHANGE
   G. After all she did for him, Idia never saw her son again!
   H. While Idia gained power and prestige, she never saw her son again.
   J. Although it may seem harsh that Idia never saw her son again, at least she wasn't beheaded.

13. **A.** NO CHANGE
   B. their sons, the obas',
   C. their sons, the obas,
   D. their sons', the obas',

Questions 14 and 15 refer to the preceding passage as a whole.

---

14. Upon reviewing this essay and realizing that some information had been left out, the writer composes the following sentence, incorporating that information:

   Benin, in what is now Nigeria, was a regional power, and the civil war had devastating effects.

   The most logical and effective place to add this sentence would be after the last sentence in Paragraph:

   F. 1.
   G. 2.
   H. 4.
   J. 5.

15. Suppose the writer had decided to write an essay discussing the role of women in Africa during the 15th century. Would this essay successfully fulfill the writer's goal?

   A. Yes, because the essay explains the role of women during times of conflict in the kingdom of Benin.
   B. Yes, because the essay provides detailed information about the lives of certain women that allows the reader to determine the roles of most women in that time and place.
   C. No, because the essay explains only what happened to the women whose sons became kings in one specific country.
   D. No, because the essay focuses on modern roles for women instead of their traditional roles.

GO ON TO THE NEXT PAGE.

Passage II

Can You Sing the World's Oldest Song?

[1]

Music seems eternal, it is: an art form that transcends
———
16
time and distance despite shifts in styles and fashion. After

all, people today still flock to hear the works of Mozart,

Beethoven, Ellington, and a growing list of aging rock stars.

Tunes by notable composers like Gershwin and folk
———
17
musicians whose names have been lost to history are

woven around the fabric of cultures worldwide.
———
18

[2]

[1] Where did it all begin? [2] Unfortunately, no

traces of those songs remain. [3] No one knows for sure,

though archaeological digs have turned up primitive bone

and ivory flutes that date back some 43,000 years. [4]

Certainly the musicians who played these instruments, and

others lost to the ages, played songs. 19

[3]

In conclusion, the oldest known sample of musical
———
20
notations dates from just 4,000 years ago—a mere

fragment on a Sumerian clay tablet. Most historians agree

that the oldest known written melody in existence is "Hurrian

16. **F.** NO CHANGE
    G. eternal; it is: an
    H. eternal; it is an
    J. eternal—it is—an

17. Which of the following is the LEAST acceptable
    alternative to the underlined portion?
    A. Ditties
    B. Music
    C. Tracks
    D. Songs

18. **F.** NO CHANGE
    G. weaving in and out of
    H. woven into
    J. weaving through

19. For the sake of the logic and coherence of Paragraph 2,
    Sentence 2 should be placed:
    A. where it is now.
    B. before Sentence 1.
    C. after Sentence 3.
    D. after Sentence 4.

20. **F.** NO CHANGE
    G. In summary
    H. In fact
    J. Nevertheless

GO ON TO THE NEXT PAGE.

Hymn No. 6," which is intended to be played on a nine-
      _____
                         21

stringed lyre.
_____
      21

[22] The clay tablets were found in Syria in the 1950s and

include instructions for how to play the song on a type of

lyre.

[4]

However, because Hurrian Hymn No. 6 is just a

fragment, some experts to claim that it cannot be considered
               _____
                        23
the oldest known musical composition. That distinction,

we insisted, belongs to the so-called Seikilos Epitaph.
_____
      24

[5]

The Seikilos Epitaph is engraved on a marble

column, or stele, marking the grave of a Turkish woman.

The stele includes complete lyrics in Greek and musical

notations, which was why those who favor it claim it is a
             _____
              25

21. Given that all of the choices are true, which one is most relevant to the focus of this paragraph?

   A. NO CHANGE
   B. which modern musicians have attempted to reconstruct and play.
   C. which can be transcribed in several ways depending on interpretations of its symbols.
   D. which was composed in cuneiform around the 14th century B.C.

22. At this point, the writer has decided to insert additional information physically describing the clay tablet on which the Hurrian Hymn was inscribed. Which sentence best accomplishes that goal?

   F. Hurrian Hymn No. 6 was written in cuneiform writing in the Hurrian language, which is not completely understood today.
   G. The hymn was inscribed on a tablet that, while cracked and partially illegible, was the most complete of a group of 36 such tablets.
   H. Clay tablets were used before the invention of paper to record business transactions, literature, and—apparently—music.
   J. Cuneiform symbols were pressed into the clay tablet.

23. A. NO CHANGE
    B. experts claiming
    C. experts claim
    D. experts having claimed

24. F. NO CHANGE
    G. we insist,
    H. I insist,
    J. they insist,

25. A. NO CHANGE
    B. has been
    C. is
    D. would be

GO ON TO THE NEXT PAGE.

complete composition. The lyrics and notes facilitate the
26

ability of modern scholars to translate the words, and
26

modern musicians play the song in full, unlike the Hurrian
27

Hymn. Perhaps because the lyrics are so poignant. The
28

music is so plaintive, a number of recordings 29 have
28

been made of the Seikilos Epitaph. It is after all hard to
30

resist a song that proclaims, "While you live, shine / Have

no grief at all / Life exists only for a short while / And time

demands its toll."

26. F. NO CHANGE
    G. open the door to
    H. create a possibility for
    J. enable

27. A. NO CHANGE
    B. to play
    C. playing
    D. played

28. F. NO CHANGE
    G. poignant: the music
    H. poignant and the music
    J. poignant. Because the music

29. At this point, the writer is considering adding the
    following parenthetical phrase:

    —you can listen to some recordings online—

    Would this phrase be a relevant addition to the
    paragraph?

    A. Yes, because hearing the actual song would
       provide more information to the reader than simply
       reading the passage does.
    B. Yes, because in order to fully understand a song it
       is necessary to hear it.
    C. No, because the passage focuses mainly on the
       Hurrian Hymn No. 6, and additional information
       about the Seiklos Epitaph is distracting.
    D. No, because information about where the reader
       can hear the epitaph is an unnecessary addition to
       the point that recordings have been made.

30. F. NO CHANGE
    G. It is after all, hard
    H. It is, after all hard
    J. It is, after all, hard

GO ON TO THE NEXT PAGE.

Passage III

Mr. Jones: An American Writer

[1]

In 1952, James Jones won the National Book Award for his first published novel. Based on his experience during World War II, *From Here to Eternity* is set in Hawaii

just before the Japanese attacked Pearl Harbor, an event it witnessed. It was the first book in what would eventually

become known as Jones's war trilogy. 34

[2]

[1] Born in Robinson, Illinois, in 1921, James Jones enlisted in the U.S. Army in 1939 and served in the 25th Infantry Division, 27th Infantry Regiment. [2] Having taken some classes at the University of Hawaii while awaiting his

combat assignment; Jones resumed his studies at New York University after leaving the military; he eventually returned to Robinson where he worked on his writing. [3] His first published story appeared in *Atlantic Monthly* in 1948. [4] He saw combat on Guadalcanal, where he was injured, and he was discharged in 1944. 36

31. A. NO CHANGE
　B. novel, based on
　C. novel based on
　D. OMIT the underlined portion.

32. F. NO CHANGE
　G. him
　H. they
　J. Jones

33. A. NO CHANGE
　B. became
　C. becomes
　D. will become

34. The writer is considering deleting the preceding sentence. If the writer were to make this deletion, the essay would primarily lose information that:
　F. places a novel in the context of other works.
　G. provides details about an author's military background.
　H. provides supporting evidence for a key argument.
　J. repeats a key idea for emphasis.

35. A. NO CHANGE
　B. assignment: Jones
　C. assignment, Jones
　D. assignment—Jones

36. For the sake of the logic and coherence of Paragraph 2, Sentence 4 should be placed:
　F. where it is now.
　G. before Sentence 1.
　H. before Sentence 2.
　J. before Sentence 3.

GO ON TO THE NEXT PAGE.

[3]

The book portrays the enlisted men and officers of
‾‾‾‾‾‾‾‾‾‾‾‾‾‾‾‾‾‾‾‾‾‾‾‾‾‾‾‾‾‾‾‾‾‾‾‾
                    37
the Army, named one of the 100 Best Novels of the 20th
‾‾‾‾‾‾‾‾‾‾‾‾‾‾‾‾‾‾‾‾‾‾‾‾‾‾‾‾‾‾‾‾‾‾‾‾
                    37
century by the Modern Library Board, not as heroes, but as
‾‾‾‾‾‾‾‾‾‾‾‾‾‾‾‾‾‾‾‾‾‾‾‾‾‾‾‾‾‾‾‾‾‾‾‾
                    37
flawed human beings struggling to find their way in a world
‾‾‾‾‾‾‾‾‾‾‾‾‾‾‾‾‾‾‾‾‾‾‾‾‾‾‾‾‾‾‾‾‾‾‾‾
                    37
that is about to be torn asunder by war. *From Here to*
‾‾‾‾‾‾‾‾‾‾‾‾‾‾‾‾‾‾‾‾‾‾‾‾‾‾‾‾‾
                    37

Eternity was such a victory on the reading public that it was
                    ‾‾‾‾‾‾‾‾‾‾‾
                         38
made into a movie starring Burt Lancaster, Deborah Kerr,

Montgomery Clift, and Frank Sinatra in 1953.

[4]

After the success of *From Here to Eternity*, Jones

wrote and published *Some Came Running*, which was not
                    ‾‾‾‾‾‾‾‾‾‾‾‾‾‾‾‾‾‾‾‾‾‾‾‾‾‾
                                39

as critically acclaimed as *From Here to Eternity* but also
‾‾‾‾‾‾‾‾‾‾‾‾‾‾‾‾‾‾
       40
became a bestseller. Following his marriage to

Gloria Mosolino, Jones relocated to France, where he
                    ‾‾‾‾‾‾‾‾‾
                       41

37. **A.** NO CHANGE
    B. The book portrays the enlisted men and officers of the Army not as heroes, but as flawed human beings struggling to find their way in a world that is about to be torn asunder by war, named one of the 100 Best Novels of the 20th century by the Modern Library Board.
    C. The book portrays the enlisted men and officers of the Army not as heroes, but as flawed human beings, named one of the 100 Best Novels of the 20th century by the Modern Library Board, struggling to find their way in a world that is about to be torn asunder by war.
    D. Named one of the 100 Best Novels of the 20th century by the Modern Library Board, the book portrays the enlisted men and officers of the Army not as heroes, but as flawed human beings struggling to find their way in a world that is about to be torn asunder by war.

38. **F.** NO CHANGE
    G. an impact on
    H. a success with
    J. a triumph over

39. **A.** NO CHANGE
    B. *Some Came Running* was not
    C. *Some Came Running*, it was not
    D. *Some Came Running*, was not

40. **F.** NO CHANGE
    G. critical acclaim
    H. critically acclaim
    J. critical acclaimed

41. Which choice is the LEAST acceptable alternative to the underlined portion?
    A. proceeded to
    B. left for
    C. immigrated to
    D. resettled in

GO ON TO THE NEXT PAGE.

write *The Thin Red Line* in 1962, the second book in his war
——
42
trilogy.

[5]

Jones was close to completing the third book of his

war trilogy, *Whistle*, when he passed away in 1977. Jones
——
43
left instructions for another writer, Willie Morris, to
——
43
complete the final novel in his war trilogy, which was
——
43
posthumously published in 1978.
——
43

42. **F.** NO CHANGE
    G. wrote
    H. writes
    J. had written

43. Given that all of the choices are true, which one would most effectively conclude this essay?
    A. NO CHANGE
    B. Jones's novels were informed by his own experience—characters in *From Here to Eternity* were based on his platoon—but they also contained fictionalized elements.
    C. In addition to his book awards, Jones was awarded the Purple Heart for his injuries in World War II.
    D. Jones's early work had been supported by a "writer's colony," a place established to provide for the needs of writers while they practice their craft.

Questions 44 and 45 refer to the preceding passage as a whole.

---

44. For the sake of logic and coherence, Paragraph 1 should be placed:
    F. where it is now.
    G. after Paragraph 2.
    H. after Paragraph 3.
    J. after Paragraph 4.

45. Suppose the writer's primary purpose had been to explain the importance of Jones's contributions in helping to shape the genre of war literature. Would this essay accomplish that purpose?
    A. Yes, because it focuses on how James Jones based his war trilogy on his own experiences of war.
    B. Yes, because it describes how James Jones's war trilogy influenced future authors.
    C. No, because the essay mainly focuses on James's life and only briefly mentions Jones's war trilogy.
    D. No, because the essay does not place Jones's writing in a broader context of war literature.

GO ON TO THE NEXT PAGE.

Passage IV

Peddling Yarns

[1]

I once worked at a small company that sold wool and yarn online. When I started the job, because I didn't realize how many different fibers were used in yarns and fabrics.

But here I was selling the stuff I had to learn fast!

[2]

One of the first fibers I got to know wasn't wool at all: it is acrylic.

Acrylic, kind of plastic. It's turned into a spinnable fiber through a process called "extrusion." Extrusion is used to make a variety of synthetic fibers, including Kevlar fibers, which are woven into Kevlar cloth. These are spun into yarns. Acrylic yarn is inexpensive, strong, and elastic.

46. **F.** NO CHANGE
    G. although
    H. whereas
    J. OMIT the underlined portion.

47. **A.** NO CHANGE
    B. was selling: the stuff I had
    C. was; selling the stuff I had
    D. was, selling the stuff; I had

48. **F.** NO CHANGE
    G. was
    H. had been
    J. will be

49. **A.** NO CHANGE
    B. Acrylic: a kind of plastic.
    C. Acrylic is a kind of plastic.
    D. Kind of plastic.

50. Given that all of the choices are true, which one is most relevant to the focus of the paragraph?

    F. NO CHANGE
    G. The plastic is melted, then forced through tiny holes to form thin strands of spinnable fibers.
    H. In addition to plastics, extrusion is also used to process natural cellulose from trees and bamboo.
    J. Extrusion is used in the food industry to create a variety of products including pasta, sausages, and cereals, but in the textile industry it is used to create spinnable fibers.

51. **A.** NO CHANGE
    B. possesses the attributes of being inexpensive, strong, and elastic.
    C. has the following characteristics: inexpensiveness, strength, and elasticity.
    D. is characterized by inexpensiveness, strength, and elasticity.

GO ON TO THE NEXT PAGE.

Unfortunately, it's also very *déclassé*—we sold high-end
fibers, and I only learned about acrylic because our
customers needed to be assured that we weren't using it.

[3]

After learning what we didn't like, I learned about
a fiber we loved: merino wool. There are many different
kinds of sheep and they produce wools with slightly
different characteristics. 53 Merino sheep produce merino
wool, which is soft, somewhat elastic, and very squishy.

The first time I heard this, I was a little confused: how can
wool be "squishy?" To understand how "squishy" describes
the texture of wool, just grab a ball and give it a squeeze: a
ball of squishy wool doesn't offer much resistance, and
bounces back after you squeeze it. Squishiness makes wool
ideal for garments that have to take a lot of wear-and-tear,
but also need to be comfortable—like socks. We sold to a lot
of sock knitters, merino our most popular product.

52. Which of the following alternatives to the underlined
portion would be LEAST acceptable?

F. However,
G. Indeed,
H. Regrettably,
J. Alas,

53. At this point, the writer is considering adding the
following sentence:

White or lightly colored wool is often dyed in an
array of dazzling colors.

Should the writer make this addition?

A. Yes, because it provides interesting additional
information about merino wool.
B. Yes, because it helps to explain how different
breeds of sheep can produce wool with different
qualities by providing a specific example.
C. No, because it does not specify the color of wool
provided by merino sheep.
D. No, because it does not develop the idea that
different breeds of sheep produce different kinds of
wool.

54. F. NO CHANGE
G. how can wool be "squishy!"
H. how can wool be "squishy."
J. how can wool be "squishy:"

55. A. NO CHANGE
B. knitters, merino was
C. knitters, so merino was
D. knitters; merino,

GO ON TO THE NEXT PAGE.

[4]

[1] We also sold some very expensive luxury fibers,
$\underline{}$
                          56
like cashmere and silk blends, but my personal favorite was

alpaca wool. [2] Alpaca wool is incredibly soft. [3] Alpaca

wool is also warmest than sheeps' wool, so garments like
         $\underline{}$
              57
scarves and gloves can be made from a finer yarn and still

provide just as much warmth as thicker, scratchier sheeps'

wool garments. [4] It's never prickly, like some sheeps' wool

can be. [58]

[5]

I don't sell wool anymore, but I still like it: a hand-

knit alpaca wool scarf is one of my most prized
                                $\underline{}$
                                     59
possessions.
$\underline{}$
    59

56. **F.** NO CHANGE
    G. expensively
    H. expense
    J. expensiveness

57. **A.** NO CHANGE
    B. warmer
    C. warm
    D. most warm

58. For the sake of the logic and coherence of Paragraph 4, Sentence 4 should be:
    F. placed where it is now.
    G. placed before Sentence 1.
    H. placed after Sentence 2.
    J. OMITTED, because the paragraph focuses on alpaca wool, not sheeps' wool.

59. **A.** NO CHANGE
    B. things that I like
    C. highly valued holdings
    D. articles of clothing

> Question 60 refers to the preceding passage as a whole.

60. Suppose the writer's primary purpose had been to describe some of what he learned from a work experience. Would this essay accomplish that goal?
    F. Yes, because it describes how the writer learned to manufacture several varieties of fiber from a kind of plastic.
    G. Yes, because it explains what the writer learned about a variety of fibers by selling them.
    H. No, because it focuses on providing general information about fibers without explaining how the writer learned the information.
    J. No, because it provides information about fibers and yarn rather than the business knowledge that a person gains through work.

GO ON TO THE NEXT PAGE.

Passage V

Who is El Niño?

[1]

[1] Weather forecasters often use the term "El
Niño." [2] However, most people have no idea what the term
really means. [3] The name, Spanish for "the boy child,"
arose, because South American fishermen noticed that
coastal waters sometimes warmed up around Christmas. [4]
This linked the event with the child Christ, or "El Niño." 62

[2]

El Niño is actually one of three states of a single
climate phenomenon known as the El Niño Southern
Oscillation, or ENSO. ENSO includes La Niña, which is a
cooling of the ocean surface, and the neutral state, during
which the temperature of the tropical Pacific is close to
average. The simplest explanation of what happens during
the phase is that the ocean surface warms up, and that
warming affects wind patterns and ocean currents.

[3]

[1] El Niño can cause droughts in western Pacific
countries from Southeast Asia to Australia, while at the
same time bringing potentially severely rain to areas that are
normally dry, like Peru and Ecuador. [2] East African

61. A. NO CHANGE
　　B. child," arose
　　C. child" arose
　　D. child" arose,

62. For the sake of the logic and coherence of Paragraph 1,
Sentence 4 should be placed:
　　F. where it is now.
　　G. before Sentence 1.
　　H. after Sentence 1.
　　J. after Sentence 2.

63. A. NO CHANGE
　　B. it
　　C. El Niño
　　D. this

64. F. NO CHANGE
　　G. potentially severe
　　H. potential severe
　　J. potential severely

GO ON TO THE NEXT PAGE.

countries experience unusually wet conditions, while South
African countries are drier. [3] During El Niños, winters in
the northern U.S., Canada, and Europe are warmer and drier
than average, while the southern portions of North America
and Europe are cooler and wetter. [4] Though hurricanes are
suppressed in the Atlantic, there's a rise in tropical cyclones
throughout the Pacific. 66

[4]

Naturally, these changes in global weather patterns
have global effects. El Niño is linked to increases in
mosquito populations and mosquito-borne diseases like
malaria and dengue fever. Economic impacts are also
significant: changes in rain patterns had affected everything
from crops to hydroelectric dams, and the prices of
everything—from food prices to electricity prices. Some

65. A. NO CHANGE
    B. have some pretty damp days,
    C. see it raining cats and dogs,
    D. are totally soaked,

66. The writer is considering deleting a sentence from this paragraph to improve its focus on the effects that El Niño has on different nations of the world. To best accomplish this goal, the writer should delete:
    F. Sentence 1.
    G. Sentence 2.
    H. Sentence 3.
    J. Sentence 4.

67. Which of the following choices is the LEAST acceptable alternative to the underlined portion?
    A. Obviously,
    B. Of course,
    C. Conversely,
    D. OMIT the underlined portion and capitalize the first letter of the next word.

68. F. NO CHANGE
    G. global effects, El Niño
    H. global effects El Niño
    J. global effects, El Niño,

69. A. NO CHANGE
    B. affected
    C. will affect
    D. affect

70. F. NO CHANGE
    G. and the prices of food, and nearly everything else, including the price of electricity.
    H. and everything from food prices to electricity prices, as a result of the effects on things such as crops and dams.
    J. and the prices of everything from food to electricity.

GO ON TO THE NEXT PAGE.

studies have even claimed that the risk of social <u>problems,</u>

<u>even civil wars increases, with El Niño's arrival.</u>

71

[5]

Not all of <u>El Niño's effects</u> are negative: in areas

72

where El Niño reduces rain, rates of mosquito-borne disease

<u>actually was falling,</u> and in many regions some crop yields

73

actually increase. Whatever the effects on a particular

<u>region. It's good</u> for us to know about them in advance and

74

plan for El Niño's arrival. 75

71. A. NO CHANGE
   B. problems—even civil wars—increases
   C. problems; even civil wars increases
   D. problems: even civil wars, increases

72. F. NO CHANGE
   G. El Niños effects
   H. El Niños effect's
   J. El Niño's effect's

73. A. NO CHANGE
   B. falls,
   C. has fallen,
   D. fall,

74. F. NO CHANGE
   G. region it's good
   H. region it's good,
   J. region, it's good

> Question 75 refers to the preceding passage as a whole.

75. Suppose the writer's primary purpose had been to argue that future generations should work to mitigate the negative effects of climate phenomena like El Niño. Would this essay accomplish that goal?

   A. Yes, because the passage concludes by indicating that we should make plans based on weather patterns.

   B. Yes, because the passage warns about many of the severe consequences of El Niño.

   C. No, because the writer does not suggest that there is any way for future generations to prevent El Niño.

   D. No, because the author focuses primarily on describing El Niño, rather than making any argument.

END OF TEST 1.

STOP! DO NOT TURN THE PAGE UNTIL YOU ARE TOLD TO DO SO.

Mathematics Test

60 Minutes—60 Questions

DIRECTIONS: For each problem, solve for the correct answer, select your choice and fill in the corresponding bubble on your answer document.

Some problems may take a longer time to solve, but do not take too much time on any single problem. Solve the easier questions first, then return to the harder questions in the remaining time for this test.

A calculator is allowed on this test. While you may be able to solve some problems without a calculator, you are allowed to use a calculator for all of the problems on this test.

Note: Unless otherwise directed, all of the following statements are considered correct.

1. All drawn figures are NOT necessarily drawn to scale.
2. All geometric figures are in a plane.
3. The word *line*, when used, is the same as a straight line.
4. The word *average*, when used, is the same as arithmetic mean.

---

1. For all nonzero values of x, the expression $-3x^3 \cdot 6x^{-2}$ is equivalent to:

   A. $3x$

   B. $3x^{-6}$

   C. $-18x^{-6}$

   D. $-18x$

   E. $18x$

2. A mole is a unit of measurement in chemistry. If 1 mole contains 6.02×10^{23} particles, how many particles are in $\frac{1}{2}$ of a mole?

   F. $3.01 \times 10^{11.5}$

   G. 3.01×10^{23}

   H. 6.02×10^{23}

   J. $6.02 \times 10^{11.5}$

   K. 3.01×5^{23}

3. 20% of x is 15. What is x% of 120?

   A. 3

   B. 24

   C. 30

   D. 45

   E. 90

4. Maria drives to her aunt's house at an average speed of 50 miles per hour. If her trip takes 5 hours and 15 minutes, how many miles does she drive?

   F. 227.5

   G. 257.5

   H. 262.5

   J. 266.5

   K. 275.5

5. A customer uses a coupon to get 16% off the cost of a jacket. Due to an in-store promotion, she receives an additional 10% off of the sale price at the register. If the jacket originally cost $237, how much does she pay, to the nearest cent?

   A. $173.94

   B. $175.38

   C. $179.17

   D. $199.08

   E. $213.30

6. What is the lowest common denominator of $\frac{1}{17}, \frac{1}{12}, \frac{1}{4}$, and $\frac{1}{6}$?

   F. 204

   G. 408

   H. 816

   J. 3,264

   K. 780,336

GO ON TO THE NEXT PAGE.

Practice Tests

7. If $x = -2$, what is the value of $(x^3 + 6)(x^2 - 3)$?

   A.   −14

   B.   −3

   C.   −2

   D.   −1

   E.   14

8. 3 points are shown below on a standard (x,y) coordinate plane.

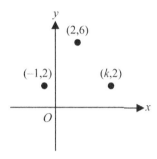

If 3 lines are drawn to connect each of the points, an isosceles triangle is formed. Which of the following is a possible value of k?

   F.   5

   G.   3

   H.   2

   J.   1

   K.   0

9. Which values of x satisfy the equation $x^2 - 16x = 0$?

   A. $x = 4$ and $x = -4$

   B. $x = 0$ and $x = 16$

   C. $x = 0$ and $x = -16$

   D. $x = 0$

   E.   There are no real solutions to the equation.

10. Which of the following expressions is equivalent to $3(5x - 2y) + 8\left(\dfrac{1}{2}y - 2x\right)$?

   F. $-x - 2y$

   G. $-2x - 2y$

   H. $-8x + 4y$

   J. $12x - 16y$

   K. $19x - 22y$

11. An artist is constructing a triangular frame out of metal for the City of Calgary. His blueprint is a triangular frame with a ratio of side lengths that is exactly 8:10:15. If the longest side of the real structure is 45 meters, what is the total length of the metal needed to build the triangular frame, to the nearest meter?

   A.   186

   B.   120

   C.   99

   D.   63

   E.   33

12. The distance d, in meters, traveled by a moving object is given by the equation $d = vt + \dfrac{1}{2}at^2$, where v is the velocity in meters per second, a is the acceleration in meters per second per second, and t is the elapsed time in seconds. If an object with velocity 15 meters per second travels 61 meters in 3 seconds, what is its acceleration, a, in meters per second per second?

   F.   0

   G. $\dfrac{9}{32}$

   H. $\dfrac{32}{3}$

   J. $\dfrac{32}{9}$

   K. $\dfrac{212}{9}$

13. A dry cleaning business charges a fee of $9 for its services, plus $5 per shirt and $6 per jacket. Kristin drops off s shirts and j jackets for dry cleaning. Which of the following expressions represents the cost, in dollars, that Kristin must pay for her dry cleaning?

   A. $5j + 6s + 9$

   B. $5s + 6j + 9$

   C. $5s + 6j$

   D. $20(s + j)$

   E. $11(s + j) + 9$

GO ON TO THE NEXT PAGE.

14. What is the sum of the 2 roots in the function shown in the graph below?

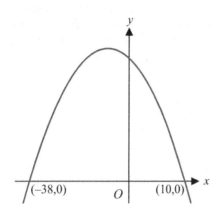

(−38,0)   O   (10,0)

F. −28

G. −3

H. 0

J. 3

K. 28

15. What is the *y*-intercept of a line that passes through the points (−2,0) and (1,6)?

A. −4

B. −2

C. 0

D. 2

E. 4

16. Let $b = x^a$. What happens to the value of *b* if *x* is equal to 2 and *a* is increased by 1?

F. It increases by 2.

G. It doubles.

H. It increases by *a*.

J. It increases by a^2.

K. It is unchanged.

17. Alex owns 5 shirts, 5 pants, 3 sweaters, and 4 pairs of sandals. A complete outfit consists of a shirt, a pair of pants, a sweater, and a pair of sandals. If he loses a pair of sandals and a shirt, how many complete outfit options does he lose?

A. 120

B. 180

C. 300

D. 360

E. 540

18. Which of the following inequalities is the solution for the inequality $23 \geq -(17 + 5x)$?

F. $x \geq -8$

G. $x \leq -8$

H. $x \geq 8$

J. $x \geq -40$

K. $x \leq -40$

19. In the figure shown below, each pair of intersecting line segments meets at a right angle, and all the lengths are given in meters. What is the perimeter, in meters, of the figure?

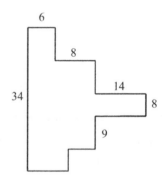

6
8
34   14
8
9

A. 62

B. 79

C. 118

D. 124

E. 952

20. The ratio of *x* to 3 is *x*:3. If this ratio of *x*:3 is equal to 7:10, what is the value of *x*?

F. 1.0

G. 2.1

H. 2.8

J. 4.3

K. 23.3

GO ON TO THE NEXT PAGE.

Practice Tests

21. A mover lowers a piano from a window using a rope, keeping the piano at a right angle to the ground. At the window, the rope bends at a 40° angle, as shown in the figure below. At what angle, with respect to the ground, must the mover hold the rope?

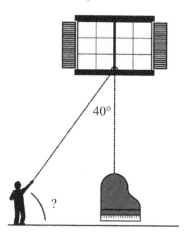

A. 35°

B. 40°

C. 45°

D. 50°

E. 90°

22. What is the correct order of the following fractions, from smallest to largest?

$$\frac{2}{3}, \frac{5}{2}, \frac{11}{12}, \frac{4}{7}$$

F. $\frac{2}{3}, \frac{4}{7}, \frac{5}{2}, \frac{11}{12}$

G. $\frac{2}{3}, \frac{5}{2}, \frac{4}{7}, \frac{11}{12}$

H. $\frac{2}{3}, \frac{4}{7}, \frac{11}{12}, \frac{5}{2}$

J. $\frac{2}{3}, \frac{11}{12}, \frac{4}{7}, \frac{5}{2}$

K. $\frac{4}{7}, \frac{2}{3}, \frac{11}{12}, \frac{5}{2}$

23. If $x^2 - 1 = y$ and $x + y = 1$, which of the following is a possible value for x?

A. −1

B. 0

C. 1

D. 2

E. 3

24. The function $f(x)$ is shown in the standard (x,y) coordinate plane.

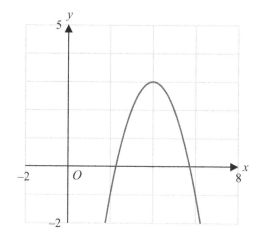

If the point $(4,y)$ lies on the curve of the function $-f(x)$, what is the value of y?

F. 3

G. 2

H. 0

J. −2

K. −3

25. If $3^x = 81^7$, $x = ?$

A. 4

B. 11

C. 10

D. 28

E. 30

26. If the arc length of a sector of a circle with radius 1 is $\frac{\pi}{2}$, what is the measure of the sector's angle, in degrees?

F. 270°

G. 180°

H. 115°

J. 90°

K. 45°

GO ON TO THE NEXT PAGE.

27. A library allows borrowers to keep books for 21 days. If a borrower returns a book 22 days after borrowing it, they are charged a late fee of $0.25. Each subsequent day, the late fee is doubled. If the late fee is greater than the cost of replacing the book, the library will replace the book and charge the borrower the replacement cost instead of a late fee. If a book costs $6.00 to replace, how many days does a borrower have to return the book before it is replaced?

- **A.** 22
- **B.** 23
- **C.** 24
- **D.** 25
- **E.** 26

28. $|9 - 21| - |8 + 3 - 16| = ?$

- **F.** -17
- **G.** -7
- **H.** 7
- **J.** 8
- **K.** 17

29. What is the value of $\dfrac{\sin \beta}{\cos \beta}$ in the figure below?

- **A.** $\dfrac{1}{2}$
- **B.** $\dfrac{3}{4}$
- **C.** 1
- **D.** $\dfrac{4}{3}$
- **E.** $\dfrac{212}{9}$

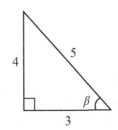

30. A number is doubled, then tripled, and then divided by 4. If n is the original number, which of the following is equal to the new number?

- **F.** $\dfrac{n}{4}$
- **G.** $\dfrac{n}{2}$
- **H.** $\dfrac{3n}{2}$
- **J.** $4n$
- **K.** $6n$

31. What is the value of $\log_2 128 - \log_2 64$?

- **A.** 4
- **B.** 3
- **C.** 2
- **D.** 1
- **E.** 0

32. John is buying candy and soda for a party. Candy costs $4 per bag, and soda costs $3 per bottle. If John has a combined total of 40 bags and bottles, and he spends $130, how many bottles does he buy?

- **F.** 5
- **G.** 10
- **H.** 20
- **J.** 30
- **K.** 40

33. The graph below represents which of the following equations?

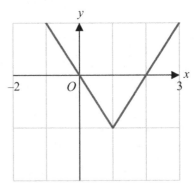

- **A.** $y = (x - 1)^2 - 1$
- **B.** $y = |x - 1| - 1$
- **C.** $y = |x - 1| + 1$
- **D.** $y = 2x - 2$ and $y = -\dfrac{1}{2}x - 1$
- **E.** $y = -2x - 2$ and $y = \dfrac{1}{2}x - 1$

GO ON TO THE NEXT PAGE.

Practice Tests

34. $\begin{bmatrix} -1 & 2 \\ 2 & 4 \end{bmatrix} + \begin{bmatrix} 4 \\ 2 \end{bmatrix} = ?$

   F. $\begin{bmatrix} 4 \\ 16 \end{bmatrix}$

   G. $\begin{bmatrix} 16 \\ 4 \end{bmatrix}$

   H. $\begin{bmatrix} -4 & 8 \\ 8 & 8 \end{bmatrix}$

   J. $\begin{bmatrix} 8 & 8 \\ -4 & 8 \end{bmatrix}$

   K. The resulting matrix is undefined.

35. Five consecutive integers add up to 105. What is the smallest of these integers?

   A. 18
   B. 19
   C. 20
   D. 21
   E. 22

Use the following information to answer questions 36-37.

Every day, Fred and Angela make daily deposits, in dollars, into their savings accounts, as shown in the table below.

Day	Fred	Angela
June 1	25	1
June 2	30	2
June 3	35	4
June 4	40	8
June 5	45	16

36. If Fred's deposits continue to increase at the same daily rate, how much money will he have after 10 days?

   F. $70
   G. $250
   H. $350
   J. $475
   K. $950

37. Both Fred and Angela's deposits continue increasing at the same rate. What is the first day on which Angela will deposit more money than Fred?

   A. June 6
   B. June 7
   C. June 8
   D. June 9
   E. October 6

38. A tent uses cables that are 13 feet long to support its structure. If the tent is erected perpendicular to the ground and the cables are secured 5 feet from the base of the tent, as shown below, how tall is the tent in feet?

   F. 4
   G. 8
   H. 12
   J. 15
   K. 18

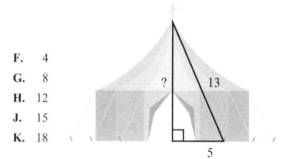

39. Jennifer asks Corwin what his favorite number is. Corwin responds, "If you add 2 to my favorite number, then find the square root of the result, the end result is 5." What is Corwin's favorite number?

   A. –27
   B. 5
   C. 23
   D. 25
   E. 27

40. The function $(x - 15)^2 + (y - 4)^2 = 81$ is graphed on a standard (x,y) coordinate plane. How many times does the function intersect the x-axis?

   F. 0
   G. 1
   H. 2
   J. 3
   K. 4

GO ON TO THE NEXT PAGE.

41. Vector $\overrightarrow{BC}$ is shown in the standard (x,y) coordinate plane below. Which of the following is the component form of $\overrightarrow{BC}$?

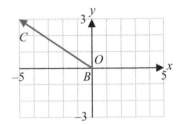

   A. $\langle -5, -3 \rangle$

   B. $\langle -5,\ 3 \rangle$

   C. $\langle\ 3, -3 \rangle$

   D. $\langle\ 5, -3 \rangle$

   E. $\langle\ 5,\ 5 \rangle$

42. If $16^x = 4$, $x = 16^y$, what is the value of xy?

   F. $-\dfrac{1}{8}$

   G. $-\dfrac{1}{4}$

   H. $-\dfrac{1}{2}$

   J. $\dfrac{1}{2}$

   K. 1

43. The volume of a sphere can be expressed by the equation $V = \dfrac{4}{3}\pi r^3$, where r is the radius. What would happen to the volume of a sphere if its radius were tripled?

   A. It would increase by a factor of 6.

   B. It would increase by a factor of 9.

   C. It would increase by a factor of 27.

   D. It would decrease by a factor of 6.

   E. If would decrease by a factor of 27.

44. If $f(x) = 2x^2 + 1$ and $g(x) = \dfrac{1}{x}$, what is $f(g(2))$?

   F. 9

   G. $\dfrac{3}{2}$

   H. $\dfrac{2}{3}$

   J. $\dfrac{1}{2}$

   K. 0

45. Two of the vertices of a square graphed on the standard (x,y) plane are at the points $(-2,3)$ and $(2,-1)$. Which of the following coordinates is NOT a possible vertex of the square?

   A. $(\ 6,\ 3)$

   B. $(\ 3,\ 6)$

   C. $(\ 2,\ 3)$

   D. $(-2, -1)$

   E. $(-6, -1)$

46. In the quadrilateral shown below, what is the value of x?

   F. 100

   G. 105

   H. 110

   J. 115

   K. 120

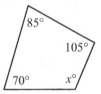

47. A line $\overline{AD}$ is shown below.

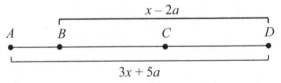

What is the length of $\overline{AB}$?

   A. $2x + 7a$

   B. $-x + 3a$

   C. $-2x + 7a$

   D. $-2x - 3a$

   E. $-4x - 3a$

GO ON TO THE NEXT PAGE.

48. What is the length of the hypotenuse of the isosceles right triangle shown below?

F. $\dfrac{10}{\sqrt{2}}$

G. $5\sqrt{2}$

H. 10

J. $10\sqrt{2}$

K. 20

$\dfrac{10}{\sqrt{2}}$

50. Caleb decides to string a clothesline along the diagonal from one end of the garden to the other. The clothesline starts 1 foot off the ground at one end, and ends 6 feet off the ground at the other end of the diagonal. What is the total length of the clothesline, in feet?

F. 10

G. $10\sqrt{2}$

H. 15

J. 20

K. 26

Use the following information to answer questions 49-51.

Caleb is planting a 10-foot-by-10-foot garden with different flowers, as shown in the figure below. He decides to plant daffodils (D), lilies (L), and pansies (P).

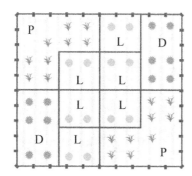

49. What is the area, to the nearest square foot, in which Caleb can plant pansies?

A. 17

B. 25

C. 38

D. 45

E. 75

51. Caleb no longer wants daffodils or lilies and hires Miu, a carpenter, to build rectangular wooden decks over the daffodils and lilies in his garden. She plans to cover the areas with planks of wood that are 0.2 feet high by 0.5 feet wide by 2.5 feet long to make the deck. What is the minimum number of planks that she will need?

A. 10

B. 20

C. 25

D. 30

E. 50

52. What is the measure of each interior angle in the regular hexagon shown below?

F. 60°

G. 80°

H. 100°

J. 110°

K. 120°

GO ON TO THE NEXT PAGE.

53. If $\dfrac{a}{b} = \dfrac{x - \frac{1}{2}}{x + \frac{1}{3}}$ and $x \neq -\frac{1}{3}$, which of the following expressions is equal to ab?

I. $x^2 - \dfrac{1}{6}x - \dfrac{1}{6}$

II. $x^2 - \dfrac{1}{6}$

III. $x^2 + \dfrac{1}{2}x - \dfrac{1}{6}$

A. I only
B. II only
C. III only
D. I and II
E. II and III

54. The diagram of a circular target is shown below. The center circle has a radius of 5 cm, and each larger circle has a radius 1 cm larger than the previous circle. Which area is the smallest?

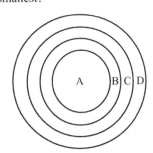

F. A
G. B
H. C
J. D
K. The three outer areas are equal in size.

55. Points A, B, C, and D lie on a line. A man starts at point A and walks to point B. He then continues 300 m to point C. After, he walks 400 m back past point B to point D. If his total trip was 900 m, how far apart are points A and D?

A. 100 m
B. 200 m
C. 300 m
D. 500 m
E. 1000 m

56. If $\tan\theta = \sqrt{3}$ and $\cos\theta = \frac{1}{2}$, what is $\sin\theta$?

F. $\dfrac{\sqrt{3}}{2}$

G. $\dfrac{2}{\sqrt{3}}$

H. $2\sqrt{3}$

J. $\sqrt{\dfrac{3}{2}}$

K. $\sqrt{3}$

57. Alan has a square backyard with an area of 64 square meters. He wants to build the largest possible circular pool in this backyard. What is the area, in square meters, of the largest possible pool that Alan can build?

A. 4π
B. 8π
C. 16π
D. 32π
E. 64π

58. A local band releases their latest album on cassette tape. They decorate each tape with a sticker that covers the entire surface except for the circular shaded regions, shown in the figure below. If the measurements are in inches, what is the area of the sticker to the nearest tenth of an inch?

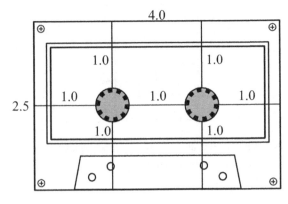

F. 8.4
G. 9.2
H. 9.6
J. 9.8
K. 10.0

GO ON TO THE NEXT PAGE.

Practice Tests

59. Which of the following number lines represents the solution of the inequality $1 < \dfrac{1}{x}$?

A.

B.

C.

D.

E.

60. Both of the curves graphed below are variants of the same base function, $y = a \cdot \sin[k(x - d)] + c$. What changes were made to $f(x)$ to yield $g(x)$?

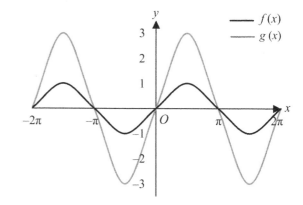

F. a increases

G. a decreases

H. c increases

J. k increases

K. d decreases

END OF TEST 2.

STOP! DO NOT TURN THE PAGE UNTIL YOU ARE TOLD TO DO SO.

DO NOT RETURN TO THE PREVIOUS TEST.

Reading Test
35 Minutes—40 Questions

DIRECTIONS: There are multiple passages in this test. Each one is accompanied by several questions. After reading a passage, choose the best answer to every question and fill in the matching circle on your scoring sheet. You can refer back to the passages as often as necessary.

Passage I

Prose Fiction: This passage is adapted from the story "David's Haircut" by Ken Elkes. The story depicts a boy going to get his haircut with his father accompanying him (©2016 Ken Elkes).

When David steps out of the front door he is blinded for a moment by the white, fizzing sunlight and reaches instinctively for his dad's hand.

It's the first really warm day of the year, an
5 unexpected heat that bridges the cusp between spring and summer. Father and son are on their way to the barbershop, something they have always done together.

Always, the routine is the same. "It's about time we got that mop of yours cut," David's dad will say.
10 "Perhaps I should do it. Where are those shears, Janet?"

Sometimes his dad chases him round the living room, pretending to cut off his ears. When he was young David used to get too excited and start crying, scared that maybe he really would lose his ears, but he has long
15 since grown out of that.

Mr. Samuels' barbershop is in a long room above the chip shop, reached by a steep flight of stairs. There is a groove worn in each step by the men who climb and descend in a regular stream. David follows his father,
20 annoyed that he cannot make each step creak like his old man can.

David loves the barbershop—it's like nowhere else he goes. Black and white photographs of men with various out-of-fashion hairstyles hang above a picture
25 rail at the end of the room, where two barber's chairs are bolted to the floor. They are heavy, old-fashioned chairs with foot pumps that hiss and chatter as Mr. Samuels adjusts the height of the seat. At the back of the room sit the customers.

30 When it is David's turn for a cut, Mr. Samuels places a wooden board covered with a piece of oxblood

red leather across the arms of the chair, so that the barber doesn't have to stoop to cut the boy's hair. David scrambles up onto the bench.

35 "The rate you're shooting up, you won't need this soon, you'll be sat in the chair," the barber says.

"Wow," says David, squirming round to look at his dad, forgetting that he can see him through the mirror. "Dad, Mr. Samuels said I could be sitting in the chair
40 soon, not just on the board!"

"So I hear," his father replies, not looking up from the paper. "I expect Mr. Samuels will start charging me more for your hair then."

"At least double the price," says Mr. Samuels,
45 winking at David.

Finally David's dad looks up from his newspaper and glances into the mirror, seeing his son looking back at him. He smiles.

"Wasn't so long ago when I had to lift you onto that
50 board because you couldn't climb up there yourself," he says.

"They don't stay young for long do they, kids," Mr. Samuels declares. All the men in the shop nod in agreement. David nods too.

55 In the mirror he sees a little head sticking out of a long nylon cape that Mr. Samuels has swirled around him and folded into his collar with a wedge of cotton wool. Occasionally he steals glances at the barber as he works. He smells a mixture of stale sweat and aftershave
60 as the barber moves around him, combing and snipping, combing and snipping.

David feels like he is in another world, noiseless except for the scuffing of the barber's shoes on the linoleum and the snap of his scissors. In the reflection
65 from the window he can see the barber's careful movements.

GO ON TO THE NEXT PAGE.

Sleepily, his eyes drop to the front of the cape where his hair falls with the same softness as snow, and he imagines sitting in the chair just like the men and older
70 boys, the special bench left leaning against the wall in the corner.

When Mr. Samuels has finished, David hops down from the seat, rubbing the itchy hair from his face. Looking down he sees his own thick, blonde hair
75 scattered among the browns, greys, and blacks of the men who have sat in the chair before him. For a moment he wants to reach down and gather up the broken blonde locks, to separate them from the others, but he does not have time.

80 The sun is still strong when they reach the pavement outside the shop, but it is less fiery now, already beginning to drop from its zenith.

"I tell you what, lad, let's get some fish and chips to take home, save your mum from cooking tea," says
85 David's dad and turns up the street.

The youngster is excited and grabs his dad's hand. The thick-skinned fingers close gently around his and David is surprised to find, warming in his father's palm, a lock of his own hair.

1. Within the passage, the father's statements, "Perhaps I should do it. Where are those shears, Janet?" (line 10) suggest that:

A. David's father usually cuts David's hair.
B. David's mother usually cuts David's hair.
C. David's father usually jokes that he will cut David's hair.
D. David's mother usually takes David to the barber's to get his hair cut.

2. As it is used in line 13, the word *excited* most nearly means:

F. enthusiastic.
G. thrilled.
H. angry.
J. worked up.

3. It can reasonably be inferred that David is "annoyed that he cannot make each step creak" because David:

A. wants to be like his father.
B. is a naturally irritable person.
C. has always dreamt of being tall and athletic.
D. finds the sound of steps creaking satisfying.

4. David's attitude toward his father can best be characterized as:

F. cautious and intrepid.
G. polite and distant.
H. admiring and fond.
J. reverent and fearful.

5. The passage suggests that David nods in line 54 because he:

A. agrees with Mr. Samuels' insight.
B. seeks to copy the older men in the shop.
C. is lost in thought.
D. wants Mr. Samuels to resume cutting his hair.

6. Details in the passage suggest that, for David, Mr. Samuels' barbershop is:

F. a new place that intimidates him.
G. a memorable place that has grown a bit dull.
H. a novel place that fills him with curiosity.
J. a familiar place that has maintained its wonder.

7. The passage describes Mr. Samuels with the repeated phrase "combing and snipping, combing and snipping" (lines 60-61) to suggest that Mr. Samuels:

A. combed and snipped David's hair exactly twice.
B. worked on David's hair with expressive gestures.
C. cut David's hair with repetitive and practiced movements.
D. was becoming drowsy as he was cutting David's hair.

8. The comparison between David's hair and snow is included to imply that, like snow, David's hair:

F. is light in color.
G. feels cold to the touch.
H. is plentiful.
J. falls lightly.

9. The author details how David's father's "thick-skinned fingers close gently around his" (line 87) primarily to:

A. suggest David's father's age and maturity in comparison to David's.
B. characterize David's father as tough and resilient.
C. identify a physical trait that David and David's father share.
D. indicate David's father's physical weakness.

GO ON TO THE NEXT PAGE.

10. The author's purpose at the end of the passage in depicting David's father holding a lock of David's hair could be to show all of the following about David's father EXCEPT that he:

   F. becomes attached to items easily.

   G. is sentimental about David's young age.

   H. anticipates that David will not always be young.

   J. appreciates their father-son haircut outings as much as David does.

Passage II

Social Science: This passage is adapted from the article "An Early Expression of Democracy, the U.S. Patent System is Out of Step with Today's Citizens" by Shobita Parthasarathy (©2015 Shobita Parthasarathy).

The U.S. patent system, first established in the late 18th and early 19th centuries, was made to be fair and equal—particularly compared to the European patent systems of the time. The U.S. encouraged great
5 participation in the system by keeping patent application fees low and creating public displays of patented technologies to inspire others to create, too.

The U.S. system, in other words, made patents, innovation, and entrepreneurship a possibility for every
10 citizen. The idea was to increase innovation, which would help the economy and eventually society as a whole. In many ways, these efforts were successful. Patent application rates grew through the 19th and 20th centuries, and in 2014, the U.S. gave out more than
15 300,000 patents, for things ranging from photocopiers to solar panels. Indeed, many industries have said they owe their success to this early patent system.

This approach has also gone global, buoyed by international legal agreements intended to make it easier
20 for inventions to travel, for inventors to collect rewards across borders, and for markets to span nations. This system has held for hundreds of years and is built on the idea that encouraging innovation through patents will ultimately be good for everyone. It sees every citizen as
25 a potential inventor, and believes that if laws help inventors, they automatically help the public.

But the relationship between the patent system and the people has changed in recent decades. Public health activists have launched lawsuits saying that, rather than
30 making technology easier to get to, patents create monopolies that make good health unaffordable for a lot of people. In 2013, a group of patients, health care workers, and scientists challenged patents on genes linked to breast and ovarian cancer at the U.S. Supreme

35 Court. They argued the patents had led to expensive and low-quality genetic tests available only through one company. Meanwhile, small farmers have organized protests against seed patents, suggesting they speed up big-company control of agriculture in ways that are bad
40 for their businesses, for innovation, for buyers, and for the environment.

Other groups have prompted legal hearings and media campaigns arguing that patents justify working with and earning money from morally controversial
45 areas of research. These campaigns began as early as the 1980s, when environmental activists, animals rights groups, and religious leaders challenged the patenting of genetically engineered animals. They worried that by turning these animals into products, the patent system
50 would change our relationship with the natural environment.

Patent system officials and lawyers tend to view these criticisms as seriously missing the point. They argue that these citizen critics do not understand how the patent
55 system works: the system is focused simply on recognizing the novelty, creativity, and usefulness of inventions. This attitude is also built into the rules and processes of the system, which make it nearly impossible for average citizens to participate, except by applying for
60 patents.

Is it possible to change the system to take into account the newly engaged public? Consider, for example, the pan-European patent system, which is in many ways quite similar to the U.S. patent system. In
65 recent years, it has been open to public participation in its official proceedings, and considered moral and social-economic concerns in its decisions. It has been particularly sensitive to citizens' concerns about patents on software and biotechnology.

70 In 2007, the European Patent Office invited a group of its critics to participate in developing a report that identified the challenges and opportunities it would face over the next 30 years. In response, governments across Europe have followed and taken steps to limit patent
75 monopolies that might hurt public health and agriculture.

It is worth recognizing that while the U.S. system was first created to be a democratic improvement on the European systems of the time, today's pan-European patent system is far ahead of the U.S. patent system in
80 terms of its public engagement and its attention to the issues that citizens care about. If the U.S. patent system wants to keep the public's trust, it has to realize that the 21st-century citizen is very different from the 18th-

GO ON TO THE NEXT PAGE.

century citizen. Today's citizen cares about the moral
85 and social-economic consequences of patents and the
technologies they cover, and is not satisfied to assume
that the system's benefits eventually make their way to
the majority of the population. She also wants to have an
active role in making decisions.

90   Taking this citizen seriously will require significant
patent system reforms, including increasing opportunities
for the public to participate in patent decision-making,
allowing more legal and bureaucratic challenges on behalf
of the public interest, and including more emphasis on
95 moral and social-economic implications into our patent
laws.

11. What is the main purpose of the passage?

     A. To demonstrate the excellence of the U.S. patent
        system

     B. To compare and contrast the U.S. patent system
        with several European patent systems

     C. To emphasize that the U.S. patent system should
        respond to public concerns

     D. To show how patent systems commonly fail to
        satisfy public demands

12. According to the passage, the late 18th and early 19th
century U.S. patent system accomplished all of the
following EXCEPT:

     F. making patents affordable by keeping application
        fees low.

     G. encouraging economic growth.

     H. championing a select few highly capable inventors.

     J. inspiring later international patent agreements.

13. The term *buoyed* in line 18 most nearly means:

     A. floated.

     B. supported.

     C. uplifted.

     D. emboldened.

14. Both health care professionals and small farmers protest
the current U.S. patent system because it contributes to:

     F. patented material being shared too widely with
        other businesses.

     G. heavy control of patents by a limited number of
        patent-holders.

     H. violations of guaranteed natural rights.

     J. irreparable damage to the environment.

15. The main function of the fourth and fifth paragraphs
(lines 27-51) is to:

     A. prove that U.S. citizens in the late 18th and 19th
        century had concerns about the patent system.

     B. emphasize how the current U.S. patent system
        honors the principles of the earlier U.S. patent
        system.

     C. assert that the U.S. patent system and medicine are
        fundamentally incompatible.

     D. show reasons for and examples of public resistance
        to the current U.S. patent system.

16. It is reasonable to infer that patent system officials and
lawyers would respond to criticisms about the moral
implications of the U.S. patent system by saying that:

     F. improvements to the patent system will take time to
        implement.

     G. such criticisms misunderstand the structure and
        goals of the patent system.

     H. critics should take up their concerns by producing
        written complaints.

     J. moral concerns are completely irrelevant to law.

17. As it is used in line 68, the word *sensitive* means:

     A. responsive.

     B. tender.

     C. touchy.

     D. sentient.

18. The author's tone can be characterized as one of:

     F. skeptical disdain.

     G. thoughtful interest.

     H. frenzied concern.

     J. detached observation.

19. The author suggests that compared to the U.S. patent
system, the pan-European patent system is:

     A. an improvement that better takes into account the
        public's moral and social concerns.

     B. a near-identical system that also struggles with
        addressing public opinions.

     C. an inefficient attempt to build on the basics of the
        U.S. patent system.

     D. an institution that further alienates the public.

GO ON TO THE NEXT PAGE.

20. By stating that a possible reform to the U.S. patent system could start "allowing more legal and bureaucratic challenges on behalf of the public interest" (lines 93-94), the author suggests that the U.S. patent system should:

F. take into account the opinions of non-American politicians.

G. be more difficult to decipher for the average person.

H. allow public concerns about patent law to have more influence.

J. feature more prominently in the government's public speeches.

Passage III

Humanities: This passage is adapted from the article "Picasso the…sculptor? Disputed purchase brings attention to lesser-known aspect of his art" by Enrique Mallen (©2016 Enrique Mallen).

A bust of Picasso's mistress, Marie-Thérèse Walter, is currently being exhibited at New York's Museum of Modern Art. Beyond the astronomical (disputed) sale price—upwards of $106 million—it's also significant
5　news because it's relatively rare for attention to be lavished upon one of Picasso's sculptures.

Pablo Picasso's sculptures remain a mystery to many. The prolific Picasso is probably best known as a painter, although his drawings, ceramics, engravings,
10　and lithographs are also often highlighted in museums, exhibitions, and auctions. What hasn't been very well publicized is the substantial contribution to modern art that Picasso made as a sculptor. In fact, *Picasso Sculpture*, an ongoing exhibition at New York's
15　Museum of Modern Art, is the first time in nearly 20 years that a museum is directing attention squarely on the artist's sculptures.

While nearly all his early experience, training, and prodigious energy went into painting, some have even
20　argued that Picasso was more naturally a sculptor. Admittedly, Picasso's sculptures make up a small fraction of the estimated 50,000 works the artist produced in his lifetime. There's still debate over how many Picasso produced. The famous Picasso biographer
25　Roland Penrose included 284 entries in his extensive exhibition of Picasso sculptures, and Picasso scholar Werner Spies identified 664 items in his catalogue raisonné. Meanwhile, the Online Picasso Project contains 796 sculptures.

30　One reason Picasso's sculptures remain a mystery to many is that the artist was averse to selling them. According to Trinity College professor Michael Fitzgerald, "trained as a painter, [Picasso] rarely hesitated to sell his paintings." On the other hand, "He
35　developed a deep fondness for his sculptures, and treasured them as if they were members of his family." In fact, Picasso didn't agree to a full-scale exhibition of his sculptures until 1966, when he participated in the large Paris retrospective *Hommage à Picasso*, which
40　would go on to London and New York in 1967. Only then did the public fully realize that Picasso had been creating—and experimenting—in this medium.

"This is the moment Picasso agrees for the first time to let his sculptures depart from his studio en masse,"
45　Anne Umland, curator of painting and sculpture at New York's Museum of Modern Art, explained at the time. "It's the first time the public has the chance to see the scope and range of his sculptures." Because Picasso wasn't willing to exhibit his sculptures until later in his
50　life, they often went undocumented in the (purportedly) comprehensive publications of his work.

While Picasso had been formally trained as a painter (and earned most of his income from selling paintings), sculpture was a medium where the artist could
55　experiment freely and break established rules without fear of damaging his reputation or hurting his bottom line. His Cubist sculptures of 1912–1913 were particularly innovative. As *The Guardian*'s Jason Farago put it, they were a "thunderclap," with the artist upending
60　what, at the time, was the traditional method of sculpture: chiseling away at a block of material to achieve a new form. Instead, by fusing pieces of cardboard, Picasso "built" his *Guitare* (1912). Constructing objects from sheets of common materials like cardboard, metal, or
65　wood, the artist was able to connect his art to the everyday world, blurring the boundaries between art and life.

For art historian Yve-Alain Bois, the role played by this sculpture lies precisely in its full exploration of the
70　nonrepresentational value of sculpture. In other words, he was able to use arbitrary objects and materials to create pictorial signifiers. As the artist once declared, he wanted to "trick the mind"—not simply fool the eye.

In the 1950s, Picasso would return to planar
75　sculptures. These would also start with paper or cardboard models that the artist would cut out and fold. He would then have them transferred to sheet metal, which he would either paint or leave unpainted, with the

GO ON TO THE NEXT PAGE.

surface of the metal exposed. The play of folds, hollow
80 spaces, and polychromatic tones serves to suggest relief.
Folding and cutting allowed Picasso to superimpose
different points of view and still retain the frontal view;
meanwhile, depth is suggested by the contrast between
filled and empty spaces.

85   Judging by the critics' glowing reception of the
current New York exhibition featuring Picasso, we may
start to see Picasso's sculptures getting the attention they
truly deserve. Perhaps Picasso's sculptures will go the
route of his revolutionary paintings from the late 1960s
90 and early 1970s, including works like *Le vieil homme
assis*, which were widely panned when they were first
exhibited at Avignon's Palais des Papes in 1973.
Nonetheless, these would go on to have a profound
influence on later generations of artists. Today, they're
95 some of the most sought-after Picassos in the world.

21. The main purpose of the passage can best be described
as:

A. arguing that Picasso's sculptures are superior to his
paintings.

B. detailing the sales processes for Picasso's various
sculptures.

C. highlighting a lesser-known area of Picasso's body
of work.

D. discussing some of Picasso's most well-known
sculptures.

22. The author's attitude toward Picasso's sculptures can
best be characterized as:

F. enthusiastic.

G. baffled.

H. dismissive.

J. amused.

23. The author believes Picasso's sculptures did not first
achieve success primarily because:

A. they were inferior in form to his paintings.

B. Picasso was initially hesitant to sell them.

C. art critics were more interested in his paintings.

D. not enough exhibits were open to displaying
sculptures.

24. According to the sixth paragraph (lines 52-67),
compared to his work with paintings, Picasso's work
with sculptures:

F. was not yet ready for public consumption and
criticism.

G. allowed for greater experimentation with less risk.

H. was a much more lucrative if less enjoyable
endeavor.

J. took more time and energy but offered fewer
payoffs.

25. As it is used in line 44, the phrase *depart from his studio
en masse* most nearly refers to:

A. Picasso's destruction of the majority of his
sculptures.

B. the widespread private sale of Picasso's sculptures
after an exhibition.

C. Picasso's participation in a public exhibition.

D. the decision Picasso made to focus primarily on
paintings.

26. The passage claims that Picasso's sculptures differed
from more traditional forms in that his sculptures:

F. focused on everyday rather than religious subjects.

G. involved conversion of a block of material into a
new form.

H. incorporated paintings into their display.

J. consisted of a fusion of different materials.

27. As it is used in line 85, the word *glowing* most nearly
means:

A. lighted.

B. enthusiastic.

C. incandescent.

D. radiant.

28. According to the passage, like some of his paintings,
Picasso's sculptures may:

F. attain recognition even if not immediately hailed
for their achievements.

G. cycle between fame and obscurity for a significant
amount of time.

H. face disproportionate criticism that eventually
destroys their potential sales.

J. achieve immediate fame upon initial presentation
in art galleries.

GO ON TO THE NEXT PAGE.

29. The author calls the sale price of one of Picasso's sculptures "astronomical" in line 3 because it:

   A. is extraordinarily high for a piece of artwork.

   B. sold for a price greater than any other Museum of Modern Art piece.

   C. is disproportionate to the quality of the piece.

   D. reflects an unsustainable price that later fell through.

30. The passage identifies Picasso's sculptures as being both:

   F. shocking and overpraised.

   G. revolutionary and underappreciated.

   H. conventional and obscure.

   J. inexpensive and popular.

Passage IV

Natural Science: Passage A is adapted from the article "Primed for Battle: Helping Plants Fight Off Pathogens by Enhancing Their Immune Systems" by Jeannette Rapicavoli (©2015 by Jeannette Rapicavoli). Passage B is adapted from "Hacking Plant 'Blood Vessels' Could Avert Food Crisis" by John Runions (©2013 by John Runions).

Passage A by Jeannette Rapicavoli

A novel area of research in the war against plant pathogens focuses on enhancing the plant's natural immune system. If a plant can fight off an infection on its own, we can reduce the amount of pesticides needed.
5 Just as children are vaccinated to protect against future diseases, plants can be "immunized" against pathogens by plant pathologists, who aim to strengthen the plants' immune defenses against invaders. This method of priming plants' immune systems could be a safe and
10 effective way to save some of the global harvest currently lost to diseases.

Plants are naturally exposed to a variety of pathogenic microbes, such as bacteria, fungi, and viruses. Plants have a multi-tiered immune system that
15 helps them fight off these microorganisms. It works in a manner very similar to the human immune system. Plants detect pathogens by recognizing microbial "patterns." These are unique characteristics of the type of microbe that the plant has evolved to recognize as "non-self."

20 One of our major research goals is to harness these patterns to prime the plant immune system, creating enhanced protection against pathogenic microbes, in lieu of traditional chemical control methods. The principle of "defense priming" is very similar to how we develop

25 vaccines to treat human diseases. A vaccine works by acting as a pathogen impostor. It tricks the immune system into thinking it's being attacked, which stimulates defense responses, such as the production of antibodies. This creates a defense memory, allowing the
30 immune system to remember a particular pathogen if the body encounters it in the future. It can then respond swiftly and robustly, thanks to its primed memory from the vaccine.

We can apply this same principle to a plant-
35 pathogen relationship. For example, once we've identified a pathogen's pattern of interest, we work to isolate and purify it. This step is like manufacturing the vaccine. We can then inoculate the plant with the purified pattern—for instance, by injecting it into the
40 stem or leaves with a syringe. The goal is to stimulate the plant's natural immune response, resulting in a faster or stronger defense response the next time the plant encounters that pathogen.

Primed plants display enhanced tolerance to
45 infection, which is often characterized by fewer symptoms and reduced pathogen populations within the plant. Although primed plants haven't yet been implemented on a large-scale basis in commercial agriculture, scientists are actively conducting research on the use of defense priming
50 in both greenhouse and field settings for protection against bacteria, viruses, and fungi.

Furthermore, the primed state is durable and can be maintained long after the initial stimulus. Current research has also shown that plants can pass on this defense
55 memory to their descendants, providing multigenerational protection without any genetic modification. Further research is needed to improve our understanding of the molecular mechanisms behind this phenomenon, but defense priming looks likely to be a valuable and
60 promising tool in the future of sustainable agriculture.

Passage B by John Runions

In a recent paper, some of the world's leading plant biologists show that, by hacking how plants transport key nutrients into plant cells, we could solve the impending food crisis.

65 Each plant is made of billions of cells, all of which are surrounded by membranes. The pores in these membranes are lined with membrane transporters, which ferry nutrients that plants capture from soil with the help of roots. What scientists have learned is that if such
70 membrane transporters are tweaked, they can enhance plant productivity. When these tweaks are applied to crops, they can produce plants that are high in calories,

GO ON TO THE NEXT PAGE.

rich in certain nutrients, or able to better fight pests. All these methods increase food production while using
75 fewer resources.

For example, over two billion people suffer from iron or zinc deficiency in their diets. Simple genetic modification increases the amount of membrane transporters that ferry these minerals. Such plants, when
80 ready for harvest, can have as much as four times the concentration of iron, compared to that of common crop variety.

Another key issue is that disease-causing microorganisms, pathogens, manipulate a plant's
85 functioning and consume the sucrose it produces for energy. Most crops have membrane transporters called SWEETs that move sucrose made by leaves from photosynthesis to other regions where it may be stored. Plant pathogens have evolved to manipulate SWEET
90 genes so that sugars are moved to cells where the pathogens can feed on the goods.

Now scientists have found a way of disrupting this pathogen-induced manipulation by a method called RNA-silencing. This reduces or eliminates the
95 pathogens' ability to feed on the plants' hard work, and in turn helps increase plant productivity.

Researchers have been quietly chugging away in labs working on making such radical improvements to crops. Breeding of plants, a form of untailored genetic
100 modification that bestowed most of the benefits to agriculture a generation ago, is not able to keep up with the pace of change required for an ever-increasing demand for food. That is why it is important that we understand the science behind the process of tinkering
105 with specific genes before making any rash judgments.

Questions 31-34 ask about Passage A.

31. The primary purpose of Passage A is to:

A. argue for using more sustainable agricultural techniques in the future.

B. discuss the benefits of defense priming in protecting plants.

C. show the mechanisms by which most pathogens attract plants.

D. demonstrate the resilience of plants in the face of pesticides.

32. The language of the first paragraph of Passage A, including "war," "fight off," and "invaders," is most likely intended to convey a sense of:

F. the violence of different plant species towards one another in nature.

G. the possible military uses for the scientists' research.

H. the high stakes involved for plants defending against pathogens.

J. the sophisticated inner machinery of plant pathogens.

33. As it is used in line 1, the word *novel* most closely means:

A. new.

B. literary.

C. narrative.

D. unique.

34. Which of the following best summarizes one of the goals of the researchers mentioned in Passage A?

F. Help plants use their natural immune system to protect against pathogens

G. Improve the chemical control methods of plant protection to ensure good harvests

H. Determine why some plant pathogens are more susceptible to viruses than others

J. Study how plants pass on defense memory to their offspring

---

Questions 35-38 ask about Passage B.

35. According to Passage B, one reason that scientists may manipulate plant genes is to:

A. ensure that plants obtain the proper nutrients from the soil.

B. increase the value of crops so farmers can make a greater profit.

C. produce plants that have increased nutritional value.

D. help protect plants against natural predators like birds.

GO ON TO THE NEXT PAGE.

36. The author of Passage B uses the example of iron and zinc deficiency to:

    F. show that genetic modifications cannot solve all hunger problems.

    G. highlight an issue with which many plants suffer.

    H. underline the author's previous research into ways that plant modifications affect vitamin uptake.

    J. demonstrate one potential area where genetic manipulation of plants may be helpful.

37. The final paragraph of Passage B serves primarily to:

    A. summarize the author's point that plants have a variety of defenses against pathogens.

    B. argue that global hunger is the most pressing issue of the modern era.

    C. suggest why scientists must study and comprehend the genetic modification of plants.

    D. explain the mechanisms behind recent developments in genome editing.

38. The word *ferry*, as it is used in line 68, most nearly means:

    F. ship.

    G. pack.

    H. transport.

    J. travel.

Questions 39 and 40 ask about both passages.

---

39. Both Passage A and Passage B view potential modifications of plants:

    A. warily.

    B. favorably.

    C. skeptically.

    D. joyously.

40. Passage A and Passage B both discuss:

    F. the impact of genetic modifications on the food supply.

    G. recent policies surrounding genetic modifications.

    H. economic considerations connected to genetically modified crops.

    J. manipulation of plants to protect against pathogens.

END OF TEST 3.

STOP! DO NOT TURN THE PAGE UNTIL YOU ARE TOLD TO DO SO.

DO NOT RETURN TO THE PREVIOUS TEST.

Science Test

35 Minutes—40 Questions

DIRECTIONS: There are several passages in this test, and each is accompanied by several questions. After reading a passage, choose the best answer to each question and fill in the corresponding oval on your answer document. You may refer to the passages as often as necessary.

You are NOT permitted to use a calculator on this test.

Passage I

Sound is a *mechanical wave*, a vibration that moves through a medium at a certain velocity. Students measured the velocity of sound in various media and at different temperatures to determine a relationship between medium, temperature, and the velocity of sound.

Experiment 1

A cylindrical tank with a length of 20 cm and a radius of 4 cm was filled with 1 L of a given liquid at 20°C. A sound velocity probe was inserted into one end of the tank. A sound pulse generator was inserted in the other end. The tank was plugged after it was filled. Ten sound pulses were sent through each given liquid and the average velocity was calculated (see Table 1). The tank was washed with distilled water before this process was repeated with each liquid.

Table 1	
Medium	Velocity (m/s)
Acetic acid	1150
Water	1482
Salt water	1522
Kerosene	1320
Mercury	1438
Octane	1171
Oil	1461

Experiment 2

Experiment 1 was repeated with a cylinder of a given solid at 20°C, with a length of 20 cm and a radius of 4 cm. A sound velocity probe was connected to one end of the cylinder and a sound pulse generator to the other. Ten sound pulses were sent through each given solid and the average velocity was calculated (see Table 2).

Table 2	
Medium	Velocity (m/s)
Brick	4208
Cork	400
Quartz	5980
Glass	3962
Copper	4589
Rubber	100
Hardwood	3954

Experiment 3

Experiment 1 was repeated with 1 L of air in the same cylindrical tank. A thermometer was also inserted into one end of the tank before it was plugged. The air in the tank was heated by immersion in a water bath or cooled in an ice bath. Ten sound pulses were sent through the tank of air at each given temperature and the average velocities were calculated (see Figure 1).

GO ON TO THE NEXT PAGE.

Practice Tests

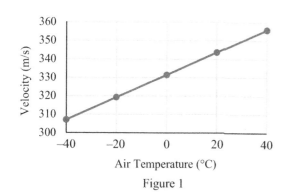

Figure 1

Experimental design adapted from Martin Greenspan and Carroll E. Tschiegg, "Speed of Sound in Water by a Direct Method." ©1957 by JRNIStand 59.4.

1. Based on Experiment 3, as air temperature increases, sound velocity:

    A. increases only.

    B. decreases only.

    C. increases, then decreases.

    D. decreases, then increases.

2. A *sound dampener* is a material that reduces sound velocity. Which of the following media would be the most effective sound dampener?

    F. Quartz

    G. Air

    H. Rubber

    J. Oil

3. The students conclude from their results that sound travels faster in solids than in liquids. According to Experiments 1 and 2, which two media are the exceptions to the students' conclusion?

    A. Oil and salt water

    B. Salt water and cork

    C. Cork and rubber

    D. Quartz and rubber

4. Assuming that water is frozen at 0°C and is gaseous at 100°C, at which of the following temperatures would the velocity of sound in water be the greatest?

    F. 120°C

    G. 80°C

    H. 40°C

    J. −20°C

5. *Elasticity* (E) is the ability of a material to recover its shape after deformation due to vibration, pressure, or other forces. *Density* (ρ) is the mass per unit volume of a material. The *velocity* of sound (v) in a given medium can be given by the following equation:

$$v = \sqrt{\frac{E}{\rho}}$$

If the density of copper is 8950 kg/m³ and the density of acetic acid is 1049 kg/m³, then the velocity of sound in copper is higher than the velocity of sound in acetic acid because copper:

    A. has a much lower density than acetic acid.

    B. has a much lower elasticity than acetic acid.

    C. has a much greater density than acetic acid.

    D. has a much greater elasticity than acetic acid.

6. Suppose Students A and B stand 50 m from Student C. Students B and C each hold a copper cup, and the two cups are attached by a copper wire measuring 50 m. If Student A shouts at Student C and Student B shouts into the copper cup, who will Student C hear first?

    F. Student C will hear Student A first.

    G. Student C will hear Student B first.

    H. Student C will hear Student A and Student B at the same time.

    J. Student C will hear Student A but will not hear Student B.

7. Suppose that another group of students attempts to replicate the results of Experiment 1. This group of students forgets to plug the cylindrical tank. Were the average velocities higher in the original or in the replicated Experiment 1?

    A. In the original, because the sound traveled through liquid and no gas, and the velocity of sound is higher in liquid than in gas.

    B. In the original, because the sound traveled through liquid and some gas, and the velocity of sound is lower in liquid than in gas.

    C. In the replication, because the sound traveled through liquid and no gas, and the velocity of sound is higher in liquid than in gas.

    D. In the replication, because the sound traveled through liquid and some gas, and the velocity of sound is lower in liquid than in gas.

GO ON TO THE NEXT PAGE.

Passage II

Researchers studied heavy metals in the water, soil, and root systems of mangrove forests to determine if the metals posed ecological risks.

Study 1

The mangrove forests bordered a *mud flat*, which is an area of seafloor left uncovered at low tide. Researchers used the unvegetated mud flat as a control. The mangrove forest was divided into two habitats, each dominated by one species of mangrove: white or black (see Diagram 1). For each habitat, researchers established three sample locations where they collected 15 overlying water samples in acid-washed plastic jars, 15 soil sediment samples in acid-washed plastic pipes, 12 seedling samples, and 15 root samples by plastic scraper. The samples were filtered and tested to determine the pH and conductivity of the overlying water, the soil sediment, and the root systems (see Table 1).

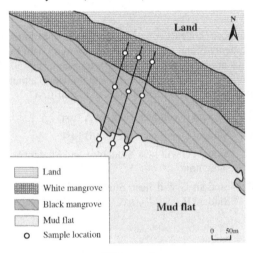

Land
White mangrove
Black mangrove
Mud flat
o   Sample location

Diagram 1

Table 1			
Mangrove habitat	White	Black	Mud flat
Overlying water			
pH	8.21	7.98	8.25
Conductivity (S/m)	1.66	1.44	1.64
Soil sediment			
pH	6.55	6.86	7.06
Conductivity (S/m)	0.51	0.33	0.36
Root system			
pH	6.95	7.18	n/a
Conductivity (S/m)	0.70	0.46	n/a

Note: S/m = Siemens/meter = $kg^{-1}m^{-3}s^3A^2$

Study 2

The same samples tested in Study 1 were tested using mass spectroscopy to determine the concentrations of five heavy metals: chromium (Cr), nickel (Ni), copper (Cu), arsenic (As), and cadmium (Cd). The concentrations (in μg/g) for each heavy metal in each habitat are shown in Table 2.

Table 2			
Mangrove habitat	White	Black	Mud flat
Overlying water			
Cr	20	10	10
Ni	11	10	9
Cu	10	11	9
As	10	14	4
Cd	0.01	0.02	0.05
Soil sediment			
Cr	90	43	74
Ni	52	24	38
Cu	102	52	74
As	98	76	52
Cd	0.96	0.88	0.67
Root system			
Cr	60	50	n/a
Ni	23	18	n/a
Cu	25	51	n/a
As	36	29	n/a
Cd	0.32	0.18	n/a

Study 3

The researchers collected the following data to determine whether the concentrations of heavy metals (in μg/g) in the mangrove forests would have adverse effects on the organisms in each habitat (see Table 3). The *probable effect level* is the concentration above which adverse effects on organisms are frequently observed.

Table 3					
	Cr	Ni	Cu	As	Cd
Background Level	38.80	19.83	9.98	5.90	0.03
Probable Effect Level	111	48.60	149	33	4.98

Data adapted from Ruili Li et al, "Distribution, Fraction, and Ecological Assessment of Heavy Metals in Sediment-Plant System in Mangrove Forest, South China Sea." ©2016 by PLoS One. 10.1371/journal.pone.0147308

GO ON TO THE NEXT PAGE.

8. Which of the following mangrove habitats had the most alkaline pH, and in which part of the habitat was that pH found?

    F. Black; root system
    G. White; overlying water
    H. White; soil sediment
    J. Mud flat; overlying water

9. Why was there no data for the mud flat's root system?

    A. There was no vegetation in the mud flat.
    B. There were many different types of plants in the mud flat.
    C. There were no samples of any kind taken in the mud flat.
    D. There was animal activity in the mud flat.

10. According to Study 2, as the distance between mangrove forests and the mud flat increased, the concentration of arsenic in the soil sediment:

    F. increased only.
    G. decreased only.
    H. increased, then decreased.
    J. decreased, then increased.

11. Researchers performed Study 2 on a new sample of soil sediment. If the heavy metal profile, in μg/g, for the samples are given in the table below, from which mangrove habitat did the researchers most likely take their sample?

Cr	50
Ni	25
Cu	51
As	76
Cd	0.88

    A. Land
    B. Mud flat
    C. Black mangrove
    D. White mangrove

12. Why did the researchers wash their sample collection equipment with acid?

    F. To lower the pH of the samples
    G. To attract heavy metals to the equipment
    H. To destroy bacteria in the soil and water
    J. To ensure no contaminants were introduced to the sample

13. It was discovered that the researchers who performed the mass spectroscopy used contaminated sample containers that released trace levels of copper into the samples. Which of the following measures would correct this error?

    A. Calculate the copper concentration due to the contaminated sample containers and add it to the copper concentrations of the samples.
    B. Calculate the copper concentration due to the contaminated sample containers and subtract it from the copper concentrations of the samples.
    C. Repeat the experiment, using the contaminated samples but different sampling equipment.
    D. Repeat the experiment, using the contaminated sampling equipment but different samples.

14. The roots of the white mangrove are ground into a powder and used as an oral medicine. Based on Studies 2 and 3, is it safe to use the roots of the white mangroves found in this region as a medicine?

    F. Yes; the concentration of arsenic found in the root systems of the white mangroves did not exceed its probable effect level.
    G. Yes; all of the concentrations of heavy metals found in the root systems of the white mangroves did not exceed their probable effect levels.
    H. No; the concentration of arsenic found in the root systems of the white mangroves exceeded its probable effect level.
    J. No; all of the concentrations of heavy metals found in the root systems of the white mangroves exceeded their probable effect levels.

GO ON TO THE NEXT PAGE.

Passage III

A *satellite* is any object that orbits another object in space. Over 2,000 human-made satellites are now orbiting Earth.

All satellites orbit in an *ellipse*—an elongated circle with two focal points—and they orbit faster when they are closer to the object they are orbiting (see Figure 1). The object orbited by the satellite is usually at one of the two focal points of the satellite's elliptical orbit.

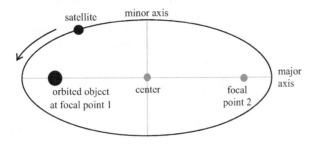

Figure 1

The *orbital period* is the time it takes the satellite to complete one orbit. The *semi-major axis* is half the length of the *major axis*, which is the distance across the long side of the elliptical orbit. For any two satellites, Kepler's Third Law states that the relationship between the orbital period (P) in years and the length of the semi-major axis (A) in Astronomical Units (AU) is constant according to the following equation:

$$\left(\frac{P_1}{P_2}\right)^2 = \left(\frac{A_1}{A_2}\right)^3$$

Students categorized six known satellites in terms of mass, average orbital height, and orbital period (see Table 1).

Table 1			
Satellite	Mass (kg)	Height (AU)	Period (yr)
ISS	4.20×10^5	2.74×10^{-6}	1.71×10^{-4}
GPS	1.47×10^3	1.35×10^{-4}	1.37×10^{-3}
Hubble	1.11×10^4	3.74×10^{-6}	1.81×10^{-4}
Spektr-R	3.60×10^3	2.01×10^{-3}	2.43×10^{-2}
Glonass-M	1.48×10^3	1.28×10^{-4}	1.28×10^{-3}

Note: 1 AU = 1.50×10^8 km.

15. According to Table 1, which of the following satellites has the greatest mass?

    A. ISS
    B. GPS
    C. Hubble
    D. Spektr-R

16. Satellites are classified in three categories based on their average orbital height: Low Earth Orbit, less than 1.34×10^{-5} AU; Medium Earth Orbit, between 1.34×10^{-5} and 5.35×10^{-4} AU; and High Earth Orbit, greater than 5.35×10^{-4} AU. Which of the following satellites would be classified as High Earth Orbit?

    F. GPS
    G. Spektr-R
    H. Glonass-M
    J. Hubble

17. According to Table 1, what is the relationship between satellite mass and orbital period?

    A. As satellite mass increases, orbital period increases.
    B. As satellite mass increases, orbital period decreases.
    C. As satellite mass increases, orbital period increases then decreases.
    D. There is no relationship between satellite mass and orbital period.

18. Suppose the students want to use Table 1 to test Kepler's Third Law. Based on the given equation and Table 1, is their approach correct?

    F. Yes; the given equation only requires the mass, which is given in Table 1.
    G. Yes; the given equation requires the period and the mass, both of which are given in Table 1.
    H. No; the given equation requires the period and the semi-major axis, and only the period is given in Table 1.
    J. No; the given equation requires the period and the height, and only the height is given in Table 1.

GO ON TO THE NEXT PAGE.

19. Suppose the orbit of the moon is analogous to Figure 1, with the moon at the position of the satellite and Earth at focal point 1. The *apogee* is the point of the moon's orbit when it is farthest from Earth. According to Figure 1, the moon's apogee is located:

   A. at the left of the ellipse along the major axis.

   B. at the right of the ellipse along the major axis.

   C. at the top of the ellipse along the minor axis.

   D. at the bottom of the ellipse along the minor axis.

20. If the moon has an average orbital period of 7.40×10^{-2} years, approximately how many times greater is the orbital period of the moon than the orbital period of the satellite with the longest orbital period in Table 1?

   F.   3

   G.   30

   H.   300

   J.   3,000

GO ON TO THE NEXT PAGE.

Passage IV

Heat tolerance is a highly desirable trait in crop plants. Researchers attempted to improve the heat tolerance of cotton and tobacco plants by introducing the heat shock protein 101 (*AtHSP101*) from the plant species *Arabidopsis thaliana*.

Study 1

Pollen are small grains that carry reproductive material from one plant to another. High temperatures inhibit the ability of tobacco pollen to produce a pollen tube, which transfers reproductive material. Researchers created 3 strains of tobacco containing *AtHSP101* in different locations in the genome (G1, G2, and G3). For comparison, they also used 2 strains of tobacco that did not contain *AtHSP101* (N1 and N2). The pollen tubes were grown from pollen grains in glass dishes filled with water. The researchers measured the lengths of the pollen tubes generated by the 5 different tobacco strains at a normal growing temperature (30°C) and at a higher temperature (60°C). The average tube lengths are shown in Figure 1.

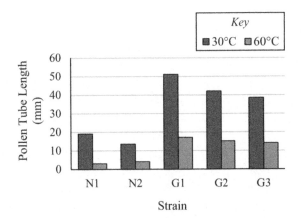

Figure 1

Study 2

Cotton plants produce *bolls*, rounded capsules that, upon opening, release cotton seeds. The researchers studied boll and seed production under high temperatures by conducting a field experiment using 1 unaltered strain of cotton plants (S1) and 1 strain of cotton plants that had the *AtHSP101* gene (S2). The researchers grew 20 plants from each strain and measured the number of bolls per plant, the number of open bolls per plant, the number of seeds per open boll, and the number of closed bolls per plant. The data were collected from Day 1 to Day 46. Daily high and low temperatures over this period are shown in Figure 2. Average boll and seed production data from each strain are shown in Table 1.

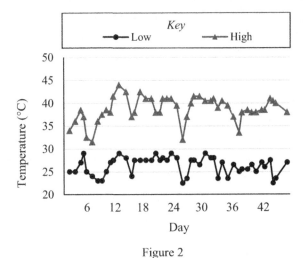

Figure 2

Table 1				
Plant Strain	Bolls/ plant	Open bolls/plant	Seeds/open boll	Closed bolls/plant
S1	22.4	11.75	18.09	10.65
S2	30.35	12.95	18.54	17.4

GO ON TO THE NEXT PAGE.

Practice Tests

21. According to Figure 2, from Day 1 to Day 46, the daily high temperature:

    A. remained the same.

    B. decreased only.

    C. increased only.

    D. fluctuated, but with no clear trend.

22. According to Figure 1, which of the following correctly orders the 5 pollen strains from shortest average pollen tube at 30°C to longest average pollen tube at 30°C?

    F. G1, G2, G3, N1, N2

    G. N2, N1, G3, G2, G1

    H. N1, N2, G3, G2, G1

    J. N1, G1, N2, G2, G3

23. In Study 2, the researchers measured the number of seeds produced by each open boll because:

    A. seeds produce energy for the plant by absorbing sunlight.

    B. seeds absorb water for the plant.

    C. seeds allow the plant to reproduce.

    D. seeds protect the plant from predation.

24. Suppose that, while observing the pollen grains in Study 1, one of the researchers notices that the water levels in the 60°C growth dishes are significantly lower than those in the 30°C growth dishes. In order to ensure that both groups of pollen grains have equal water availability, the best solution would be to:

    F. increase the temperature of the 60°C growth dishes.

    G. remove all water from both sets of dishes.

    H. cover the dishes so that the water cannot evaporate.

    J. move the pollen grains from the 60°C growth dishes into the 30°C growth dishes and vice versa.

25. If the researchers from Study 1 had grown pollen grains at a third temperature of 80°C, the average pollen tube length of the G1 strain would most likely have been:

    A. less than 20 mm.

    B. between 20 mm and 40 mm.

    C. between 40 mm and 50 mm.

    D. greater than 50 mm.

26. One researcher hypothesizes that S2 cotton plants grown in an environment with an average daily high temperature between 35°C and 40°C will, on average, produce fewer than 38 bolls. Do the data from Study 2 support this hypothesis?

    F. Yes, because the average daily high temperature from Study 2 fell between 35°C and 40°C.

    G. Yes, because the S2 plants produced more than 38 bolls on average.

    H. No, because the average daily high temperature from Study 2 fell between 35°C and 40°C.

    J. No, because the S2 plants produced more than 38 bolls on average.

27. The *reproductive efficiency* of a cotton plant is defined as the total number of seeds released by a cotton plant divided by the number of bolls produced. The researchers conclude that S2 plants have a lower average reproductive efficiency than S1 plants. Which of the following could explain this observation?

    A. On average, S2 plants produced more bolls that did not open.

    B. S2 plants produced fewer seeds per open boll than S1 plants.

    C. The pollen grains produced by S2 plants produced longer pollen tubes than pollen grains produced by S1 plants.

    D. On average, S2 plants produced fewer bolls.

GO ON TO THE NEXT PAGE.

Passage V

Denaturation is a process by which the two strands of a DNA molecule separate, destroying the structure of the DNA and rendering it functionless. Scientists studied the stability of DNA molecules in the organic solvent dimethylformamide (DMF), which is used in laboratories to dissolve DNA.

First, the scientists measured the amount of UV light absorbed by DNA dissolved in various concentrations of DMF. As DNA becomes less stable and begins to denature, it absorbs more UV light. The scientists tested the UV absorbance of both a linear DNA segment and a circular DNA segment at 25°C. The results are shown in Figure 1.

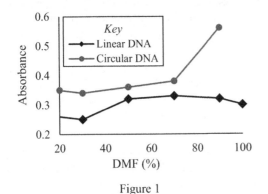

Figure 1

Next, the scientists used UV absorbance to investigate the behavior of circular DNA in DMF solvent at various temperatures. Typically, as temperature increases, DNA stability decreases, and eventually denatures. The scientists measured the UV absorbance of circular DNA in 3 different concentrations of DMF solvent at temperatures between 20°C and 65°C. The results are shown in Figure 2.

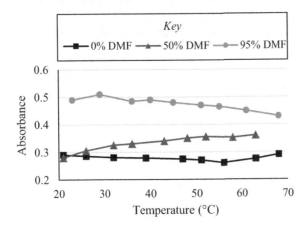

Figure 2

28. According to Figure 1, in which solution did linear DNA have the lowest UV absorbance?

F. 10% DMF

G. 20% DMF

H. 30% DMF

J. 40% DMF

29. According to Figure 1, as the concentration of DMF increased from 30% to 90%, the UV absorbance of circular DNA:

A. decreased only.

B. increased only.

C. increased, then decreased.

D. decreased, then increased.

30. Based on Figure 2, if the scientists had measured the UV absorbance of circular DNA in 95% DMF at 75°C, the absorbance would most likely have been:

F. lower than 0.2.

G. between 0.2 and 0.35.

H. between 0.35 and 0.5.

J. greater than 0.5.

31. A scientist hypothesizes that when concentrations of DMF increase, the UV absorbance of both types of DNA increases as well. Do the data in Figure 1 support this hypothesis?

A. Yes, because the UV absorbance of circular DNA increases with increasing DMF concentration.

B. Yes, because the UV absorbance of linear DNA does not have a clear relationship with DMF concentration.

C. No, because the UV absorbance of circular DNA increases with increasing DMF concentration.

D. No, because the UV absorbance of linear DNA does not have a clear relationship with DMF concentration.

GO ON TO THE NEXT PAGE.

32. The backbone of the DNA molecule is negatively charged. If a DNA molecule were placed between a negatively charged surface and a positively charged surface, the molecule would:

    F. remain stationary between the two surfaces.

    G. move toward the negatively charged surface.

    H. move toward the positively charged surface.

    J. move erratically, with no particular direction.

33. DNA is considered to be completely denatured if its UV absorbance is greater than 0.4. According to Figure 1 and Figure 2, in which of the following situations would a DNA segment NOT be completely denatured?

    A. Circular DNA in 85% DMF at 25°C

    B. Circular DNA in 95% DMF at 70°C

    C. Circular DNA in 95% DMF at 20°C

    D. Circular DNA in 25% DMF at 25°C

GO ON TO THE NEXT PAGE.

Passage VI

Atoms are a unit of matter, and combinations of atoms form molecules such as water (H_2O) and carbon dioxide (CO_2). Because atoms are very small, it can be difficult to study their structure. Three theories of atomic structure are outlined below.

Theory 1

Atoms are the smallest units of matter. Matter is composed of elements, each of which comprises atoms of a single, unique type. Atoms are indivisible, which means that there are no smaller subunits that compose an atom. Atoms cannot be destroyed or created, but they can be combined in different whole-number ratios to form molecules. Because atoms are indivisible, mass is always conserved during a chemical reaction. All atoms have an overall, uniformly distributed neutral electric charge.

Theory 2

Atoms are divisible. They consist of small, negatively charged particles called *electrons*, which are spread throughout a cloud of positive charge. The electrons are held within the cloud because of the attraction between positive and negative charges. The electrons are free to float within the cloud, but they cannot escape it. As electrons float farther from the center of the atom, the attractive force acting on them increases linearly. Overall, atoms have a neutral charge due to equal positive and negative charges from the cloud and the electrons, respectively.

Theory 3

Atoms are divisible. At the center of the atom lies the *nucleus*, a small, dense cluster of positively charged particles called *protons* and neutral particles called *neutrons*. The attractive forces between the negatively charged electrons and positively charged protons keep the atom together. Electrons are constrained to particular orbits around the nucleus, though they can jump between orbits. As electrons jump to orbits farther from the nucleus, the attractive force acting on them decreases in steps. Protons and electrons have equal and opposite charges, so an atom with an overall neutral charge has equal numbers of protons and electrons. Atoms can gain or lose electrons, thereby becoming negatively or positively charged.

34. According to Theory 3, which of the following conditions are *possible*?

    I. The number of protons in an atom equals the number of electrons.

    II. The number of protons in an atom is greater than the number of electrons.

    III. The number of protons in an atom is less than the number of electrons.

    F. I only
    G. II only
    H. II and III
    J. I, II, and III

35. A researcher discovers a particle that is smaller than the smallest known atom. Which of the 3 theories is contradicted by this evidence?

    A. Theory 1
    B. Theory 2
    C. Theory 3
    D. None of the theories are contradicted by the evidence.

36. In an experiment, positively charged particles were fired at a thin sheet of atoms. Most of the particles passed through the sheet, but some bounced off in different directions. A proponent of Theory 3 would most likely explain this phenomenon by arguing that:

    F. the positively charged particles usually pass through the nucleus. The occasional deflections occur when the particles are repelled by an electron.

    G. the positively charged particles usually pass through the space around the nucleus. The occasional deflections occur when the particles are repelled by the nucleus.

    H. the positively charged particles usually pass through the cloud of positive charge. The occasional deflections occur when the particles are repelled by free-floating electrons.

    J. the positively charged particles usually pass between atoms. The occasional deflections occur when the particles hit an indivisible atom.

GO ON TO THE NEXT PAGE.

37. According to Theory 2 and Theory 3, which of the following pairs of graphs could represent the relationship between an electron's distance from the center of the atom and the attractive force acting upon that electron?

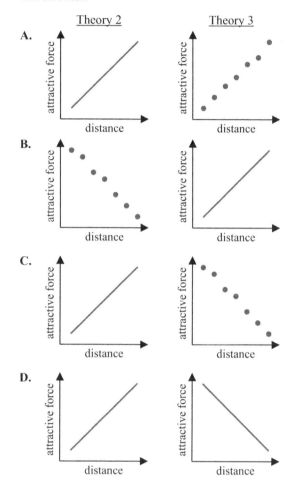

38. With which of the following statements would a proponent of Theory 2 be LEAST likely to agree?

   F. An atom's stability depends on the attractive force between positive and negative charges.

   G. An atom's negative charge exists in small pockets dispersed throughout a larger space.

   H. An atom's positive charge exists in a dispersed cloud.

   J. An atom can gain or lose electrons, thus altering its overall charge.

39. A researcher discovers that the distribution of charge throughout an atom is not uniform. How does this evidence affect the strength of the 3 theories?

	Theory 1	Theory 2	Theory 3
A.	strengthen	strengthen	strengthen
B.	strengthen	weaken	weaken
C.	weaken	strengthen	strengthen
D.	weaken	weaken	weaken

40. Which of the following best describes the forces between positively charged particles and negatively charged particles?

   F. Positive particles and negative particles are attracted to each other due to electrostatic forces.

   G. Positive particles and negative particles are attracted to each other due to frictional forces.

   H. Positive particles and negative particles are repelled from each other due to gravitational forces.

   J. Positive particles and negative particles are repelled from each other due to electrostatic forces.

END OF TEST 4.

STOP! DO NOT TURN THE PAGE UNTIL YOU ARE TOLD TO DO SO.

DO NOT RETURN TO THE PREVIOUS TEST.

Writing Test
40 Minutes—1 Prompt

Directions: This is a test of your writing ability. You'll have 40 minutes to read the prompt, plan your response, and write your essay. Before you begin, read all of the material in this test section carefully and make sure you understand what is being asked of you.

You should write your essay on the lined pages included in your answer sheet. Only your writing on those pages will be scored. Your work on these pages will not be scored.

Your essay will be graded based on the evidence it provides and your ability to:

- analyze and evaluate different perspectives on complicated issues
- express and develop your own perspective on the issue
- explain and support your arguments with logical reasoning and detailed examples
- clearly and logically organize your ideas in an essay
- effectively communicate your point of view in English

Stop writing and put down your pencil as soon as time is called.

DO NOT BEGIN THE WRITING TEST UNTIL YOU ARE TOLD TO DO SO.

How Much Homework?

A recent study from Spain suggested that the optimal amount of homework for teenagers was about one hour per day. Statistics collected in the United States show that most American high schoolers also do about an hour of homework every day, if not more. Proponents of more homework hope that students will be better prepared for the workloads of postsecondary programs. Critics of assigning more homework cite the many ways teenagers might use more free time: work, volunteering, extracurricular activities, hobbies, or even just relaxing with their friends. Should high schools be assigning more homework, or less?

Read and carefully consider these perspectives. Each suggests a particular way of thinking about the amount of homework assigned by high schools.

Perspective 1	**Perspective 2**	**Perspective 3**
We must prepare young people for the amounts of homework they'll encounter in college or university. High schools should assign more homework.	The amount of homework assigned is just right. Students who do about an hour of homework a day will be prepared for higher education. However, they'll also have ample free time to use as they see fit.	Adolescence is a time of personal growth and self-discovery, but high schoolers will miss out on this if they have too much homework. Schools should assign less homework, making up for any gaps by prioritizing more rigorous in-class work.

Essay Task

Write a unified, coherent essay in which you evaluate multiple perspectives on the amount of homework assigned by high schools. In your essay, be sure to:

- analyze and evaluate the perspectives given
- state and develop your own perspective on the issue
- explain the relationship between your perspective and those given

Your perspective may be in full agreement with any of the others, in partial agreement, or wholly different. Whatever the case, support your ideas with logical reasoning and detailed, persuasive examples.

Planning Your Essay

Your work on these prewriting pages will not be scored.

Use the space below and on the back cover to generate ideas and plan your essay. You may wish to consider the following as you think critically about the task:

Strengths and weaknesses of the three given perspectives

- What insights do they offer, and what do they fail to consider?
- Why might they be persuasive to others, or why might they fail to persuade?

Your own knowledge, experience, and values

- What is your perspective on this issue, and what are its strengths and weaknesses?
- How will you support your perspective in your essay?

Note

- Your practice Writing Test includes scratch paper and four lined sheets for your essay.
- Your official ACT exam will include a test booklet with space for planning and four lined sheets to write your essay.
- Review Answers and Scoring for instructions on how to grade your exam.

Practice Test 2

The ACT

This practice test contains tests in English, Math, Reading, and Science. These tests measure skills and abilities related to high school course work and college preparedness. **You can use a calculator on the math test only.**

The questions in each test are numbered, and the suggested answers for each question are lettered. On the answer sheet, the rows are numbered to match the questions, and the circles in each row are lettered to correspond to the suggested answers.

For each question, choose the best answer and fill in the corresponding circle on your answer document. Use a soft lead pencil and make your marks heavy and black. **Do not use a ballpoint pen.**

Fill in only one answer to each question. If you change your mind about an answer, completely erase your first mark before filling in your new answer. For each question, make certain that you mark in the row of ovals with the same number as the question.

Only responses marked on your answer sheet will be scored. Your score on each test will be based only on the number of questions you answer correctly during the time allowed for that test. You will NOT be penalized for guessing. **Even if you are unsure about an answer, you should make a guess.**

You may work on each test ONLY when your proctor tells you to do so. If you complete a test before the end of your allotted time, use the extra minutes to check your work on that section only. Do NOT use the time to work on another section. Doing this will disqualify your scores.

Put down your pencil immediately when time is called at the end of each test. You are not allowed to continue answering questions after the allotted time has run out. This includes marking answers on your answer sheet that you previously noted in your test booklet.

You are not allowed to fold or tear the pages of your test booklet.

Do Not Open This Booklet Until You Are Told to Do So.

NAME: _____

DATE: _____

TEST 1

1 Ⓐ Ⓑ Ⓒ Ⓓ	14 Ⓕ Ⓖ Ⓗ Ⓙ	27 Ⓐ Ⓑ Ⓒ Ⓓ	40 Ⓕ Ⓖ Ⓗ Ⓙ	53 Ⓐ Ⓑ Ⓒ Ⓓ	66 Ⓕ Ⓖ Ⓗ Ⓙ
2 Ⓕ Ⓖ Ⓗ Ⓙ	15 Ⓐ Ⓑ Ⓒ Ⓓ	28 Ⓕ Ⓖ Ⓗ Ⓙ	41 Ⓐ Ⓑ Ⓒ Ⓓ	54 Ⓕ Ⓖ Ⓗ Ⓙ	67 Ⓐ Ⓑ Ⓒ Ⓓ
3 Ⓐ Ⓑ Ⓒ Ⓓ	16 Ⓕ Ⓖ Ⓗ Ⓙ	29 Ⓐ Ⓑ Ⓒ Ⓓ	42 Ⓕ Ⓖ Ⓗ Ⓙ	55 Ⓐ Ⓑ Ⓒ Ⓓ	68 Ⓕ Ⓖ Ⓗ Ⓙ
4 Ⓕ Ⓖ Ⓗ Ⓙ	17 Ⓐ Ⓑ Ⓒ Ⓓ	30 Ⓕ Ⓖ Ⓗ Ⓙ	43 Ⓐ Ⓑ Ⓒ Ⓓ	56 Ⓕ Ⓖ Ⓗ Ⓙ	69 Ⓐ Ⓑ Ⓒ Ⓓ
5 Ⓐ Ⓑ Ⓒ Ⓓ	18 Ⓕ Ⓖ Ⓗ Ⓙ	31 Ⓐ Ⓑ Ⓒ Ⓓ	44 Ⓕ Ⓖ Ⓗ Ⓙ	57 Ⓐ Ⓑ Ⓒ Ⓓ	70 Ⓕ Ⓖ Ⓗ Ⓙ
6 Ⓕ Ⓖ Ⓗ Ⓙ	19 Ⓐ Ⓑ Ⓒ Ⓓ	32 Ⓕ Ⓖ Ⓗ Ⓙ	45 Ⓐ Ⓑ Ⓒ Ⓓ	58 Ⓕ Ⓖ Ⓗ Ⓙ	71 Ⓐ Ⓑ Ⓒ Ⓓ
7 Ⓐ Ⓑ Ⓒ Ⓓ	20 Ⓕ Ⓖ Ⓗ Ⓙ	33 Ⓐ Ⓑ Ⓒ Ⓓ	46 Ⓕ Ⓖ Ⓗ Ⓙ	59 Ⓐ Ⓑ Ⓒ Ⓓ	72 Ⓕ Ⓖ Ⓗ Ⓙ
8 Ⓕ Ⓖ Ⓗ Ⓙ	21 Ⓐ Ⓑ Ⓒ Ⓓ	34 Ⓕ Ⓖ Ⓗ Ⓙ	47 Ⓐ Ⓑ Ⓒ Ⓓ	60 Ⓕ Ⓖ Ⓗ Ⓙ	73 Ⓐ Ⓑ Ⓒ Ⓓ
9 Ⓐ Ⓑ Ⓒ Ⓓ	22 Ⓕ Ⓖ Ⓗ Ⓙ	35 Ⓐ Ⓑ Ⓒ Ⓓ	48 Ⓕ Ⓖ Ⓗ Ⓙ	61 Ⓐ Ⓑ Ⓒ Ⓓ	74 Ⓕ Ⓖ Ⓗ Ⓙ
10 Ⓕ Ⓖ Ⓗ Ⓙ	23 Ⓐ Ⓑ Ⓒ Ⓓ	36 Ⓕ Ⓖ Ⓗ Ⓙ	49 Ⓐ Ⓑ Ⓒ Ⓓ	62 Ⓕ Ⓖ Ⓗ Ⓙ	75 Ⓐ Ⓑ Ⓒ Ⓓ
11 Ⓐ Ⓑ Ⓒ Ⓓ	24 Ⓕ Ⓖ Ⓗ Ⓙ	37 Ⓐ Ⓑ Ⓒ Ⓓ	50 Ⓕ Ⓖ Ⓗ Ⓙ	63 Ⓐ Ⓑ Ⓒ Ⓓ	
12 Ⓕ Ⓖ Ⓗ Ⓙ	25 Ⓐ Ⓑ Ⓒ Ⓓ	38 Ⓕ Ⓖ Ⓗ Ⓙ	51 Ⓐ Ⓑ Ⓒ Ⓓ	64 Ⓕ Ⓖ Ⓗ Ⓙ	
13 Ⓐ Ⓑ Ⓒ Ⓓ	26 Ⓕ Ⓖ Ⓗ Ⓙ	39 Ⓐ Ⓑ Ⓒ Ⓓ	52 Ⓕ Ⓖ Ⓗ Ⓙ	65 Ⓐ Ⓑ Ⓒ Ⓓ	

TEST 2

1 Ⓐ Ⓑ Ⓒ Ⓓ Ⓔ	11 Ⓐ Ⓑ Ⓒ Ⓓ Ⓔ	21 Ⓐ Ⓑ Ⓒ Ⓓ Ⓔ	31 Ⓐ Ⓑ Ⓒ Ⓓ Ⓔ	41 Ⓐ Ⓑ Ⓒ Ⓓ Ⓔ	51 Ⓐ Ⓑ Ⓒ Ⓓ Ⓔ
2 Ⓕ Ⓖ Ⓗ Ⓙ Ⓚ	12 Ⓕ Ⓖ Ⓗ Ⓙ Ⓚ	22 Ⓕ Ⓖ Ⓗ Ⓙ Ⓚ	32 Ⓕ Ⓖ Ⓗ Ⓙ Ⓚ	42 Ⓕ Ⓖ Ⓗ Ⓙ Ⓚ	52 Ⓕ Ⓖ Ⓗ Ⓙ Ⓚ
3 Ⓐ Ⓑ Ⓒ Ⓓ Ⓔ	13 Ⓐ Ⓑ Ⓒ Ⓓ Ⓔ	23 Ⓐ Ⓑ Ⓒ Ⓓ Ⓔ	33 Ⓐ Ⓑ Ⓒ Ⓓ Ⓔ	43 Ⓐ Ⓑ Ⓒ Ⓓ Ⓔ	53 Ⓐ Ⓑ Ⓒ Ⓓ Ⓔ
4 Ⓕ Ⓖ Ⓗ Ⓙ Ⓚ	14 Ⓕ Ⓖ Ⓗ Ⓙ Ⓚ	24 Ⓕ Ⓖ Ⓗ Ⓙ Ⓚ	34 Ⓕ Ⓖ Ⓗ Ⓙ Ⓚ	44 Ⓕ Ⓖ Ⓗ Ⓙ Ⓚ	54 Ⓕ Ⓖ Ⓗ Ⓙ Ⓚ
5 Ⓐ Ⓑ Ⓒ Ⓓ Ⓔ	15 Ⓐ Ⓑ Ⓒ Ⓓ Ⓔ	25 Ⓐ Ⓑ Ⓒ Ⓓ Ⓔ	35 Ⓐ Ⓑ Ⓒ Ⓓ Ⓔ	45 Ⓐ Ⓑ Ⓒ Ⓓ Ⓔ	55 Ⓐ Ⓑ Ⓒ Ⓓ Ⓔ
6 Ⓕ Ⓖ Ⓗ Ⓙ Ⓚ	16 Ⓕ Ⓖ Ⓗ Ⓙ Ⓚ	26 Ⓕ Ⓖ Ⓗ Ⓙ Ⓚ	36 Ⓕ Ⓖ Ⓗ Ⓙ Ⓚ	46 Ⓕ Ⓖ Ⓗ Ⓙ Ⓚ	56 Ⓕ Ⓖ Ⓗ Ⓙ Ⓚ
7 Ⓐ Ⓑ Ⓒ Ⓓ Ⓔ	17 Ⓐ Ⓑ Ⓒ Ⓓ Ⓔ	27 Ⓐ Ⓑ Ⓒ Ⓓ Ⓔ	37 Ⓐ Ⓑ Ⓒ Ⓓ Ⓔ	47 Ⓐ Ⓑ Ⓒ Ⓓ Ⓔ	57 Ⓐ Ⓑ Ⓒ Ⓓ Ⓔ
8 Ⓕ Ⓖ Ⓗ Ⓙ Ⓚ	18 Ⓕ Ⓖ Ⓗ Ⓙ Ⓚ	28 Ⓕ Ⓖ Ⓗ Ⓙ Ⓚ	38 Ⓕ Ⓖ Ⓗ Ⓙ Ⓚ	48 Ⓕ Ⓖ Ⓗ Ⓙ Ⓚ	58 Ⓕ Ⓖ Ⓗ Ⓙ Ⓚ
9 Ⓐ Ⓑ Ⓒ Ⓓ Ⓔ	19 Ⓐ Ⓑ Ⓒ Ⓓ Ⓔ	29 Ⓐ Ⓑ Ⓒ Ⓓ Ⓔ	39 Ⓐ Ⓑ Ⓒ Ⓓ Ⓔ	49 Ⓐ Ⓑ Ⓒ Ⓓ Ⓔ	59 Ⓐ Ⓑ Ⓒ Ⓓ Ⓔ
10 Ⓕ Ⓖ Ⓗ Ⓙ Ⓚ	20 Ⓕ Ⓖ Ⓗ Ⓙ Ⓚ	30 Ⓕ Ⓖ Ⓗ Ⓙ Ⓚ	40 Ⓕ Ⓖ Ⓗ Ⓙ Ⓚ	50 Ⓕ Ⓖ Ⓗ Ⓙ Ⓚ	60 Ⓕ Ⓖ Ⓗ Ⓙ Ⓚ

TEST 3

1 Ⓐ Ⓑ Ⓒ Ⓓ	8 Ⓕ Ⓖ Ⓗ Ⓙ	15 Ⓐ Ⓑ Ⓒ Ⓓ	22 Ⓕ Ⓖ Ⓗ Ⓙ	29 Ⓐ Ⓑ Ⓒ Ⓓ	36 Ⓕ Ⓖ Ⓗ Ⓙ
2 Ⓕ Ⓖ Ⓗ Ⓙ	9 Ⓐ Ⓑ Ⓒ Ⓓ	16 Ⓕ Ⓖ Ⓗ Ⓙ	23 Ⓐ Ⓑ Ⓒ Ⓓ	30 Ⓕ Ⓖ Ⓗ Ⓙ	37 Ⓐ Ⓑ Ⓒ Ⓓ
3 Ⓐ Ⓑ Ⓒ Ⓓ	10 Ⓕ Ⓖ Ⓗ Ⓙ	17 Ⓐ Ⓑ Ⓒ Ⓓ	24 Ⓕ Ⓖ Ⓗ Ⓙ	31 Ⓐ Ⓑ Ⓒ Ⓓ	38 Ⓕ Ⓖ Ⓗ Ⓙ
4 Ⓕ Ⓖ Ⓗ Ⓙ	11 Ⓐ Ⓑ Ⓒ Ⓓ	18 Ⓕ Ⓖ Ⓗ Ⓙ	25 Ⓐ Ⓑ Ⓒ Ⓓ	32 Ⓕ Ⓖ Ⓗ Ⓙ	39 Ⓐ Ⓑ Ⓒ Ⓓ
5 Ⓐ Ⓑ Ⓒ Ⓓ	12 Ⓕ Ⓖ Ⓗ Ⓙ	19 Ⓐ Ⓑ Ⓒ Ⓓ	26 Ⓕ Ⓖ Ⓗ Ⓙ	33 Ⓐ Ⓑ Ⓒ Ⓓ	40 Ⓕ Ⓖ Ⓗ Ⓙ
6 Ⓕ Ⓖ Ⓗ Ⓙ	13 Ⓐ Ⓑ Ⓒ Ⓓ	20 Ⓕ Ⓖ Ⓗ Ⓙ	27 Ⓐ Ⓑ Ⓒ Ⓓ	34 Ⓕ Ⓖ Ⓗ Ⓙ	
7 Ⓐ Ⓑ Ⓒ Ⓓ	14 Ⓕ Ⓖ Ⓗ Ⓙ	21 Ⓐ Ⓑ Ⓒ Ⓓ	28 Ⓕ Ⓖ Ⓗ Ⓙ	35 Ⓐ Ⓑ Ⓒ Ⓓ	

TEST 4

1 Ⓐ Ⓑ Ⓒ Ⓓ	8 Ⓕ Ⓖ Ⓗ Ⓙ	15 Ⓐ Ⓑ Ⓒ Ⓓ	22 Ⓕ Ⓖ Ⓗ Ⓙ	29 Ⓐ Ⓑ Ⓒ Ⓓ	36 Ⓕ Ⓖ Ⓗ Ⓙ
2 Ⓕ Ⓖ Ⓗ Ⓙ	9 Ⓐ Ⓑ Ⓒ Ⓓ	16 Ⓕ Ⓖ Ⓗ Ⓙ	23 Ⓐ Ⓑ Ⓒ Ⓓ	30 Ⓕ Ⓖ Ⓗ Ⓙ	37 Ⓐ Ⓑ Ⓒ Ⓓ
3 Ⓐ Ⓑ Ⓒ Ⓓ	10 Ⓕ Ⓖ Ⓗ Ⓙ	17 Ⓐ Ⓑ Ⓒ Ⓓ	24 Ⓕ Ⓖ Ⓗ Ⓙ	31 Ⓐ Ⓑ Ⓒ Ⓓ	38 Ⓕ Ⓖ Ⓗ Ⓙ
4 Ⓕ Ⓖ Ⓗ Ⓙ	11 Ⓐ Ⓑ Ⓒ Ⓓ	18 Ⓕ Ⓖ Ⓗ Ⓙ	25 Ⓐ Ⓑ Ⓒ Ⓓ	32 Ⓕ Ⓖ Ⓗ Ⓙ	39 Ⓐ Ⓑ Ⓒ Ⓓ
5 Ⓐ Ⓑ Ⓒ Ⓓ	12 Ⓕ Ⓖ Ⓗ Ⓙ	19 Ⓐ Ⓑ Ⓒ Ⓓ	26 Ⓕ Ⓖ Ⓗ Ⓙ	33 Ⓐ Ⓑ Ⓒ Ⓓ	40 Ⓕ Ⓖ Ⓗ Ⓙ
6 Ⓕ Ⓖ Ⓗ Ⓙ	13 Ⓐ Ⓑ Ⓒ Ⓓ	20 Ⓕ Ⓖ Ⓗ Ⓙ	27 Ⓐ Ⓑ Ⓒ Ⓓ	34 Ⓕ Ⓖ Ⓗ Ⓙ	
7 Ⓐ Ⓑ Ⓒ Ⓓ	14 Ⓕ Ⓖ Ⓗ Ⓙ	21 Ⓐ Ⓑ Ⓒ Ⓓ	28 Ⓕ Ⓖ Ⓗ Ⓙ	35 Ⓐ Ⓑ Ⓒ Ⓓ	

Use a soft lead No. 2 pencil only. Do NOT use a mechanical pencil, ink, ballpoint, or felt-tip pens.

Begin WRITING TEST here.

_____

_____

_____

_____

_____

_____

_____

_____

_____

_____

_____

_____

_____

_____

_____

_____

_____

_____

_____

_____

_____

_____

_____

If you need more space, please continue on the next page.

1

WRITING TEST

_____

_____

_____

_____

_____

_____

_____

_____

_____

_____

_____

_____

_____

_____

_____

_____

_____

_____

_____

_____

_____

_____

_____

_____

_____

_____

_____

If you need more space, please continue on the back of this page.

WRITING TEST

_____

_____

_____

_____

_____

_____

_____

_____

_____

_____

_____

_____

_____

_____

_____

_____

_____

_____

_____

_____

_____

_____

_____

_____

_____

_____

_____

_____

If you need more space, please continue on the next page.

WRITING TEST

_____

_____

_____

_____

_____

_____

_____

_____

_____

_____

_____

_____

_____

_____

_____

_____

_____

_____

_____

_____

_____

_____

_____

_____

_____

_____

_____

_____

STOP!

4

English Test
45 Minutes—75 Questions

DIRECTIONS: In the five passages that follow, certain words and phrases are underlined and numbered. In the right-hand column, you will find alternatives for the underlined part. In most cases, you are to choose the one that best expresses the idea, makes the statement appropriate for standard written English, or is worded most consistently with the style and tone of the passage as a whole. If you think the original version is best, choose "NO CHANGE." In some cases, you will find in the right-hand column a question about the underlined part. You are to choose the best answer to the question.

You will also find questions about a section of the passage, or about the passage as a whole. These questions do not refer to an underlined portion of the passage, but rather are identified by a number or numbers in a box.

For each question, choose the alternative you consider best and fill in the corresponding circle on your answer document. Read each passage through once before you begin to answer the questions that accompany it. For many of the questions, you must read several sentences beyond the question to determine the answer. Be sure that you have read far enough ahead each time you choose an alternative.

Passage I

Study of an Unusual Vermeer

[1]

Although, the Dutch painter Johannes Vermeer was considered only modestly successful during his lifetime, he is now considered one of the most important artists of the Dutch Golden Age. Part of the reason Vermeer was underestimated during his lifetime may have been that he did not paint as much at that time as his contemporaries, a group that included Frans Hals and Rembrandt. However, such works as *The Milkmaid* and *The Girl with a Pearl Earring* have been studied intensely and continue to earned Vermeer acclaim to this day.

[2]

[1] One painting that has long fascinated art critics and art historians is his *Study of a Young Woman*. [2] This piece is an example of a Dutch form called the "tronie,"

1. A. NO CHANGE
    B. Although, the Dutch painter Johannes Vermeer,
    C. Although the Dutch painter Johannes Vermeer
    D. Although the Dutch painter, Johannes Vermeer

2. F. NO CHANGE
    G. was underestimated may have been that he did not paint as much
    H. was underestimated during his lifetime is he did not paint as much during his lifetime
    J. was underestimated may have been partly that he did not paint as much

3. A. NO CHANGE
    B. earning
    C. earns
    D. earn

GO ON TO THE NEXT PAGE.

painted sometime between 1665 and 1667, a painting of
$\overline{}$

the head and face of a figure thought to be unusual or

striking. [3] This painting is of particular interest, in part,

because the dark background of the painting is very

different than Vermeers usual vividly-lit and richly-detailed
$\overline{}$

backgrounds. 6

[3]

It is also notable that, while the subject of the

painting is certainly striking, I would not call her
$\overline{}$

conventionally beautiful. This young woman's gaze is
$\overline{}$

steady and a slight smile tugs at their lips, hinting at a sort of
$\overline{}$

confidence. Yet she seems to have no eyebrows or

eyelashes. Eyes set extremely wide. That may be the
$\overline{}$

point, in *Study of a Young Woman,* Vermeer seems to be
$\overline{}$

more interested in exploring and representing aspects of his

subject's character and expression rather than representing

conventional forms of beauty.

4. The best placement for the underlined phrase would be:
   F. where it is now.
   G. after the word *piece* (revising the punctuation accordingly).
   H. after the word *figure.*
   J. after the word *form.*

5. A. NO CHANGE
   B. Vermeers'
   C. Vermeers's
   D. Vermeer's

6. If the writer were to delete Sentence 2, the essay would primarily lose details that:
   F. describe the form of a painting, giving the reader an idea of what Vermeer painted.
   G. suggest that Dutch painters were mostly concerned with unusual or striking faces of figures.
   H. raise the question of why Vermeer decided to use such an unusual model for his painting.
   J. continue to develop the idea that Vermeer's paintings are widely acclaimed.

7. A. NO CHANGE
   B. we would not regard her as conventionally beautiful.
   C. conventionally beautiful is not what she was.
   D. she is not conventionally beautiful.

8. F. NO CHANGE
   G. one's
   H. her
   J. its

9. A. NO CHANGE
   B. Her eyes are extremely wide-set.
   C. Her eyes being extremely wide-set.
   D. The eyes, set extremely wide.

10. F. NO CHANGE
    G. point: in
    H. point, in,
    J. point in

GO ON TO THE NEXT PAGE.

[4]

The painting itself, likewise, is beautiful. There
<u>   </u>
           11

is a gradual transition from light to shadow on the

<u>young woman's face; which is echoed by the subtle shifts of</u>
                 12

tone in the folds of cloth draped over her shoulder.

<u>Vermeer's exploration of the effect of light on this</u>
              13

<u>extraordinary face</u> creates the sense that he has somehow
    13

illuminated a dream of moving beyond mere beauty toward

a more authentic engagement with the world.

11. **A.** NO CHANGE
    B. however,
    C. therefore,
    D. in the meantime,

12. **F.** NO CHANGE
    G. young woman's face which is
    H. young woman's face which is;
    J. young woman's face, which is

13. Given that all the choices are true, which one most effectively introduces this sentence by describing what technique Vermeer used?

    A. NO CHANGE
    B. Vermeer's use of color
    C. The fact that there are no distracting details like a window or furniture
    D. The use of bold, broad brushstrokes in the painting

Questions 14 and 15 ask about the preceding passage as a whole.

---

14. Upon reviewing notes for this essay, the writer comes across the following true statement:

    Some scholars claim the model for *Study of a Young Woman* was Vermeer's daughter.

    The writer is considering adding the sentence. The most logical choice for the writer is to:

    F. add it at the end of paragraph 1.
    G. add it at the end of paragraph 2.
    H. add it at the end of paragraph 3.
    J. OMIT the sentence, because it is not a relevant addition to any paragraph.

15. Suppose the writer's goal had been to write an essay focusing on the reasons Vermeer is held in such high esteem by art critics and historians. Would this essay fulfill that goal?

    A. Yes, because the essay explains in detail why Vermeer's paintings are considered masterpieces.
    B. Yes, because the essay focuses on Vermeer's use of richly-detailed backgrounds.
    C. No, because the essay does not provide enough detail about Vermeer's life.
    D. No, because the essay does not explain the reasons art critics and historians believe Vermeer should be considered an important artist.

GO ON TO THE NEXT PAGE.

Passage II

What Is Music? The Brain Knows.

[1] Though research has found that even the most ancient cultures made music. The reasons behind this universal drive remain unexplained. [2] However, until recently they have been unable to verify this theory. [3] Scientists have long assumed that there must be a neural basis for our love of music, and they have searched for evidence using conventional brain-scanning technology. [4] Now, though, researchers at the Massachusetts Institute of Technology (MIT) have devised a weird trick for brain imaging that seems to support this long-held hypothesis. 19

These MIT researchers, performed mathematical analyses of scans of the auditory cortex and found that specific groups of neurons in this region, which is located in the temporal lobes, fires in response to music.

16. F. NO CHANGE
    G. made music, and the reasons
    H. made music; however, the reasons
    J. made music, the reasons

17. A. NO CHANGE
    B. Scientists have long assumed, using conventional brain-scanning technology, that there must be a neural basis for our love of music, and they have searched for evidence.
    C. Using conventional brain-scanning technology, scientists have long assumed that there must be a neural basis for our love of music, and they have searched for evidence.
    D. Scientists have long assumed that there must be a neural basis for our love of music using conventional brain-scanning technology, and they have searched for evidence.

18. F. NO CHANGE
    G. new approach to
    H. cool new method of
    J. mode of action concerning

19. For the sake of the logic and coherence of this paragraph, Sentence 2 should be placed:
    A. where it is now.
    B. before Sentence 1.
    C. after Sentence 3.
    D. after Sentence 4.

20. F. NO CHANGE
    G. These, MIT researchers,
    H. These, MIT researchers
    J. These MIT researchers

21. A. NO CHANGE
    B. fire
    C. has fired
    D. is firing

However, they found a part of the brain that is dedicated
22

to distinguishing music from noise in general. They also
23

found that this area is able to recognize music as distinctly
23

separate from speech. During testing, neurons in the area
23

fired in response to everything from Bach to bluegrass and

hip-hop but stayed unmoved by other sounds. Different parts

of the auditory cortex responded to such sounds as running

water and falling trees. 24

After gathering a library of easy recognizable sounds,
25

the researchers scanned the brains of a group of volunteers

who listened to the sound clips. Researchers matched the

activation patterns in the brain to the sounds that were

played. And determined that four basic response patterns
26

were linked to such properties as pitch, rhythm, and
26

frequency.
26

Though researchers still can't say which exact
27

acoustic features in music stimulate the music-sensitive

---

22. **F.** NO CHANGE
    G. Insofar as,
    H. In other words,
    J. Therefore,

23. **A.** NO CHANGE
    B. general. This area, they found, also recognizes music as different.
    C. general, or from such specific other noises as speech.
    D. general and from speech.

24. The writer is considering deleting the preceding sentence from this paragraph. If the writer made this deletion, the paragraph would primarily lose:
    F. information explaining how parts of the brain recognize music, speech, and other sounds.
    G. examples of non-musical sounds processed by different parts of the brain than those that process music.
    H. scientific proof of the statement that brain scanning technology is effective.
    J. evidence that the sound of running water is not music.

25. **A.** NO CHANGE
    B. easy recognizably
    C. easily recognizably
    D. easily recognizable

26. **F.** NO CHANGE
    G. They determined that four basic response patterns were linked to such properties as pitch, rhythm, and frequency.
    H. And four basic response patterns were linked to such properties as pitch, rhythm, and frequency.
    J. Four basic response patterns were linked.

27. **A.** NO CHANGE
    B. researchers' still can't
    C. researchers still cant
    D. researchers' still cant

GO ON TO THE NEXT PAGE.

areas of the brain, <u>but it's clear that the brain recognizes</u>
₂₈

<u>music when it hears it. Of course, a number of questions</u>
₂₉

<u>remain, including such questions as</u> why humans have music
₂₉

to begin with and why some music moves us to dance. This

discovery, however, opens up the possibility of finally

finding the answers.

28. **F.** NO CHANGE
    G. and it is
    H. but it is
    J. it's

29. **A.** NO CHANGE
    B. Of course, a number of questions remain, including
    C. Of course, questions remain, such as those of
    D. A number of questions remain, of course,

Question 30 asks about the preceding passage as a whole.

30. Suppose the writer's primary purpose had been to describe how a specific study sheds light on a bigger question. Would this essay accomplish that goal?

    F. Yes, because it shows how a study of the brain has revealed music-sensitive areas that may help to answer bigger questions about why we enjoy music.

    G. Yes, because it shows how a study of the brain reveals the areas of the brain that make us respond to music with joy and dance.

    H. No, because it describes a study that ultimately fails to answer any big questions.

    J. No, because it begins by posing questions about why we like music, but focuses instead on how we perceive it.

Passage III

A Very Important Person

[1] A V.I.P. was coming to <u>visit, I had no idea what</u>
₃₁
that meant, but everyone else in my family seemed very

excited. [2] The house was <u>subjected to</u> an extra-deep
₃₂
cleaning, a menu was planned, and the phone kept ringing

with people wanting to be invited over on the red-letter day.

[3] My mother apologized to every caller, explaining that

although our guest was a V.I.P., he was also my father's

cousin, and his visit would be strictly a family affair.

31. **A.** NO CHANGE
    B. visit I had no
    C. visit. I had no
    D. visit, I had no,

32. Which of the following alternatives to the underlined portion would be the LEAST acceptable?
    F. put through
    G. imperiled by
    H. exposed to
    J. made to endure

GO ON TO THE NEXT PAGE.

[4] Of course, that didn't stop my mother from making me practice curtsying. Or reminding my brother about the
_____
33
importance of making eye contact when shaking hands.
[5] I have to admit I was a little disappointed when the V.I.P. turned out to be an ordinary man. [6] He was wearing khakis and a blue sports coat just like my dad. [7] The only thing that set him apart from most men I knew was his mustache. 34

"It's just a guy," I whispered to my brother, who

gave me a hard nudge in the ribs with his elbow. He smiled
_____
35
when I curtsied and asked if I greeted all our guests this way.

I blurted out that, I was only curtsying because he was the
_____
36

V.I.P. I heard my mother gasp as a result of this comment.
_____
37
But the man laughed and asked me, "What is your favorite thing to do?" I told him that my favorite thing was getting

piggyback rides, he laughed again, got down on one knee,
_____
38

33. **A.** NO CHANGE
B. curtsying or
C. curtsying;
D. curtsying; or

34. The writer has decided to divide this opening paragraph into two. The best place to add the new paragraph break would be at the beginning of Sentence:
F. 4, because at this point the focus shifts to the narrator's mother's expectations.
G. 4, because at this point the emphasis shifts from the narrator's mother to the narrator.
H. 5, because at this point the essay shifts from describing the guest as important to describing him as unimportant.
J. 5, because at this point the essay shifts from events before the VIP's arrival to the event of his arrival.

35. **A.** NO CHANGE
B. The V.I.P.
C. My brother
D. She

36. **F.** NO CHANGE
G. that I was only,
H. that I was only
J. that, I was only,

37. **A.** NO CHANGE
B. As a result of this comment, my mother gasped.
C. The fact that I made this comment is what made my mother gasp.
D. This comment made my mother gasp.

38. **F.** NO CHANGE
G. rides, and he laughed
H. rides he laughed
J. rides, and he laughed;

GO ON TO THE NEXT PAGE.

and told me to climb up. In fact, before my mother could
<u>   </u>
39

lodge a <u>protest; he</u> galloped across the lawn with me on
              40

his back.

     Eventually we were called to lunch. My mother

was inside <u>had set</u> the dining room table with the good
                  41

china and silverware. Having been carefully coached in

table etiquette, I noticed the V.I.P. break the rules several

times—but <u>of upsetting her, instead, this actually seemed</u>
                                              42

<u>to make my mother feel more relaxed!</u>
                    42

<u>It turned out that the V.I.P was a regular person like us,</u>
                                        43

and the day was truly my <u>families'</u> affair. I will never forget
                                          44

the day the U.S. Ambassador to France gave me a piggyback

ride.

39. **A.** NO CHANGE
    B. However
    C. Then
    D. Finally

40. **F.** NO CHANGE
    G. protest—he
    H. protest, he
    J. protest: he

41. **A.** NO CHANGE
    B. sets
    C. set
    D. setting

42. **F.** NO CHANGE
    G. more relaxed, instead of upsetting her, this actually seemed to make my mother feel!
    H. this seemed to, instead of upsetting her, more relaxed make my mother feel!
    J. instead of upsetting her, this actually seemed to make my mother feel more relaxed!

43. **A.** NO CHANGE
    B. Despite his status, this man was clearly of an egalitarian disposition,
    C. See, he was just a regular guy,
    D. We realized that he wasn't special,

44. **F.** NO CHANGE
    G. family's
    H. family
    J. families

Question 45 asks about the preceding passage as a whole.

45. Suppose the writer's goal had been to write an essay focusing on the behavior of ambassadors when they are off-duty. Would this essay fulfill that goal?

    A. Yes, because the essay focuses on a day when a U.S. ambassador was visiting with family.
    B. Yes, because the essay indicates that ambassadors are just normal people.
    C. No, because the essay primarily focuses on just one person on a specific day.
    D. No, because the essay focuses more on the narrator's opinions than the ambassador's behavior.

GO ON TO THE NEXT PAGE.

Passage IV

Will You Be My Valentine?

[1]

February 14th is widely celebrated as Valentine's Day, an occasion for sharing cards, flowers, gifts; chocolates, and romantic candlelit dinners. Today over 1 billion Valentine's Day cards are sent each year.

The origins of this holiday, however, are shrouded in mystery. Who was St. Valentine, and why is he's day so romantic?

[2]

[1] Simply knowing that the date celebrates St. Valentine does little to clarify things. [2] There are, after all, three different martyred saints bearing the name. [49]

[3] The most widely held legend is that the one we celebrate was a priest named Valentine living in Rome during the third century. [4] At that time, the Roman Emperor Claudius II outlawed marriage for young men

46. F. NO CHANGE
G. sharing cards, flowers; gifts, chocolates—and romantic candlelit dinners.
H. sharing cards, flowers, gifts chocolates, and romantic—candlelit dinners.
J. sharing cards, flowers, gifts, chocolates, and romantic candlelit dinners.

47. Which of the following alternatives to the underlined portion would be LEAST acceptable?
A. though
B. in addition
C. meanwhile
D. nevertheless

48. F. NO CHANGE
G. it's
H. his
J. its

49. If the writer were to delete the preceding sentence, the essay would primarily lose:
A. an introduction of several historical figures who will each be discussed further.
B. a fact that helps to explain why the origin of Valentine's Day is shrouded in mystery.
C. an interpretation of historical events that refutes the common wisdom about Valentine's Day.
D. a possible answer to the questions surrounding the origin of Valentine's Day.

50. F. NO CHANGE
G. whose name was Valentine
H. by the name of Valentine
J. OMIT the underlined portion

GO ON TO THE NEXT PAGE.

because he believed, single soldiers were better soldiers.
_____
51

[5] Valentine defied what he saw as an unjust decree

by continuing to perform marriages for young lovers.

[6] When this was discovered. Claudius had Valentine
                        _____
                            52

put to death. [53]

[3]

Why celebrate St. Valentine on February 14th! The
                                            _____
                                               54
simplest answer is that this is supposedly the anniversary

of the date when they was either executed or buried.
                    _____
                        55
However, some scholars claim that it was because the

Christian church sought to replace the pagan fertility festival
                             _____
                                 56
of Lupercalia with its own celebration. Lupercalia was
   _____
       56
celebrated until the end

of the fifth century when Pope Gelasius, who was the pope
                        _____
                            57
at that time, outlawed the festival and declared February
_____
    57
14th St. Valentine's Day.

51. **A.** NO CHANGE
    B. because he, believed
    C. because he believed
    D. because, he believed

52. **F.** NO CHANGE
    G. discovered, Claudius
    H. discovered; Claudius
    J. discovered, and Claudius

53. For the sake of the logic and coherence of this paragraph, Sentence 4 should be placed:
    A. where it is now.
    B. after Sentence 1.
    C. after Sentence 2.
    D. after Sentence 6.

54. **F.** NO CHANGE
    G. 14th. The
    H. 14th, the
    J. 14th? The

55. **A.** NO CHANGE
    B. he was
    C. it was
    D. they were

56. Given that all of the choices are true, which one provides the most logical cause for the action described in the statement immediately following this underlined portion?
    F. NO CHANGE
    G. to give converts a chance to celebrate a romantic holiday.
    H. to require former pagans to learn about St. Valentine.
    J. to create another joyous Winter holiday to keep morale up until Spring.

57. **A.** NO CHANGE
    B. when Pope Gelasius
    C. when the pope at that time, Gelasius,
    D. when the pope at that time, named Gelasius,

GO ON TO THE NEXT PAGE.

[4]

<u>During the Middle Ages, tales of romance flourished.</u>
                                                    58
The date was also believed to be the beginning of birds'

mating season, which also <u>might had lead</u> to the day being
                                        59
associated with romance.

[5]

By the 19th century, the combination of mass-

produced cards and inexpensive postage made exchanging

Valentine's Day greetings very popular. Today, it is second

only to Christmas in the number of cards exchanged for the

holiday.

58. Given that all the choices are true, which one provides the best opening to this paragraph?

   F. NO CHANGE

   G. St. Valentine became popular during the Middle Ages.

   H. Perhaps because of his dedication to young lovers, St. Valentine's day became associated with romance during the Middle Ages, a time when tales of romance flourished.

   J. Perhaps because the Middle Ages were a time of upheaval and young romance, St. Valentine became very popular during that time.

59. A. NO CHANGE

   B. might have led

   C. might have lead

   D. might led

Question 60 asks about the preceding passage as a whole.

---

60. Upon reviewing notes for this essay, the writer comes across the following true statement:

> The first mass-produced valentines in America were elaborate creations featuring real lace and colorful graphics made by Esther A. Howland, the "Mother of the Valentine."

If the writer were to use this sentence, the most logical place to add it would be after the first sentence in Paragraph:

   F. 1.

   G. 2.

   H. 3.

   J. 5.

GO ON TO THE NEXT PAGE.

PASSAGE V

How is Paper Made?

[1]

We are surrounded by paper. Books, newspapers, magazines, the boxes our cereal comes in, and that paper plates we use to avoid washing dishes all add up to millions of tons of paper. Even as we move toward a "paperless environment," in the U.S. alone, offices use 12.1 trillion so-called sheets of paper each year.

[63] According to one study by the American Forest & Paper

Association, Americans discarding 4 million tons of paper every year.

[2]

That's a huge amount of paper, but where do they all come from? Although paper has been made using such materials as rice, water plants, cotton, and even recycled clothing, most of the paper made today comes from pulpwood logs, recycled paper products, or by mixing logs and recycled paper into a combination of the two. No matter what material is used, the process is

---

61. **A.** NO CHANGE
    B. those
    C. them
    D. a

62. The best placement for the underlined phrase would be:
    F. where it is now.
    G. after the word *toward*.
    H. after the word *offices*.
    J. before the word *paper*.

63. Given that all the choices are true, which one provides the most relevant information at this point in the essay?
    A. Paper manufacturing also uses a large amount of water.
    B. Further, up to 95% of business information is still recorded on paper.
    C. The global average is much lower, however.
    D. Paper can be recycled up to seven times before it has to be combined with fresh wood pulp.

64. **F.** NO CHANGE
    G. while Americans discard
    H. Americans discard
    J. while Americans are discarding

65. **A.** NO CHANGE
    B. does he
    C. does it
    D. does they

66. **F.** NO CHANGE
    G. a combination of the two.
    H. by mixing the two into a combination.
    J. by mixing logs and recycled paper.

GO ON TO THE NEXT PAGE.

Practice Tests

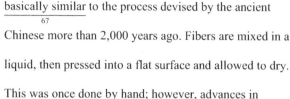

basically similar to the process devised by the ancient
_____
   67

Chinese more than 2,000 years ago. Fibers are mixed in a

liquid, then pressed into a flat surface and allowed to dry.

This was once done by hand; however, advances in

manufacturing technology had transformed papermaking
                       _____
                          68

from a fledgling industry into a large-scale industrial
_____
      69

process.

[3]

     The story begins in the forest. After harvesting trees,
   _____
      70

removing the bark, and milling the wood into lumber, there

is a lot left over. These leftovers are converted into small

wood chips, and the small wood chips are then either ground
_____
                         71

down or mixed with chemicals to create a pudding-like pulp.

Obviously, there's a lot of liquid in the pulp that must be

removed.

[4]

     So the next step is to spray it onto moving wire
                         __
                         72

screens that can be up to 20 feet wide. These screens move

67. **A.** NO CHANGE
   B. basic similarly
   C. basically similarly
   D. basic similar

68. **F.** NO CHANGE
   G. will have transformed
   H. transform
   J. have transformed

69. At this point, the writer wants to add a statement that would effectively contrast the old process of papermaking with the current process. Given that all of the choices are true, which one would best accomplish that purpose?

   A. NO CHANGE
   B. a small-scale craft
   C. a natural process
   D. an art-form

70. Given that all of the choices are true, which one would most effectively introduce this paragraph?

   F. NO CHANGE
   G. When paper is made from wood, the first step is to harvest trees.
   H. As I've already mentioned, paper can be made from recycled paper or from wood.
   J. Here, we are concerned only with paper that is made from wood.

71. **A.** NO CHANGE
   B. and those little wood chips are then either further ground
   C. which are then ground
   D. which, already small, are then either ground

72. **F.** NO CHANGE
   G. the wet paper pulp
   H. the liquid portion
   J. that

GO ON TO THE NEXT PAGE.

at speeds as fast as 60 miles per hour which forces the water
_____
73

to drop away and makes the cellulose fibers mat together to

form paper. While the paper is still damp, it is fed through

heated rollers that press and dry it.

[5]

The completed paper is wound into reels. These paper

reels can be so large it takes a crane to move them. The

paper on the reels is cut into whatever size is needed

to create the final paper product. 74

73. **A.** NO CHANGE
    B. per hour which forces,
    C. per hour, which forces,
    D. per hour, which forces

74. Which of the following sentences, if added here, would provide the best conclusion to the paragraph and make it most consistent with the main focus of the essay?

    F. Whether that product is a book or a paper plate, made of recycled paper or from a newly-cut tree, the process of creating the material from which it is made is essentially the same.

    G. The fact that paper reels are so large means that huge storage facilities must be maintained to handle it all.

    H. There are a trillion reasons to choose paper goods made from recycled paper instead of chopping down trees.

    J. Imagine what the ancient Egyptians would think about that!

Question 75 asks about the preceding passage as a whole.

75. The writer is considering combining Paragraphs 3 and 4 into a single paragraph. Should the writer make this change?

    A. Yes, because Paragraphs 3 and 4 are concerned with the same subject.

    B. Yes, because Paragraph 4 is only three sentences.

    C. No, because Paragraph 3 describes how water is removed from paper pulp, while Paragraph 4 describes how paper is stored.

    D. No, because combining the paragraphs will result in a single paragraph with more than 5 sentences.

END OF TEST 1.

STOP! DO NOT TURN THE PAGE UNTIL YOU ARE TOLD TO DO SO.

Mathematics Test

60 Minutes—60 Questions

DIRECTIONS: For each problem, solve for the correct answer, select your choice and fill in the corresponding bubble on your answer document.

Some problems may take a longer time to solve, but do not take too much time on any single problem. Solve the easier questions first, then return to the harder questions in the remaining time for this test.

A calculator is allowed on this test. While you may be able to solve some problems without a calculator, you are allowed to use a calculator for all of the problems on this test.

Note: Unless otherwise directed, all of the following statements are considered correct.

1. All drawn figures are NOT necessarily drawn to scale.
2. All geometric figures are in a plane.
3. The word *line*, when used, is the same as a straight line.
4. The word *average*, when used, is the same as arithmetic mean.

---

1. In scientific notation, $0.00000729 = ?$

   A. 7.29×10^{-8}
   B. 7.29×10^{-6}
   C. 7.29×10^{-5}
   D. 7.29×10^{-4}
   E. 0.729×10^{-3}

2. The average of 2 numbers is 184. The smaller of the 2 numbers is 170. What is the value of the larger number?

   F. 192
   G. 195
   H. 198
   J. 199
   K. 201

3. What is the greatest common factor of 72, 88, and 120?

   A. 2
   B. 3
   C. 4
   D. 6
   E. 8

4. If $6z + 2 = 5 - 11z$, then $z = ?$

   F. $\dfrac{3}{17}$
   G. $\dfrac{17}{3}$
   H. 3
   J. $\dfrac{7}{17}$
   K. $-\dfrac{7}{5}$

5. The rectangular field shown below has an area of 320,000 square feet. If the field is 400 feet wide, as shown below, what is the perimeter of the field?

   A. 800 feet
   B. 1,200 feet
   C. 1,600 feet
   D. 1,800 feet
   E. 2,400 feet

   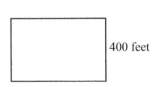

6. Which of the following ratios is equivalent to $\dfrac{2}{5} : \dfrac{1}{8}$?

   F. 1:20
   G. 2:5
   H. 8:5
   J. 16:5
   K. 5:16

GO ON TO THE NEXT PAGE.

Practice Tests

7. If $f(x) = (a^4 b^3)^{2x+1}$, what is the value of $f(2)$?

   A. $a^9 b^8$

   B. $a^{10} b^9$

   C. $a^{15} b^{20}$

   D. $a^{20} b^{15}$

   E. $a^{24} b^{18}$

8. A recipe for 5 cupcakes calls for $1\frac{1}{4}$ cups of flour. A bag of flour contains $7\frac{1}{2}$ cups. How many cupcakes can be made with 1 bag of flour?

   F. 5

   G. 6

   H. 7

   J. 25

   K. 30

9. If n is a positive integer, which of the following *must* be odd?

   A. n

   B. $n + 1$

   C. $2n$

   D. $2n + 1$

   E. $3n$

10. A student creates a circle graph to help plan her homework time over the course of 24 hours, as shown below. If she sleeps for 8 hours, which of the of the following is the closest angle measure for the time she spends on homework?

   F. 15°

   G. 30°

   H. 60°

   J. 70°

   K. 105°

11. For all x, $(x - 5)(x + 2) = ?$

   A. $x^2 + 3x - 10$

   B. $x^2 - 3x - 10$

   C. $x^2 - 3x + 10$

   D. $x^2 - 10$

   E. $x^2 - 3x$

12. If a is half of b, and c is 3 times a, how many times greater than b is c?

   F. $\frac{1}{2}$

   G. $\frac{2}{3}$

   H. $\frac{3}{2}$

   J. 2

   K. 3

13. If $|x - 5| = 3$ and $4x + 1 = y$, which of the following is a possible value for y?

   A. 42

   B. 9

   C. 0

   D. −9

   E. −33

14. A blueprint depicts the floor of a treehouse. The blueprint is a rectangle measuring 6 inches by 10 inches, and the floor's longer side measures 15 feet. To the nearest foot, what is the length of the shorter side of the floor?

   F. 4

   G. 6

   H. 9

   J. 10

   K. 15

GO ON TO THE NEXT PAGE.

15. In the figure below, *A, C,* and *E* are collinear, *B, C,* and *D* are collinear, and $\overline{AB}$ is parallel to $\overline{DE}$. What is the sum of the measures of the angles marked *x* and *y*?

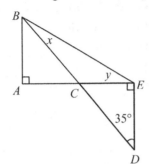

A. 35°

B. 45°

C. 55°

D. 125°

E. 135°

16. If *x* is a real number such that $\sqrt{x} = 2$, then $x^2 + x^3 = ?$

F. 4

G. 16

H. 32

J. 64

K. 80

17. In the scale model of the solar system shown below, the distance from the Sun to Jupiter is 65 cm, the distance from the Sun to Mars is 20 cm, and the distance from Mercury to Jupiter is 60 cm. What is the distance from Mercury to Mars?

Sun   Mercury   Mars   Jupiter

A. 45 cm

B. 40 cm

C. 25 cm

D. 15 cm

E. 5 cm

18. The smaller of two numbers is 6 less than 2 times the larger number. When the smaller number is subtracted from the larger number, the result is 1. If *y* is the larger number, which equation below determines the correct value of *y*?

F. $y - 2y - 6 = 1$

G. $(2y - 6) - y = 1$

H. $y - (2y - 6) = 1$

J. $2y - (2y - 6) = 1$

K. $y - (2y - 6) = 0$

19. The expression $(x^6 - x^5)^{\frac{1}{2}}$ is equivalent to:

A. 1

B. $x\sqrt{x - 1}$

C. $\sqrt{x^5 + x - 1}$

D. $x^2\sqrt{x^2 - x}$

E. $x^2\sqrt{2x - 1}$

20. A right triangle has a base of 4 units and hypotenuse of 6 units. What is its height?

F. $2\sqrt{5}$

G. $5\sqrt{2}$

H. $\sqrt{10}$

J. $2\sqrt{10}$

K. 20

Use the following information to answer questions 21-22.

Nathan budgets $100 for iced tea and spends $10 on iced tea every day.

21. Which of the following expressions represents the amount of money remaining in Nathan's iced tea budget after *w* weeks?

A. $100 + 5w$

B. $100 + 70w$

C. $100 - 50w$

D. $100 - 70w$

E. $70w$

22. Nathan decides to increase how much he spends on iced tea by $10 per day, starting on day 2 and ending when he spends 100% of his budget. During which day will Nathan run out of money?

F. Day 3

G. Day 4

H. Day 5

J. Day 6

K. Day 7

GO ON TO THE NEXT PAGE.

23. Which of the following equations represents the line below?

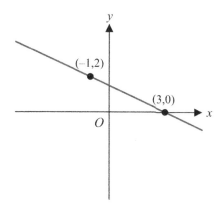

A. $y = -2x + \dfrac{3}{2}$

B. $y = -\dfrac{1}{2}x + \dfrac{3}{2}$

C. $y = \dfrac{1}{2}x + \dfrac{3}{2}$

D. $y = \dfrac{1}{2}x - \dfrac{3}{2}$

E. $y = 2x + \dfrac{3}{2}$

24. A chimpanzee receives a maximum of 63 bananas each week. Some weeks, the chimpanzee does not eat the maximum number of bananas. If b is its average daily banana consumption for a 1 week period, which of the following inequalities best describes b?

F. $b \le 9$

G. $b \ge 9$

H. $b \le 63$

J. $b \ge 63$

K. $b \ge 441$

25. Which of the following expressions is equivalent to $-\left(\dfrac{(z^2 - 4)}{16z^3 - 64z} \right)$?

A. $-\dfrac{1}{4}z$

B. $-\dfrac{1}{4}x^2z^2$

C. $-\dfrac{1}{32z}$

D. $\dfrac{1}{4z}$

E. $-\dfrac{1}{16z}$

26. A door-stopper is a triangle with a height increase of 2 inches for every 5-inch increase in the length of the horizontal base. The top corner of the door-stopper fits exactly in the 3-inch space between the bottom of a door and the floor. What is the length, in inches, of the base of the door-stopper?

F. 1.2

G. 2.5

H. 5.0

J. 7.5

K. 15.0

27. $(8x^2y^3)^2 \cdot (-2x)^3 = ?$

A. $-512x^7y^6 - 2y^3$

B. $-512x^{12}y^5 - 2y^3$

C. $-512x^{12}y^6 + 2y^3$

D. $-512x^{12}y^5 + 2y^3$

E. $-512x^7y^6$

28. Which of the following is the solution to the system of equations below?

$$y = x + 1$$
$$y = -3x - 3$$

F. $(-1, 0)$

G. $(1, 2)$

H. $\left(\dfrac{1}{2}, \dfrac{5}{4} \right)$

J. $\left(-\dfrac{1}{2}, \dfrac{3}{4} \right)$

K. There are no solutions to the system of equations.

29. In order to win an election, the top candidate must receive at least 30 votes more than the runner-up candidate. If the top candidate receives a votes, and the runner-up candidate receives b votes, which of the following expresses this rule?

A. $a - b \ge 30$

B. $a - b \le 30$

C. $a - b = 30$

D. $a - b > 30$

E. $a - b < 30$

GO ON TO THE NEXT PAGE.

30. $32^{\frac{2}{5}}$ is equivalent to which of the following?

    F. $2^{\frac{7}{5}}$

    G. 2^2

    H. $2^{\frac{5}{2}}$

    J. 2^5

    K. 2^7

31. What is the area of the parallelogram, in units squared?

    A. 20

    B. 25

    C. 32

    D. 40

    E. 120

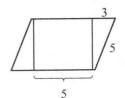

32. If the pattern below continues to increase, what will be the total number of circles in the first 9 rows?

    F. 21

    G. 63

    H. 117

    J. 130

    K. 189

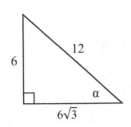

33. In the triangle below, what is the value of sin α?

    A. 3

    B. 2

    C. $\frac{5}{6}$

    D. $\frac{\sqrt{3}}{2}$

    E. $\frac{1}{2}$

34. In a drama class of 60 students, $\frac{1}{4}$ participate in musical theater. Of the students in musical theater, $\frac{1}{3}$ do not play an instrument. How many students in the class participate in musical theater and play an instrument?

    F. 15

    G. 10

    H. 8

    J. 5

    K. 3

35. A fundraiser sells cookies for $2 each. Its goal is to average $100 per day over 1 full week. On the first 6 days, the fundraiser made $52, $84, $106, $66, $94, and $98. How many cookies must be sold on the last day in order to reach this goal?

    A. 28

    B. 38

    C. 50

    D. 54

    E. 100

36. The table below shows values of x and $f(x)$ for the function $f(x) = mx + 4$. What is the value of m?

x	$f(x)$
0	4
1	7
2	10
3	13
4	16
5	19

    F. 1

    G. 2

    H. 3

    J. 4

    K. 5

37. Parallelogram $ABCD$ is divided into 4 triangles. $\triangle AED$ and $\triangle BCF$ are congruent isosceles triangles. $\triangle ABF$ and $\triangle ECD$ are congruent right triangles. If angle $\angle EDC$ measures 50°, what is the measure of $\angle FBC$?

    A. 20°

    B. 30°

    C. 45°

    D. 50°

    E. 60°

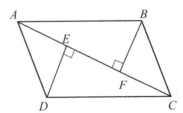

GO ON TO THE NEXT PAGE.

38. Two perpendicular lines on a standard (x,y) coordinate plane intersect at the point (2,1). If one of the lines crosses the y-axis at the origin, at what point does the other line intersect the y-axis?

   F. (0,0)

   G. (0,2)

   H. (0,5)

   J. (5,0)

   K. (2,0)

39. A local sports store sells baseballs, hockey sticks, and footballs. For every hockey stick sold, it sells 3 baseballs. For every baseball sold, it sells 5 footballs. If the store sold 720 footballs, how many hockey sticks did it sell?

   A. 43

   B. 48

   C. 90

   D. 144

   E. 240

40. A square is inscribed in another square, as shown in the figure below. What percentage of the larger square's area is the smaller square's area?

   F. 33%

   G. 43%

   H. 50%

   J. 52%

   K. 64%

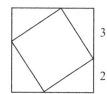

41. If $c = 2x^2 - 10x - 28$ and $d = 4x + 8$, which expression is equivalent to $\dfrac{c}{d}$?

   A. $x - 7$

   B. $\dfrac{x - 7}{2}$

   C. $x - \dfrac{7}{2}$

   D. $\dfrac{x + 7}{2(x + 2)}$

   E. $\dfrac{(x + 7)(x - 2)}{2(x + 2)}$

42. Which of the following systems of inequalities represents the shaded region on the graph below?

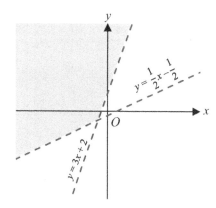

   F. $y > \dfrac{1}{2}x - \dfrac{1}{2}$ and $y > 3x + 2$

   G. $y > \dfrac{1}{2}x - \dfrac{1}{2}$ or $y < 3x + 2$

   H. $y < \dfrac{1}{2}x - \dfrac{1}{2}$ and $y < 3x + 2$

   J. $y > \dfrac{1}{2}x - \dfrac{1}{2}$ and $y < 3x + 2$

   K. $y > \dfrac{1}{2}x - \dfrac{1}{2}$ or $y > 3x + 2$

43. Given that $i^2 = -1$, what is the value of $(i + 2)(i - 2)$?

   A. 5

   B. $4 + i$

   C. -5

   D. $-4 + i$

   E. $-4 - i$

44. The unit vector notations for vectors **u** and **v** are given by **u** = 7**i** + 4**j** and **v** = 3**i** − 2**j**. What is the value of 2**u** − 3**v**?

   F. 4**i** + 6**j**

   G. 5**i** + 14**j**

   H. 8**i** + 12**j**

   J. 10**i** + 2**j**

   K. 20**i** + 6**j**

GO ON TO THE NEXT PAGE.

45. If $\sin \theta = \dfrac{1}{2}$ and $\cos \theta = \dfrac{\sqrt{3}}{2}$, $\theta = ?$

- **A.** 15°
- **B.** 30°
- **C.** 45°
- **D.** 60°
- **E.** 90°

46. A square window with a perimeter of 16 inches and a piece of colored glass is shown in the standard (x,y) coordinate plane below.

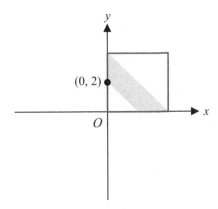

If the edge of the colored glass that connects with the point (0,2) has a slope of –1, what is the perimeter, in inches, of the colored glass?

- **F.** 12
- **G.** 8
- **H.** $6 + 2\sqrt{3}$
- **J.** $4 + 6\sqrt{2}$
- **K.** $4 + 2\sqrt{2}$

47. $x^{\log_x a} = ?$

- **A.** a
- **B.** $a \cdot \log_a x$
- **C.** 0
- **D.** 1
- **E.** $\log_x 2a$

Use the following information to answer questions 48-50.

A gold company melts gold and forms it into bars. They have 100,000 cubic centimeters of gold, and they plan to make gold bars in the shape of trapezoidal prisms, each with a volume of 1,040 cubic centimeters and an expected pure weight of approximately 12.55 kilograms, as shown in the figure below. All measurements are in centimeters.

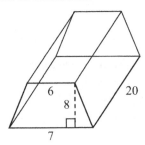

48. The company covers the bottom and top of each gold bar in wax paper to prevent scratching. To the nearest square centimeter, how much wax paper would it need to cover 1 gold bar?

- **F.** 130
- **G.** 140
- **H.** 260
- **J.** 420
- **K.** 1,040

49. After the company makes the maximum number of gold bars from its gold, what volume, in cubic centimeters, of gold will be left over?

- **A.** 96
- **B.** 100
- **C.** 160
- **D.** 320
- **E.** 884

50. The purity of gold is its actual weight divided by its expected weight. If the company makes a gold bar with the dimensions above that weighs 12.52 kg, what is its purity, to the nearest tenth of a percent?

- **F.** 52.0%
- **G.** 94.5%
- **H.** 98.9%
- **J.** 99.6%
- **K.** 99.8%

GO ON TO THE NEXT PAGE.

Practice Tests

51. Which of the following is NOT infinite?

   A. Line

   B. Line segment

   C. Ray

   D. Plane

   E. All of the above are infinite.

52. Centripetal force can be modeled by the equation $F = \dfrac{mv^2}{r}$, where m is mass, v is velocity, and r is the distance to the center of the circle. If the centripetal force is doubled and the mass and distance from the object to the center remain the same, how does the velocity change?

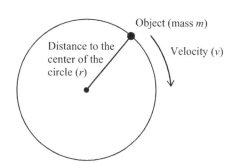

   F. v is multiplied by a factor of $\sqrt{2}$.

   G. v is multiplied by a factor of 2.

   H. v is multiplied by a factor of 4.

   J. v is divided by a factor of 2.

   K. v is divided by a factor of 4.

53. Let u, v, and w be positive integers such that $u = \dfrac{3v}{5}$ and $v = \dfrac{4}{w}$. Which of the following expresses w in terms of u?

   A. $\dfrac{12}{5u}$

   B. $\dfrac{5}{12u}$

   C. $\dfrac{4}{u}$

   D. $\dfrac{5u}{12}$

   E. $\dfrac{12u}{5}$

54. Two congruent triangles are drawn on a standard (x,y) coordinate plane, as shown below.

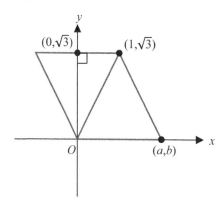

What is the value of $\dfrac{b}{a} + a$?

   F. $\dfrac{3}{2}$

   G. 0

   H. 1

   J. $\dfrac{3}{2}$

   K. 2

55. A radar on a boat records the positions of 2 islands, A and B, and the angle between them, as shown in the diagram below. If the units on the diagram are in miles, what is the distance d between islands A and B to the closest mile?

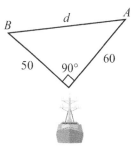

   A. 10

   B. 78

   C. 100

   D. 110

   E. 6,100

GO ON TO THE NEXT PAGE.

56. If the statement below is true, which of the following statements must also be true?

"If a wagon is red, then it is painted."

F. "If a wagon is red, then it is not painted."

G. "If a wagon is not red, then it is not painted."

H. "If a wagon is painted, then it is red."

J. "If a wagon is not painted, then it is red."

K. "If a wagon is not painted, then it is not red."

57. A pool with a base of 30 feet by 15 feet is filled to a uniform depth of 5 feet, as shown below. The walls of the pool are 5.5 feet high. Three people enter the pool and it overflows. Which of the following, to the nearest cubic foot, is the minimum volume displaced by the 3 people?

A. 2,475

B. 2,250

C. 1,650

D. 450

E. 225

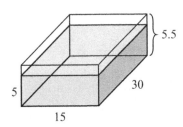

58. Which of the following graphs functions $f(x)$, $g(x)$, and $h(x)$ for $-2 < 2x \leq 2$?

$$f(x) = -x^2 - 1$$

$$g(x) = \frac{x}{2} + \frac{1}{2}$$

$$h(x) = 1 - x$$

F.

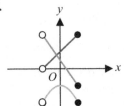

J.

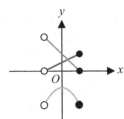

G.

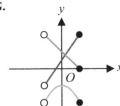

K.

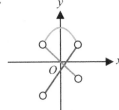

H.

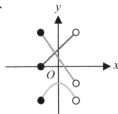

GO ON TO THE NEXT PAGE.

Practice Tests

59. A restaurant cuts a circular table so it has a flat edge that can rest against a wall, as shown in the figure below. The radius of the table is 40 centimeters, and the distance from the center to the flat edge is 32 centimeters. To the nearest centimeter, how long is the flat edge of the table?

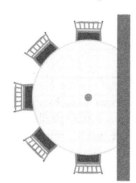

A. 24
B. 48
C. 64
D. 80
E. 96

60. An oceanographer records the height of the tides at a beach at regular intervals throughout the week. She plots the data on a graph and finds that it can be modeled by the function $y = a \cos(kx) + c$, where y is height and x is time. If the time between high tides decreased, which constant in the function would change?

F. a
G. k
H. c
J. x
K. y

END OF TEST 2.

STOP! DO NOT TURN THE PAGE UNTIL YOU ARE TOLD TO DO SO.

DO NOT RETURN TO THE PREVIOUS TEST.

Reading Test

35 Minutes—40 Questions

DIRECTIONS: There are multiple passages in this test. Each one is accompanied by several questions. After reading a passage, choose the best answer to every question and fill in the matching circle on your scoring sheet. You can refer back to the passages as often as necessary.

Passage I

Prose Fiction: This passage is adapted from the story "Metropolis" by Crystal Gail Shangkuan Koo. The story focuses on a young woman's recollection of her time in Beijing. (©2016 Crystal Gail Shangkuan Koo).

This is how you talk about a city you love. You talk about it as if it's the only place in the world where this story can happen.

The postcard I look at most often now was a picture
5 of a language university in Beijing that specialized in teaching Mandarin to foreigners. Once in the Philippines, when I was eleven, I had to recite the week's lesson from memory in Mandarin class.

Eight years later I was sent to Beijing with my
10 parents' blessings. I met my language partners every Friday in the school library, two girls who wanted to practice their English with me, but they frequently slipped back to Mandarin. *How can you be Chinese? How can you be Filipino? How can you speak English?*
15 *You speak Filipino too, right? How do you say, 'How do you do?'* Xin Feng spoke English with recklessness and confidence; Miao Ban was made of inquisitiveness, looking at Xin Feng for frequent translation.

Xin Feng and Miao Ban brought me out for dinner.
20 Across the restaurant was a frozen lake, fenceless, unwatched. I had never stood on iced water before. Figures whispered and laughed softly around me, but the lake was quiet and the world was calm.

I went walking in a *hutong* during lunch hour in
25 spring. Pots of rice and cabbage boiled outside sheds made of iron sheets. The aroma of garlic and meat coming from the makeshift vents smelled of a home.

Once, after one of my lunch hour walks, I stood before the Imperial Palace in the Forbidden City, hat in
30 my hands, waiting for a realization to engulf me. It had only been in Beijing that I learned to say 'ancestors' without feeling too self-aware. But tourists jostled around me, shoving each other to see the Imperial Throne, and the realization never came.

35 I went to parks often to escape the crowds. One of them had a small pavilion. When I reached it, a few lights were turned on softly and old fifties music was playing and middle-aged people were dancing. Some wore cocktail dresses; others office clothes. Swing, tango,
40 waltz. They would take each other's arms and twirl over the floor, lost in the sepia-colored music. Spring was turning to summer. I sat on a nearby bench, feeling the air turn humid, and a dragonfly landed on my shoulder.

Once, an old man and his wife stopped me on the
45 way back to the university. His accent was missing the Beijing growl. He said they had come to the city because his wife needed a surgical operation. The wife was moaning to herself and her husband was close to tears. They were hungry and needed money for a subway ticket
50 to the hospital.

I went to a small restaurant nearby and bought them two meals and bottled tea. Both of them were crying. I gave them money for the trip, and as the old man took the coins he whispered to his wife in a dialect before
55 thanking me and turning away.

The months passed quickly. Beijing was a detour to keep off the hunger till we reached home. That is why we write stories of it, so we won't forget. If I had found a home in Beijing, where I am a nameless unit in a sea
60 of faces, where I am finally part of the majority—until I speak and the accent reveals everything—I would have forgotten all my wonder.

Toward the end of my trip, I went to see my friend. She had been watching the sandstorm when I arrived.

65 She looked at me and asked: "So what's waiting for you after Beijing?"

"Looking for work in the Philippines, I suppose. Or maybe I'll go to Hong Kong and teach English there. Something. How are you doing?"

70 She shrugged. "I think he's going to call it quits before I leave. It's difficult. I mean, if it all just falls apart in the future, it won't be completely unexpected."

GO ON TO THE NEXT PAGE.

            Practice Tests

My friend left Beijing three days before I did. I heard from friends that she and her boyfriend did break
75 up. I wonder how he could stay there seeing everything that would remind him of her.

This is how you talk about something you love. You tell *why*. And in the end it's really all about remembering. How the sun rose above the granite and
80 concrete. How the pigeon flew above you, its tail feathers trilling. Sometimes I remember it so well I can feel the sand being crunched between my teeth.

1. The author's tone can be described as:

   A. resentful.
   B. distraught.
   C. worshipful.
   D. reflective.

2. The main purpose of the passage is to:

   F. describe a nostalgia for one's hometown.
   G. show the process of learning a language.
   H. relate the meaningfulness of a place.
   J. demonstrate a good deed.

3. It can be reasonably inferred from the passage that the narrator:

   A. grew up in Beijing, lived for a while in the Philippines, and then visited Beijing.
   B. grew up in the Philippines and visited Beijing.
   C. grew up in and still lives in Beijing.
   D. grew up in Hong Kong and visited Beijing.

4. Details in the passage suggest that the context for the narrator's meeting with Xin Feng and Miao Bian is that the three of them:

   F. are family friends.
   G. have been acquaintances since high school.
   H. met by chance in a restaurant.
   J. study at the same university.

5. The passage mentions all of the following in relation to Beijing EXCEPT:

   A. local foods.
   B. public leisure activities.
   C. art festivals.
   D. historical sites.

6. When the narrator says she is waiting for a "realization" (line 30), she means she was:

   F. waiting for her language lessons to take hold.
   G. hoping to be overtaken in a crowd.
   H. wishing to feel a profound connection to her heritage.
   J. looking for inspiration for her writing in the Forbidden City.

7. The scene where the narrator encounters the old man and his wife could have all of the following purposes EXCEPT:

   A. to contrast with the more serene picture of Beijing in the previous paragraph.
   B. to illustrate a tragic aspect of Beijing's busy atmosphere.
   C. to give a fuller impression of the narrator's emotions during her stay.
   D. to emphasize the narrator's fear of falling ill.

8. In saying that "Beijing was a detour" (line 56), the author suggests that:

   F. she only stayed in Beijing for a couple of weeks.
   G. Beijing was a popular destination spot for tourists.
   H. she felt Beijing could only be a temporary home.
   J. Beijing had many winding routes.

9. The narrator notes that not making a home in Beijing allows her to:

   A. return early to the Philippines.
   B. write a renowned story about Beijing.
   C. begin a life of luxurious travel.
   D. keep Beijing something of a mystery.

10. The story of the friend's breakup serves to:

    F. mirror the narrator's complex feelings about leaving Beijing.
    G. illustrate the romantic nature of relationships in Beijing.
    H. provide a scenario of which the author is jealous.
    J. prove that the author is a good friend.

GO ON TO THE NEXT PAGE.

Passage II

Social Science: Passage A is adapted from the article "Why Do Oil Prices Keep Going Down?" by Marcelle Arak and Scheila Tschinkel (©2016 Marcelle Arak and Scheila Tschinkel). Passage B is adapted from the article "We Need to Rethink the Financial Future of Oil" by Andreas Goldthau and Benjamin Sovacool (©2016 Andreas Goldthau and Benjamin Sovacool).

Passage A by Marcelle Arak and Scheila Tschinkel

A glut of crude oil in the global economy has led to the sharp declines in oil prices. Additional supplies of oil have ended up in storage tanks, because consumption of oil has barely budged. In tandem with price, oil revenues
5   of producing countries have dropped. If prices have fallen so much, why doesn't demand increase? It's because oil use in the short run is determined by factors that cannot be changed quickly.

Economists look at the responsiveness of demand
10 to price changes in terms of "the elasticity of demand." Demand for oil consumption in the short run is inelastic, in that it is not significantly affected by changes in price. To illustrate, a consumer driving a gas-guzzling SUV in excellent condition will not trade it in right away just
15 because prices rise. Or if you are a manufacturer and your equipment is still in good condition, you cannot quickly adjust this equipment to use less energy or buy different machines.

With demand for oil inelastic, the price decline does
20 not generate enough of an increase in sales volume to raise revenue for any seller. Nonetheless, producers and individual nations keep trying to increase revenue by producing and selling even more oil.

If demand is inelastic in the short run, would
25 withholding supply (in hopes prices will rise) lead to more revenue? If a cooperating group of sellers account for a large enough share of total sales, cutting back on supply will generate a large-enough price increase that these sellers can improve their revenue, even if sales
30 volume declines. In the 1970s, the Organization of Petroleum Exporting Countries controlled more than half of the global supply of crude oil. When it cut production, prices rose and all its members benefited. All it would take today is two or three major suppliers
35 working together to restrict supply sufficiently to raise prices by enough to increase their total revenue. This would also improve revenues of countries and producers who did not cut back.

That said, today's oil-producing countries don't

40 appear interested or even able to work together to raise prices—let alone to do so unilaterally—due in part to varying foreign policy interests and economic structures. Producers may also be thinking long-term and waiting out the lower prices in hopes of either pushing U.S.
45 marginal suppliers into bankruptcy or reversing the trend toward fuel efficiency.

In the long run, the price elasticity of demand is higher, because consumers are more responsive to price changes. If prices go up, consumers and businesses
50 eventually find ways to cut back. If prices are low, demand will eventually rise to a level commensurate with the reduced cost. Meanwhile, though, as long as supply continues to rise and demand remains inelastic or unresponsive, the price of oil is likely to continue its
55 slide.

Passage B by Andreas Goldthau and Benjamin Sovacool

The price of oil keeps moving in one direction—down. Oil assets are on the losing side and the future does not bode well for global oil. This, however, is for reasons related to climate change, not because of
60 tumbling prices. Two actors are key: the U.S. government and financial investors.

In the U.S., "independents" have become squeezed. "Independents" are small- to mid-sized companies that form the backbone of the recent shale-to-gas revolution.
65 So far, they have shown a remarkable ability to cope with an oil price spiraling downward, thanks to their innovative nature and their ability to cut costs and streamline production processes. Now, they have hit their limits, and find themselves in the red.

70 The U.S. government's decarbonization strategy, meanwhile, has a strong incentive to keep these independents alive and well. By and large the strategy relies on replacing coal with gas, in addition to implementing tougher power plant regulation. This
75 strategy has worked so far thanks to lots of additional gas coming online as a byproduct of oil production, keeping the market oversupplied and gas cheap.

The finance industry, in turn, shows signs of a serious rethink over whether oil remains as attractive for
80 investment as it has been in the past. Already in 2013, Citibank, a global financial firm, declared that global oil demand was "approaching a tipping point" and that "the end is nigh" for growth. It cited the trends of substituting natural gas for oil, coupled with improvements in the fuel
85 economy of vehicles, as the reasons.

GO ON TO THE NEXT PAGE.

Moreover, 196 world parties to the 2015 Paris Climate Conference acknowledged that humanity must, for climate reasons, manage its remaining "carbon budget." This means that it needs to limit, and eventually
90 end, the use of fossil fuels, including oil. As a consequence, many barrels of oil will need to stay in the ground as "stranded assets." Reacting to this, the global insurance companies Allianz and Axa already announced an end to investing in coal. Oil is likely to
95 follow. With the global divestment movement gaining further traction, there will be additional impetus from civil society to abandon oil. This is why some observers have already called on established international oil companies "to sell their existing oil reserves as quickly
100 as possible."

Ultimately, the future politics of oil present a fundamental and inescapable paradox. Ironically, it is the very same climate change imperatives that are helping to stabilize America's oil industry in the short
105 term that will sound its death knell in the long term.

Questions 11-14 ask about Passage A.

11. According to the passage, demand for oil in the short term is "inelastic" in response to price (line 11) because:

A. oil is a non-renewable natural resource.

B. all car models use relatively the same amount of oil.

C. consumers are slow to adjust consumption in the short term.

D. consumers actively resist economic pressures.

12. The authors would most likely characterize suppliers' efforts to increase revenue by selling still more oil as:

F. necessary.

G. inventive.

H. ineffective.

J. disastrous.

13. The passage states that decreasing oil supply sufficiently will cause:

A. a decrease in demand for oil.

B. an increase in demand for oil.

C. a decrease in price of oil.

D. an increase in revenues from oil.

14. According to the passage, all of the following are reasons countries that supply oil are unwilling to deliberately increase oil prices EXCEPT:

F. confidence that oil prices will increase naturally over time.

G. satisfaction with current strong oil revenues.

H. political relations among countries.

J. different economic structures within nations.

Questions 15-17 ask about Passage B.

15. It is reasonable to infer from the passage that the U.S. government:

A. prefers shale to gas as an energy source.

B. has policies in place to reduce uses of carbon.

C. is uninvolved with private oil companies' activities.

D. is creative in streamlining production of oil.

16. The passage mentions Citibank's declarations (lines 80-83) primarily in order to:

F. prove that automobiles use fuel more efficiently than before.

G. highlight the environmental leadership of major investors.

H. emphasize a collaboration between financial investors and the U.S. government.

J. cite an example of how investors are turning away from oil.

17. It is reasonable to infer from the passage that a paradox of lowered financial investment in oil is that:

A. investors are writing off oil, while consumers remain optimistic about it.

B. the long-term decrease in oil's value is protecting the oil industry in the short term.

C. coal is in high demand, but oil is not.

D. oil prices are going down, while oil supplier revenues are going up.

GO ON TO THE NEXT PAGE.

Questions 18-20 ask about both passages.

18. Both Passage A and Passage B are concerned with:

    F. patterns of decreasing prices of oil.

    G. trends of increasing revenues of oil suppliers.

    H. implications of climate change on oil sales.

    J. the effects oil price has on demand.

19. Which of the following is a reason for the oversupply of oil mentioned by Passage A but not by Passage B?

    A. Alternative natural sources of oil

    B. Lower financial investment in oil

    C. Oil reserves that have to be sold off

    D. Oil suppliers' efforts to increase revenues

20. The authors of Passage A suggest that in the long run, for oil, "If prices are low, demand will eventually rise to a level commensurate with the reduced cost" (lines 50-52). The authors of Passage B would most likely respond by saying that:

    F. long-term demand for oil is also inelastic.

    G. oil reserves will be used until they run out.

    H. the U.S. will mandate a ban on oil in the future.

    J. total oil usage will decline in the long run.

GO ON TO THE NEXT PAGE.

Passage III

Humanities: This passage is adapted from the article "Explainer: the History of Jazz" by Alexander Hunter (©2015 Alexander Hunter).

After more than 100 years of history, it's clear the word "jazz" means many different things to many different people. Depending on who's doing the talking, it can either mean a highly specific musical style, or almost
5 nothing. The early timeline of jazz is spotty, vague, and disputed, as one might expect of a musical movement that grew from a group that was both marginalized and exploited. Jazz evolved from the fringes of American society into one of the most influential, and enduring,
10 musical movements of the 20th century.

New Orleans in the late 1800s was a remarkably cosmopolitan city, with a more racially egalitarian society than the rest of the American south. In that city, distinct musical trends began to develop, fusing
15 elements of West African musical traditions with European harmonic structures.

Jelly Roll Morton claimed to have invented what we call "jazz" in 1902, and did much to popularize the New Orleans sound through newly available recording
20 technologies. By the time he recorded his "Black Bottom Stomp" in 1926, this new music had travelled as far as Chicago. In 1917 the cultural hub known as Storyville was closed, which coincided with The Great Migration, in which more than a million African Americans travelled
25 from rural communities in the South to major cities between 1910 and 1930. That migration, combined with recording technology and Prohibition, brought jazz to an unprecedented number of black and non-black audiences.

During this time, Louis Armstrong was at the
30 forefront of jazz. He altered the performance practice of jazz from the traditional texture in which multiple musicians play melody lines simultaneously, to what we now recognize as the individualist, soloist-plus-ensemble format. Later, the period between 1935 and
35 1946, generally referred to as the "Swing Era," saw small, soloist-plus-ensemble bands of Armstrong and others largely give way to big bands, consisting of about 18 musicians.

In the early 1940s, a schism occurred in jazz that
40 forever changed the face of pop music. Many black musicians resented the success of white bands and, led by Charlie Parker and Dizzy Gillespie, returned to the virtuosic combo setting. "Bebop" was faster and more complicated than anything that had come before it. This
45 was the first time jazz audiences sat down and listened, moving out of the dance halls and into smoky bars. Jazz

was becoming art music. Just as bebop musicians were getting the hang of their new ideas, the Musicians Union in the U.S. enforced a ban on new commercial recordings
50 as part of a dispute over royalties. For more than a year, starting in August 1942, almost no instrumental musicians were permitted to make new recordings (vocalists were exempt from the ban).

Before the ban, vocalists were special soloists with
55 big bands, and usually sang a verse or two in the middle of the song. But Tommy Dorsey's trombone, not Sinatra's voice, was the important feature. During the ban, audiences became accustomed to vocal pop music, and haven't looked back. From this split in the early 40s
60 between jazz as art music, and popular music with a vocal focus, the history of jazz follows the art branch.

Jazz musicians tend not to stay in one genre too long. Out of the rejection of the fast-paced, complex bebop emerged the late 40s new West Coast scene.
65 "Cool Jazz" had a more relaxed tempo, with less focus on soloing and a return to ensemble playing. This caused yet another reaction, resulting in what is known as "hard bop," which fuses bebop practices with R&B, Gospel, and Blues influences, and is generally
70 recognized as the default style practiced and taught around the world today.

In 1958, when bebop had taken chord progressions and virtuosity to its extreme, Miles Davis began experimenting with the other logical extreme. Jazz
75 musicians had been playing the same standard repertoire since the days of early bebop, and had become very adept at what is called "running the changes."

If bebop had the maximum number of chord changes, what might happen when there were no, or very few, chord
80 changes? Miles Davis's *Milestones* (1958) has only two chords. Davis sought to encourage melodic improvising by removing the "crutches" of complex changes. This "Modal Jazz" represented a huge shift in the techniques utilized by soloists, encouraging space in solos.

85 This focus in attention to space and melody, combined with new techniques and ideas coming out of the classical avant-garde, gave rise to a new avant-garde, and eventually "free," jazz. Starting with *The Shape of Jazz to Come* in 1959, Ornette Coleman did away with
90 chords altogether, encouraging musicians to play without being constrained by ideas of Western harmonic and melodic conventions.

As electronic instruments and funk gained in popularity, jazz musicians quickly jumped on new trends
95 and innovations, starting in 1968 with Miles Davis's

GO ON TO THE NEXT PAGE.

Filles de Kilamanjaro. As jazz moved through the 70s and 80s various elements of pop music seeped in, with just as many jazz elements seeping out.

When speaking of jazz in academia today we are
100 using the vocabulary set out by the pioneers of bebop. As with all music, jazz had to be codified, and classicized, in order to be studied, integrated into education, and understood.

21. Which of the following statements best characterizes the author's attitude toward jazz?

A. It is an impressive form of music that has remained largely uniform through its short history.

B. It is an outdated and largely forgotten form of music that should be revived.

C. It is a fascinating and multifaceted form of music with many different eras in its evolution.

D. It is a baffling form of music that achieved prominence largely because of bans on vocal music in the mid-century.

22. The passage devotes the LEAST attention to which of the following topics?

F. The history of jazz music

G. Popular jazz musicians

H. Divisions within jazz

J. Sales of jazz records

23. Which of the following developments does the passage indicate occurred first chronologically?

A. Miles Davis experiments with "Modal Jazz."

B. The cultural center of Storyville closes.

C. Elements of pop music make their way into jazz.

D. The "Swing Era" sees a shift towards larger bands.

24. What does the author name as the type of jazz that brings R&B, Gospel, and Blues infusions to bebop styles?

F. Bebop

G. Hard bop

H. Modal jazz

J. Free jazz

25. According to the passage, early precursors to jazz were influenced by:

A. The Great Migration and the cultural hub of Storyville.

B. New Orleans art and West African culture.

C. African musical traditions and European harmonic structures.

D. early R&B music and European classical music.

26. As it is used in line 28, the word *unprecedented* most nearly means:

F. irreplaceable.

G. unique.

H. exclusive.

J. record.

27. It is most reasonable to infer that in line 53 the phrase "exempt from the ban" refers to the fact that jazz vocalists:

A. could still make new recordings.

B. were still allowed to perform in bars.

C. could make use of imported music.

D. were not prevented from selling their work.

28. According to the passage, one of the effects of the ban imposed by the Musicians Union in the USA was that:

F. jazz boomed as a genre as a result of restrictions on other forms of music.

G. bebop trends started to veer more towards hard bop music.

H. vocal music gained preeminence as audiences grew familiar with it.

J. musicians moved from a focus on recordings to a focus on live performances.

29. The author notes that "free" jazz encouraged musicians to:

A. offer public performances and concerts for free.

B. shed the restrictions of traditional music conventions.

C. collaborate with musicians in other genres.

D. record songs that did not rely on contributions from vocalists.

30. The author refers to *Filles de Kilamanjaro* as an example of a work that:

F. utilized new trends like electronic instruments and funk.

G. infused classical jazz with many elements of pop music.

H. found popularity only decades after its initial release.

J. pushed the boundaries of conventional jazz with mixed results.

GO ON TO THE NEXT PAGE.

Passage IV

Natural Sciences: This passage is adapted from the article "What can beagles teach us about Alzheimer's disease?" by Elizabeth Head (©2015 Elizabeth Head).

Every 67 seconds, someone in the United States is diagnosed with Alzheimer's disease, and new estimates suggest that it may be the third leading cause of death for older people. Alzheimer's disease is associated with
5 memory loss in older people that becomes severe enough over time to interfere with normal daily functions. Other signs of Alzheimer's include changes in the ability to communicate, losses in language, decreased ability to focus and to pay attention, impairments in judgment, and
10 other behavioral changes.

People with Alzheimer's disease experience changes in their brains, which we can see in autopsies. Over the course of the disease, clumps of protein (called senile plaques) and tangles in neurons (called
15 neurofibrillary tangles) accumulate. These plaques and tangles interfere with how the brain works and disrupt connections that are important for intact learning and memory ability.

The majority of studies to develop treatments for
20 Alzheimer's disease use mice that are genetically modified to produce human proteins with mutations. But these mutations are usually present in less than 5% of people with Alzheimer's disease. This limitation can make it difficult to translate benefits of a treatment tested
25 in mouse studies to people. However, there are several animals, including dogs, that naturally develop human-like brain changes that look much like Alzheimer's disease.

Old dogs may teach us a great deal about aging. As
30 dogs get older, some develop learning and memory problems, much like we do. And like people, not all old dogs become impaired. Indeed, some old dogs remain bright and able to learn just as well as younger dogs, although they may be a little slower in reaching high
35 levels of performance.

When aged dogs show cognitive changes not caused by other systemic illnesses, they are related to brain changes that are strikingly similar to people's. For example, old dogs develop senile plaques in their brains
40 that are made of a protein that is identical to one that humans produce. This protein, called beta-amyloid, is toxic to cells in the brain. Unlike mice and rats, old dogs naturally develop significant brain pathology like we see in people. In this way, aging dogs may resemble aging

45 humans in a more natural or realistic way than mice with genetic mutations.

Dogs may be very well suited to help us understand how different lifestyle factors help our brains as we get older. Our lab initially began studying beagles in the
50 early 1990s, as there was interest in developing a drug to treat "dog dementia" based on pet owners' observations of changes in behavior in their older dogs. At that time, little was known about learning and memory changes in aging dogs (beagles over eight years of age) and our
55 earliest research was designed to find ways to systematically measure these changes.

The first step in doing this was to teach dogs to look at different objects (for example a Lego block or a toy truck) and learn that one of the two always hid a food
60 reward. When we switched the food reward to the object that was previously not rewarded, older dogs kept choosing the wrong object. Young dogs very quickly switched over to the new object.

When we counted the number of errors dogs make
65 to learn the problem, old dogs made many more errors overall. Interestingly, not all old dogs were impaired. Another subset of old dogs showed significant losses in their ability to remember information and some showed changes in their ability to be "flexible" in changing
70 behaviors.

This is very similar to people. Not everyone ages in the same way—some people remain sharp as tacks well into their older years. After measuring learning and memory changes in dogs, we next studied the brain
75 changes that were most strongly linked to these cognitive losses. We found that senile plaques in the brains of old dogs were more frequent in the animals that had learning and memory problems. In our more recent studies, we have been seeking ways to improve brain health in old
80 dogs with the hope that these approaches can translate to healthy aging in people.

For instance, in several studies of aging in beagles, we have found that a diet rich in antioxidants that includes vitamins E and C, and importantly, fruits and
85 vegetables, can lead to wonderful benefits in learning and memory ability that can be maintained for years. Dogs that had trouble remembering where they had seen a food reward (this is an example of spatial memory) showed significant improvements in their memory over
90 time when following this diet. Also, old dogs showed rapid improvements in their ability to modify their behaviors (an example of enhanced executive function)

GO ON TO THE NEXT PAGE.

when the rules had changed in the task they were
learning. In addition, providing dogs with physical
95 exercise, social enrichment, and "brain games," like the
food reward game, can also significantly improve
cognition as they get older.

If we take these factors into account, we may be
able to engage in strategies and lifestyle changes that
100 will be good for both species. If we participate in
exercise, social interaction, and learning new tricks with
our aged companion animals, the benefits will be
twofold: for them and for us.

31. In the context of the passage as a whole, it is most
reasonable to infer that the phrase "lifestyle factors"
(line 48) includes:

A. diet and exercise.
B. memory and cognition.
C. sleep and stress.
D. strength and endurance.

32. The passage implies that Alzheimer's disease can cause:

F. changes in the brain and behavior that may affect
quality of life.
G. a massive stroke due to the accumulation of
neurofibrillary tangles.
H. disruptions in long-term memory and ability to
recall childhood memories.
J. alterations in speech patterns and the favoring of
short, simple words.

33. The passage suggests that dogs may be more useful than
mice for studying Alzheimer's disease because:

A. their age-related brain changes are more similar to
humans'.
B. they are mammals and so suffer from the same
diseases.
C. most dogs remain bright and intelligent through
their old age.
D. dogs have longer life spans than mice and can be
studied for longer.

34. Which of the following findings, if true, would best
support the idea that brain games "can significantly
improve cognition" in aging dogs (lines 96-97)?

F. Dogs that consumed more vitamin E and C
outperformed others on cognitive tests.
G. Dogs that exercised outdoors with their human
owners developed better spatial memory.
H. Dogs trained with brain games showed improved
scores on tests of cognition following training.
J. Dogs that performed well on brain-related games
typically continued to do so throughout their lives.

35. As described in the passage, people who suffer from
Alzheimer's may experience all of the following
EXCEPT:

A. impairments in judgment.
B. changes in behavior.
C. loss of focus.
D. improvements in language.

36. The passage makes clear that the senile plaques humans
develop are made up of:

F. beta-amyloid.
G. vitamins E and C.
H. neurons.
J. neurofibrillary fibers.

37. According to the passage, in a study by the author, dogs
were tested on their ability to:

A. distinguish between numerous objects.
B. sniff out a hidden treat.
C. locate a food reward.
D. follow verbal commands.

38. The central idea of the hypothesis proposed by the
author is that:

F. Alzheimer's can be cured with a proper regimen of
diet and exercise.
G. dogs and humans are more alike in cognition than
previously recognized.
H. specific lifestyle changes may delay some
Alzheimer's symptoms.
J. the buildup of plaque in dogs' brains can be treated
with careful therapy.

GO ON TO THE NEXT PAGE.

39. As it is used in line 80, the word *translate* most nearly means:

A. change.

B. apply.

C. transform.

D. decode.

40. In their experiments with dogs on locating food rewards, the researchers measured their results by counting the number of:

F. food rewards found by young versus old dogs.

G. mistakes made before dogs found the reward.

H. errors made before dogs gave up on the task.

J. young dogs that performed better than old dogs.

END OF TEST 3.

STOP! DO NOT TURN THE PAGE UNTIL YOU ARE TOLD TO DO SO.

DO NOT RETURN TO THE PREVIOUS TEST.

Science Test

35 Minutes—40 Questions

DIRECTIONS: There are several passages in this test, and each is accompanied by several questions. After reading a passage, choose the best answer to each question and fill in the corresponding oval on your answer document. You may refer to the passages as often as necessary.

You are NOT permitted to use a calculator on this test.

Passage I

In honey bee colonies, there are 3 *castes*, or types of bees. The queen produces eggs at a rate of 2,000 per day. The workers care for the eggs, gather food, and defend the colony. The drones fertilize the eggs. Scientists investigated how bees maintain environmental conditions in the hive.

Experiment 1

Three honey bee colonies (Colonies 1–3) were placed in separate hives. A queen was placed in a cage in the center of each hive, and 800 worker eggs and 800 drone eggs were harvested from her over a period of 24 hrs. Worker larvae and drone larvae were taken from a different hive. Each of the 3 experimental hives contained 4 frames: one with worker eggs, one with worker larvae, one with drone eggs, and one with drone larvae. Three sensors were stripped of their plastic cases and inserted between each pair of frames. Temperature and humidity were recorded at intervals of 30 minutes over a period of 5 days (see Figure 1 and Figure 2).

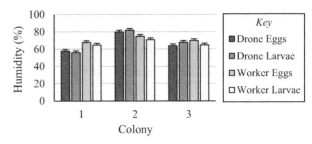

Figure 2

Experiment 2

Honeycomb—wax cells full of honey—is often found in hives. Three hives were used to study how the presence of bees and honeycomb affects hive humidity. Each hive had frames, sensors, and queens inserted as in Experiment 1. Hive 1 contained no honeycomb and no bees. Hive 2 contained honeycomb but no bees. Hive 3 contained both honeycomb and bees. Humidity was recorded in each hive at intervals of 30 minutes over a period of 24 hrs (see Figure 3).

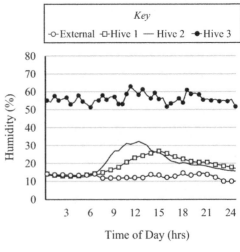

Figure 3

Data adapted from Zhiyong Li et al, "Drone and Worker Brood Microclimates Are Regulated Differently in Honey Bees, *Apis mellifera*." ©2016 by PLoS One. 10.1371/journal.pone.0148740

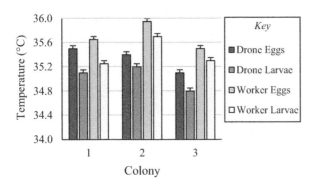

Figure 1

GO ON TO THE NEXT PAGE.

1. Based on the results of Experiment 1, frames containing which of the following had the highest average temperature?

    A. Drone eggs

    B. Drone larvae

    C. Worker eggs

    D. Worker larvae

2. In Experiment 1, did the scientists use all the eggs that each of the 3 queens could have produced that day?

    F. Yes; each queen could have produced 1,600 eggs per day.

    G. Yes; each queen could have produced 2,000 eggs per day.

    H. No; each queen could have produced 1,600 eggs per day.

    J. No; each queen could have produced 2,000 eggs per day.

3. Based on the results of Experiment 2, which of the following is the most important factor influencing humidity in the hive?

    A. Frames

    B. Sensors

    C. Combs

    D. Bees

4. The scientists place their sensor between two frames in another hive. It records an average temperature of 35.7°C and an average humidity of 65% at 30-minute intervals over a period of 5 days. If there were eggs and larvae in these frames, in which caste do they belong?

    F. Drones only

    G. Workers only

    H. Both drones and workers

    J. Neither drones nor workers

5. Which of the following claims about temperature and humidity is consistent with both Experiments 1 and 2?

    A. Temperature is dependent on caste, and humidity is dependent on the presence of bees.

    B. Temperature is dependent on the queen, and humidity is dependent on the presence of honeycomb.

    C. Humidity is dependent on caste, and temperature is dependent on the presence of bees.

    D. Humidity and temperature are both dependent on caste.

6. Which of the following is the best explanation for why the sensors were stripped of their plastic cases before they were inserted between the frames?

    F. The plastic cases were foreign to the honey bee hives.

    G. The plastic cases were too large to fit between the frames.

    H. The plastic cases increased the sensors' precision.

    J. The plastic cases increased the sensors' range.

7. When the temperature of the hive falls below 35.6°C, bees contract their thoracic muscles to heat it. When the temperature of the hive rises above 35.6°C, bees fan their wings to cool it. In Colony 2, which of these two methods would be more prevalent in the worker and drone frames?

	Drone	Worker
A.	thoracic contraction	thoracic contraction
B.	thoracic contraction	wing fanning
C.	wing fanning	thoracic contraction
D.	wing fanning	wing fanning

GO ON TO THE NEXT PAGE.

Passage II

Concrete is the most widely used building material in the world. It is relatively inexpensive but vulnerable to explosive blasts. New buildings can be reinforced against blast damage as they are built, but old buildings must be *retrofitted*—reinforced after construction with additional material.

Figure 1 shows the stress-strain curves of various materials. *Stress* is force per unit area, measured in kilopascals (kPa), and *strain* is percent deformation, which describes how much the shape of the material changes under stress. Materials fail at a certain combination of stress and strain, indicated by an *x* on the figure.

Figure 2 shows the displacement-time graph for concrete retrofitted with different 8 mm layers of spray-on polyurethane (PU) during and after the explosion of 2 kg of trinitrotoluene (TNT) from 1.6 m away over a duration of 1.05 ms. *Displacement* is the distance the material moves in response to a force.

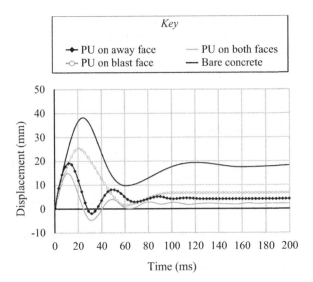

Figure 2

Figures adapted from S. N. Raman et al, "Elastomeric Polymers for Retrofitting of Reinforced Concrete Structures against the Explosive Effects of Blast." ©2012 by Advances in Materials Science and Engineering. 10.1155/2012/754142

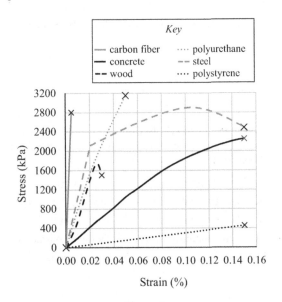

Figure 1

8. Based on Figure 2, the average displacement for bare concrete for the 200 ms during and after the explosion of 2 kg of TNT was closest to which of the following?

   F. 0 mm

   G. 12 mm

   H. 18 mm

   J. 39 mm

9. According to Figure 1, if polystyrene did not fail and its stress-strain curve had maintained its constant slope, its strain under 600 kPa of stress would most likely have been:

   A. less than 0.16%.

   B. between 0.16% and 0.20%.

   C. between 0.20% and 0.24%.

   D. greater than 0.24%.

GO ON TO THE NEXT PAGE.

10. Based on Figure 2, which of the following methods of retrofitting concrete was the most effective at reducing displacement?

 F. PU on away face

 G. PU on blast face

 H. PU on both faces

 J. Bare concrete

11. According to Figures 1 and 2, how do displacement and strain differ?

 A. Displacement is a distance, and strain is a percent change.

 B. Displacement is a percent change, and strain is a distance.

 C. Displacement is measured in kPa, and strain is a percent change.

 D. Displacement is a distance, and strain is force.

12. At the *yield point* of a given material, the relationship between stress and strain for a given material ceases to be linear. Prior to the yield point, a deformed material will return to its original shape. After the yield point, a material will maintain its deformed shape. If a steel plate experiences a stress of 2400 kPa, will it return to its original shape after deforming?

 F. Yes; this stress occurs before the yield point of steel.

 G. Yes; this stress occurs after the yield point of steel.

 H. No; this stress occurs before the yield point of steel.

 J. No; this stress occurs after the yield point of steel.

13. The *ultimate strength* of a material is the maximum amount of stress that it can bear without failing. Deformation under stress can weaken materials, however, so that they eventually fail at stresses lower than their ultimate strength. Which of the following materials has an ultimate strength that is greater than the stress at its fail point?

 I. Carbon fiber

 II. Steel

 III. Wood

 A. I only

 B. II only

 C. II and III

 D. I, II, and III

GO ON TO THE NEXT PAGE.

Passage III

Harmful oral microbes cause infections and ferment sugars into acids, which erode the minerals of the teeth. They also form *plaque*, a film that covers the teeth and can lead to tooth decay and gum disease. Students studied how various toothpastes affect the growth of these microbes.

Experiment 1

The students prepared 12 plates with a standard nutrient broth before transferring microbes and toothpaste to the plates. They prepared 3 plates for each of 3 strains of oral microbes: *Streptococcus mutans*, *Candida albicans*, and *Escherichia coli*. They also prepared 3 plates without microbes. Each plate received the same 5 treatments: 0.2 mL droplets of 4 different types of toothpaste (Toothpastes 1–4) and a 0.2 mL droplet of distilled water. The plates were then incubated at 37°C for 48 hrs to allow the microbes to grow. The diameter of the *inhibition zone*—the area around the treatment where no microbes grew—was measured for each of the 12 plates as shown in Diagram 1. The averages of the diameters of the inhibition zones for each group of 3 plates are shown in Table 1.

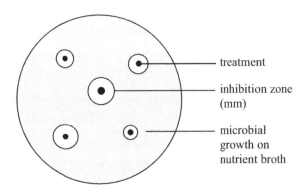

Diagram 1

Table 1

	Inhibition Zone Diameter (mm)			
	S. mutans	*C. albicans*	*E. coli*	No Microbes
Toothpaste 1	2.80	3.62	2.62	0.00
Toothpaste 2	1.25	3.21	2.00	0.00
Toothpaste 3	0.09	0.12	0.23	0.00
Toothpaste 4	2.21	1.30	1.36	0.00
Distilled Water	0.08	0.07	0.08	0.00

Experiment 2

The students repeated Experiment 1 using different dilutions of Toothpaste 1. Each plate received the same 5 treatments: 0.2 mL droplets of 4 different dilutions of Toothpaste 1 and a 0.2 mL droplet of distilled water. The dilutions were 1:2, 1:4, 1:8, and 1:16. The results are shown in Table 2.

Table 2

	Inhibition Zone Diameter (mm)			
	S. mutans	*C. albicans*	*E. coli*	No Microbes
1:2	2.49	3.14	2.31	0.00
1:4	1.41	1.78	1.32	0.00
1:8	0.86	1.20	0.75	0.00
1:16	0.40	0.55	0.38	0.00
Distilled Water	0.07	0.07	0.08	0.00

Experimental design adapted from Manupati Prasanth, "Antimicrobial Efficacy of Different Toothpastes and Mouthrinses: An In Vitro Study." © 2011 by Dental Research Journal. PMC3177399

14. According to Experiment 1, which toothpaste was most effective at inhibiting microbial growth?

   F. Toothpaste 1
   G. Toothpaste 2
   H. Toothpaste 3
   J. Toothpaste 4

15. According to Experiment 2, when the concentration of toothpaste decreased, the growth of the microbes in the treatment area:

   A. increased only.
   B. decreased only.
   C. increased, then decreased.
   D. decreased, then increased.

16. If the *corrected diameter* of the inhibition zone is the average diameter of the distilled water inhibition zone subtracted from the average diameter of the treatment inhibition zone, what was the corrected diameter of the inhibition zone for Toothpaste 4 on *C. albicans*?

   F. 1.30 mm
   G. 1.28 mm
   H. 1.23 mm
   J. 0.05 mm

GO ON TO THE NEXT PAGE.

17. Distilled water is water that:

   A. has no chemical or biological contaminants.

   B. has been added to the toothpastes.

   C. is found in glaciers.

   D. has no microbial inhibition zone.

18. Suppose that, in Experiments 1 and 2, only treatments using toothpaste were conducted. What effect would the absence of a distilled water treatment have on the results of both experiments?

   F. The students would be unable to determine the differences between toothpaste treatments.

   G. The students would be unable to determine the type of microbes affected by the toothpaste.

   H. The students would be unable to determine the type of toothpaste used.

   J. The students would be unable to determine the cause of the inhibition zone.

19. In another experiment, a student treated *E. coli* with a 1:4 dilution of Toothpaste 4. Based on the data in Tables 1 and 2, which of the following was most likely the average inhibition zone diameter in this experiment?

   A. 0.65 mm

   B. 1.01 mm

   C. 1.32 mm

   D. 1.36 mm

20. Based on the results of Experiment 1, a student concludes that Toothpaste 2 was the second-most effective toothpaste against *all* 3 types of oral microbes. Do the data from Table 1 support this conclusion?

   F. No; Toothpaste 4 produced a larger inhibition zone against *S. mutans*.

   G. No; Toothpaste 3 produced a larger inhibition zone against *S. mutans*.

   H. Yes; Toothpaste 2 produced the second-smallest inhibition zones against all 3 types of oral microbes.

   J. Yes; Toothpaste 2 produced the second-largest inhibition zones against all 3 types of oral microbes.

GO ON TO THE NEXT PAGE.

Passage IV

Chemical reactions often move in only one direction, but can also move forward and backward. Le Chatelier's Principle states that if a reactant is added to a chemical reaction, more products will be produced, and if a product is added to a chemical reaction, more reactants will be produced.

Researchers performed two experiments to investigate Le Chatelier's Principle. They studied a reaction involving observable color changes. The equation of this reaction is as follows:

$$[CoCl_4]^{2-} + 6H_2O \rightleftarrows [Co(H_2O)_6]^{2+} + 4Cl^-$$

Reactants   Products
(Clear)   (Pink)

Study 1

Researchers added 4 g of $CoCl_4{}^{2-}$ to 40 mL of water at 25°C. The resulting solution was a dark pink color. The researchers divided the solution into 5 vials (Vials 1–5) and added various amounts of hydrochloric acid (HCl), which contains Cl⁻, to each vial (excluding Vial 1, which received no HCl). The researchers measured the light absorbance of each solution at 425 nm. The researchers also noted the color of each vial. The results are shown in Table 1.

	Table 1		
Vial #	# HCl drops added	Color	Absorbance at 425nm
1	0	Dark pink	0.652
2	1	Medium pink	0.508
3	2	Light pink	0.348
4	3	Very light pink	0.211
5	4	Clear	0.046

Study 2

The researchers added 4 g of CoCl₄²⁻ to 40 mL water at 25°C. They measured the absorbance of the solution and then heated the reaction vial over a flame, measuring the absorbance of the solution at 10°C intervals. They then cooled the vial in an ice bath and measured the absorbance at temperatures below 25°C. The results are shown in Table 2.

Table 2	
Temperature (°C)	Absorbance at 425 nm
25	0.648
35	0.604
45	0.555
55	0.505
65	0.447
15	0.696
5	0.749

21. According to Table 1, as more drops of hydrochloric acid were added to the reaction, the color of the solution:

   A. became darker only.
   B. became lighter only.
   C. became darker, then lighter.
   D. did not change.

22. During Study 2, one of the researchers measured the absorbance of the solution at 50°C. The absorbance of the solution was most likely:

   F. 0.501.
   G. 0.525.
   H. 0.549.
   J. 0.576.

23. If the researchers from Study 2 had continued to heat the reaction vial to 85°C, the color of the solution would have been closest to:

   A. light pink.
   B. medium pink.
   C. dark pink.
   D. very light pink.

GO ON TO THE NEXT PAGE.

24. Suppose the researchers conducted a new study, but started with a solution heated to 45 degrees and cooled it by 10 degrees each time they added a drop of HCl. Which of the following predictions is most reasonable based on information in the passage and tables?

F. The solution would be clear initially and would remain clear as the experiment progressed.

G. The solution would be clear initially and would become darker as the experiment progressed.

H. The solution would be pink initially and would become darker as the experiment progressed.

J. The solution would be pink initially and would become lighter as the experiment progressed.

25. In Study 1, the addition of HCl to the reaction vials:

A. increased the concentration of one of the products, producing more products.

B. increased the concentration of one of the products, producing more reactants.

C. decreased the concentration of one of the reactants, producing more products.

D. decreased the concentration of one of the reactants, producing more reactants.

26. Based on the results of Study 2, one of the researchers concludes that, in this chemical reaction, heat is a product. Do the data in Table 2 support this conclusion?

F. No; as heat was added, more products were produced.

G. No; as heat was added, more reactants were produced.

H. Yes; as heat was added, more products were produced.

J. Yes; as heat was added, more reactants were produced.

27. After Study 1 was completed, it was discovered that the HCl used was contaminated with an unknown amount of pink dye, which absorbs light at 425 nm. What effect, if any, did this contamination have on the results of Study 1?

A. The pink dye increased the absorbance measurements of Vials 1, 2, 3, 4, and 5.

B. The pink dye decreased the absorbance measurements of Vials 1, 2, 3, 4, and 5.

C. The pink dye increased the absorbance measurements of Vials 2, 3, 4, and 5, but had no effect on Vial 1.

D. The pink dye had no effect on the absorbance measurements of Vials 2, 3, 4, and 5, but increased the absorbance of Vial 1.

GO ON TO THE NEXT PAGE.

Passage V

Scientists analyzed the climate change vulnerability of 82 species of fish and marine invertebrates found in the Northeast United States Continental Shelf region. Figure 1 shows a map of the region, which consists of 4 distinct sub-regions: Cape Hatteras, Mid-Atlantic Bight, Georges Bank, and the Gulf of Maine.

The scientists outlined 7 climate exposure factors to describe the extent to which a species experiences the effects of climate change. They then rated each marine species on a scale of 1–4 for each of these 7 factors. Table 1 shows the average score among all species for each factor.

The climate exposure factors were used to create an overall climate vulnerability score. The species were then divided into 6 general categories. Figure 2 shows the distributions of climate vulnerability scores for each category.

Table 1	
Climate Exposure Factor	Average Score
Surface temperature	3.95
Surface salinity	1.79
Air temperature	2.09
Precipitation	1.18
Ocean acidification	3.99
Currents	1.20
Sea level rise	1.27

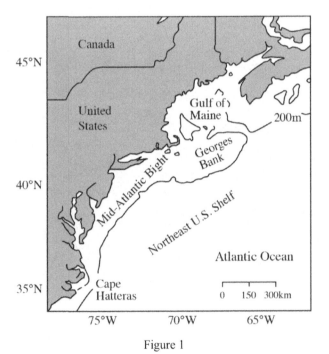

Figure 1

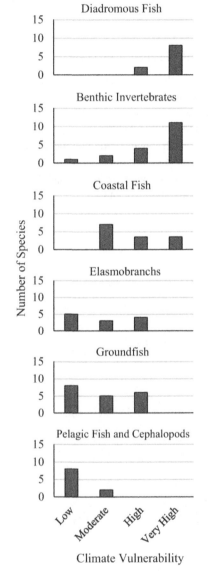

Figure 2

GO ON TO THE NEXT PAGE.

28. The witch flounder scores below average on its exposure to surface salinity. Which of the following could be the surface salinity exposure score of this species?

F. 1.00

G. 2.00

H. 3.00

J. 4.00

29. According to Figure 2, among the benthic invertebrates, which climate vulnerability score describes the largest number of species?

A. Low

B. Moderate

C. High

D. Very High

30. There were no species from Cape Hatteras that scored Very High on climate vulnerability. Which of the following categories of marine animal is LEAST likely to have been sampled from Cape Hatteras?

F. Groundfish

G. Pelagic fish and cephalopods

H. Diadromous fish

J. Elasmobranchs

31. Ocean acidification causes seawater to become more acidic. Which of the following statements best describes this phenomenon?

A. The density of the seawater increases.

B. The viscosity of the seawater decreases.

C. The pH of the seawater increases.

D. The pH of the seawater decreases.

32. A researcher hypothesizes that, because groundfish are found in the widest range of habitats, they will have the highest variability in climate vulnerability scores. Do the data from Figure 2 support this hypothesis?

F. No; the diadromous fish show a wider range of climate vulnerability scores.

G. No; the benthic invertebrates show a wider range of climate vulnerability scores.

H. Yes; the groundfish show the widest range of climate vulnerability scores.

J. Yes; the groundfish and elasmobranchs both show the widest range of climate vulnerability scores.

33. According to Figures 1 and 2, and assuming that climate change is more extreme in more northerly regions, which of the following populations is most vulnerable to climate change effects?

A. Benthic invertebrates in Georges Bank

B. Benthic invertebrates in the Gulf of Maine

C. Elasmobranchs in the Gulf of Maine

D. Groundfish in Cape Hatteras

GO ON TO THE NEXT PAGE.

Passage VI

A *supernova* is a star explosion, during which a star launches all its particles into space except its neutrons, which form a *neutron star*. Scientists debate whether neutron stars form *black holes*—objects with gravity so strong that no matter or radiation can escape them, making them difficult to detect.

(Note: The force of gravity depends on mass, and increases proportionally with it.)

Scientist A

Massive stars have too much gravity to launch all their particles into space. When a massive star explodes and forms a neutron star, some of the supernova debris accumulates on the neutron star and increases its mass. The neutron star's gravity, which pulls the debris inward, then exceeds its *neutron degeneracy* pressure, which pushes outward. The neutron star collapses into a black hole.

Black holes can be detected via distorted light, which occurs when light from stars close to a black hole is bent, forming halos, arcs of light, and duplicate star images. They can also be detected via *Hawking radiation*, which is the appearance of pairs of particles and antiparticles. These pairs negate each other and cease to exist—except when a particle appears outside a black hole and its antiparticle appears inside a black hole. The antiparticle cannot escape and negate the particle, so the particle exists and can be detected from Earth.

Scientist B

Massive stars explode with such force that all their particles are launched a great distance into space. Scientist A is incorrect in stating that the neutron star will accumulate supernova debris, because too few particles remain to accumulate on the neutron star. Therefore, it will not gain significant mass, and its gravity will not overcome its neutron degeneracy pressure. No black hole will form.

Distorted light does not indicate a black hole because galaxies and star clusters are massive enough to distort light from nearby stars. Any observed halos, arcs, or duplicate images are due to the force of gravity of galaxies or star clusters. There is no method to determine whether a particle came into existence through Hawking radiation at the edge of a black hole or elsewhere. Furthermore, single particles cannot be detected from Earth.

34. Which of the following observations would indicate the presence of a black hole, in Scientist A's view?

    F. The same star appears twice in a given region of space.
    G. A large neutron star is observed with gas and dust around it.
    H. A supernova is detected near the edge of a star cluster.
    J. A massive star orbits a neutron star.

35. Based on Scientist A's view, which of the following figures best depicts the change in mass of a massive star as it undergoes supernova and black hole formation?

    (Note: In each figure, S represents the star before the supernova occurs, N represents the time of neutron star formation, and B represents the time of black hole formation.)

    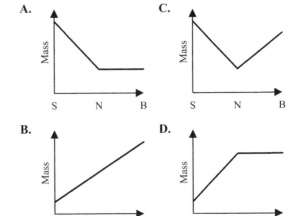

36. With which of the following statements would Scientist B be LEAST likely to agree?

    F. Neutron stars are often formed by supernova.
    G. Distorted light can be observed from Earth in the form of halos and arcs of light.
    H. Hawking radiation occurs in the universe.
    J. A neutron star's gravity always overcomes neutron degeneracy pressure.

GO ON TO THE NEXT PAGE.

37. Which scientist(s), if any, assert(s) that a neutron star will form after a massive star undergoes a supernova?

    A. Scientist A only

    B. Scientist B only

    C. Both Scientist A and B

    D. Neither Scientist A nor B

38. If a black hole were to form near a star, it would accumulate matter from that star. The accumulated matter would then emit single particles. Which scientist, if any, would be likely to claim that these particles would be observable from Earth?

    F. Scientist A only

    G. Scientist B only

    H. Both Scientist A and B

    J. Neither Scientist A nor B

39. Suppose a study of a nearby lone star, isolated from star clusters and galaxies, produced a double image and a nearby halo of light. How would this study most likely affect the scientists' viewpoints?

	Scientist A	Scientist B
A.	strengthen	strengthen
B.	strengthen	weaken
C.	weaken	strengthen
D.	weaken	weaken

40. Suppose a black hole had the same mass as the Sun. Which of the following statements accurately describes the relationship between the black hole's force of gravity and the Sun's force of gravity?

    F. The black hole's force of gravity would be smaller than the Sun's force of gravity.

    G. The black hole's force of gravity would be larger than the Sun's force of gravity.

    H. The black hole's force of gravity would be equal to the Sun's force of gravity.

    J. The black hole would not have a force of gravity.

END OF TEST 4.

STOP! DO NOT TURN THE PAGE UNTIL YOU ARE TOLD TO DO SO.

DO NOT RETURN TO THE PREVIOUS TEST.

Writing Test
40 Minutes—1 Prompt

Directions: This is a test of your writing ability. You'll have 40 minutes to read the prompt, plan your response, and write your essay. Before you begin, read all of the material in this test section carefully and make sure you understand what is being asked of you.

You should write your essay on the lined pages included in your answer sheet. Only your writing on those pages will be scored. Your work on these pages will not be scored.

Your essay will be graded based on the evidence it provides and your ability to:

- analyze and evaluate different perspectives on complicated issues
- express and develop your own perspective on the issue
- explain and support your arguments with logical reasoning and detailed examples
- clearly and logically organize your ideas in an essay
- effectively communicate your point of view in English

Stop writing and put down your pencil as soon as time is called.

DO NOT BEGIN THE WRITING TEST UNTIL YOU ARE TOLD TO DO SO.

Group Work or Individual Projects?

It's quite common for students in college and university classes to have group assignments. In a science class, several students might be responsible for a single lab experiment and report; in the humanities and social sciences, students might work together on a class presentation. Supporters of group assignments say that cooperation encourages students to share ideas and perspectives, and to get to know one another better. They also emphasize the importance of learning how to work well with others. Those who favor individual projects cite the potential for unfairness in groups, such as one or two students being given all of a group's work. Others question why particularly introverted students should be compelled to participate in group projects if they don't want to. Should college and university classes encourage group work, or should they encourage individual projects?

Read and carefully consider these perspectives. Each suggests a particular way of thinking about the merits of group work and individual projects.

Perspective 1	Perspective 2	Perspective 3
Working together is an important skill in many workplaces and academic fields. It is therefore important to encourage this behavior in undergraduates by assigning group projects.	It's more fair on students, who often have clashing schedules and differing personal investments in a class, to be given individual assignments only. This way, everyone will be judged solely on their own efforts.	Everyone is different. Some people love working in groups, and others are happiest working on their own. College and university educators should be mindful of this, and ensure that everyone's preferences are reasonably accommodated.

Essay Task

Write a unified, coherent essay in which you evaluate multiple perspectives on the merits of group work and individual projects. In your essay, be sure to:

- analyze and evaluate the perspectives given
- state and develop your own perspective on the issue
- explain the relationship between your perspective and those given

Your perspective may be in full agreement with any of the others, in partial agreement, or wholly different. Whatever the case, support your ideas with logical reasoning and detailed, persuasive examples.

Planning Your Essay

Your work on these prewriting pages will not be scored.

Use the space below and on the back cover to generate ideas and plan your essay. You may wish to consider the following as you think critically about the task:

Strengths and weaknesses of the three given perspectives

- What insights do they offer, and what do they fail to consider?
- Why might they be persuasive to others, or why might they fail to persuade?

Your own knowledge, experience, and values

- What is your perspective on this issue, and what are its strengths and weaknesses?
- How will you support your perspective in your essay?

Note

- Your practice Writing Test includes scratch paper and four lined sheets for your essay.
- Your official ACT exam will include a test booklet with space for planning and four lined sheets to write your essay.
- Review Answers and Scoring for instructions on how to grade your exam.

Practice Test 3

The ACT

This practice test contains tests in English, Math, Reading, and Science. These tests measure skills and abilities related to high school course work and college preparedness. **You can use a calculator on the math test only.**

The questions in each test are numbered, and the suggested answers for each question are lettered. On the answer sheet, the rows are numbered to match the questions, and the circles in each row are lettered to correspond to the suggested answers.

For each question, choose the best answer and fill in the corresponding circle on your answer document. Use a soft lead pencil and make your marks heavy and black. **Do not use a ballpoint pen.**

Fill in only one answer to each question. If you change your mind about an answer, completely erase your first mark before filling in your new answer. For each question, make certain that you mark in the row of ovals with the same number as the question.

Only responses marked on your answer sheet will be scored. Your score on each test will be based only on the number of questions you answer correctly during the time allowed for that test. You will NOT be penalized for guessing. **Even if you are unsure about an answer, you should make a guess.**

You may work on each test ONLY when your proctor tells you to do so. If you complete a test before the end of your allotted time, use the extra minutes to check your work on that section only. Do NOT use the time to work on another section. Doing this will disqualify your scores.

Put down your pencil immediately when time is called at the end of each test. You are not allowed to continue answering questions after the allotted time has run out. This includes marking answers on your answer sheet that you previously noted in your test booklet.

You are not allowed to fold or tear the pages of your test booklet.

Do Not Open This Booklet Until You Are Told to Do So.

Marking Directions: Mark only **one** oval for each question. Fill in response completely. Erase errors cleanly without smudging.

Correct mark: ○ ● ○ ○

Do NOT use these *incorrect* or *bad* **marks.**

Incorrect marks:
Overlapping mark:
Cross-out mark:
Smudged erasure:
Mark is too light:

NAME: _____

DATE: _____

TEST 1

1 Ⓐ Ⓑ Ⓒ Ⓓ	14 Ⓕ Ⓖ Ⓗ Ⓙ	27 Ⓐ Ⓑ Ⓒ Ⓓ	40 Ⓕ Ⓖ Ⓗ Ⓙ	53 Ⓐ Ⓑ Ⓒ Ⓓ	66 Ⓕ Ⓖ Ⓗ Ⓙ
2 Ⓕ Ⓖ Ⓗ Ⓙ	15 Ⓐ Ⓑ Ⓒ Ⓓ	28 Ⓕ Ⓖ Ⓗ Ⓙ	41 Ⓐ Ⓑ Ⓒ Ⓓ	54 Ⓕ Ⓖ Ⓗ Ⓙ	67 Ⓐ Ⓑ Ⓒ Ⓓ
3 Ⓐ Ⓑ Ⓒ Ⓓ	16 Ⓕ Ⓖ Ⓗ Ⓙ	29 Ⓐ Ⓑ Ⓒ Ⓓ	42 Ⓕ Ⓖ Ⓗ Ⓙ	55 Ⓐ Ⓑ Ⓒ Ⓓ	68 Ⓕ Ⓖ Ⓗ Ⓙ
4 Ⓕ Ⓖ Ⓗ Ⓙ	17 Ⓐ Ⓑ Ⓒ Ⓓ	30 Ⓕ Ⓖ Ⓗ Ⓙ	43 Ⓐ Ⓑ Ⓒ Ⓓ	56 Ⓕ Ⓖ Ⓗ Ⓙ	69 Ⓐ Ⓑ Ⓒ Ⓓ
5 Ⓐ Ⓑ Ⓒ Ⓓ	18 Ⓕ Ⓖ Ⓗ Ⓙ	31 Ⓐ Ⓑ Ⓒ Ⓓ	44 Ⓕ Ⓖ Ⓗ Ⓙ	57 Ⓐ Ⓑ Ⓒ Ⓓ	70 Ⓕ Ⓖ Ⓗ Ⓙ
6 Ⓕ Ⓖ Ⓗ Ⓙ	19 Ⓐ Ⓑ Ⓒ Ⓓ	32 Ⓕ Ⓖ Ⓗ Ⓙ	45 Ⓐ Ⓑ Ⓒ Ⓓ	58 Ⓕ Ⓖ Ⓗ Ⓙ	71 Ⓐ Ⓑ Ⓒ Ⓓ
7 Ⓐ Ⓑ Ⓒ Ⓓ	20 Ⓕ Ⓖ Ⓗ Ⓙ	33 Ⓐ Ⓑ Ⓒ Ⓓ	46 Ⓕ Ⓖ Ⓗ Ⓙ	59 Ⓐ Ⓑ Ⓒ Ⓓ	72 Ⓕ Ⓖ Ⓗ Ⓙ
8 Ⓕ Ⓖ Ⓗ Ⓙ	21 Ⓐ Ⓑ Ⓒ Ⓓ	34 Ⓕ Ⓖ Ⓗ Ⓙ	47 Ⓐ Ⓑ Ⓒ Ⓓ	60 Ⓕ Ⓖ Ⓗ Ⓙ	73 Ⓐ Ⓑ Ⓒ Ⓓ
9 Ⓐ Ⓑ Ⓒ Ⓓ	22 Ⓕ Ⓖ Ⓗ Ⓙ	35 Ⓐ Ⓑ Ⓒ Ⓓ	48 Ⓕ Ⓖ Ⓗ Ⓙ	61 Ⓐ Ⓑ Ⓒ Ⓓ	74 Ⓕ Ⓖ Ⓗ Ⓙ
10 Ⓕ Ⓖ Ⓗ Ⓙ	23 Ⓐ Ⓑ Ⓒ Ⓓ	36 Ⓕ Ⓖ Ⓗ Ⓙ	49 Ⓐ Ⓑ Ⓒ Ⓓ	62 Ⓕ Ⓖ Ⓗ Ⓙ	75 Ⓐ Ⓑ Ⓒ Ⓓ
11 Ⓐ Ⓑ Ⓒ Ⓓ	24 Ⓕ Ⓖ Ⓗ Ⓙ	37 Ⓐ Ⓑ Ⓒ Ⓓ	50 Ⓕ Ⓖ Ⓗ Ⓙ	63 Ⓐ Ⓑ Ⓒ Ⓓ	
12 Ⓕ Ⓖ Ⓗ Ⓙ	25 Ⓐ Ⓑ Ⓒ Ⓓ	38 Ⓕ Ⓖ Ⓗ Ⓙ	51 Ⓐ Ⓑ Ⓒ Ⓓ	64 Ⓕ Ⓖ Ⓗ Ⓙ	
13 Ⓐ Ⓑ Ⓒ Ⓓ	26 Ⓕ Ⓖ Ⓗ Ⓙ	39 Ⓐ Ⓑ Ⓒ Ⓓ	52 Ⓕ Ⓖ Ⓗ Ⓙ	65 Ⓐ Ⓑ Ⓒ Ⓓ	

TEST 2

1 Ⓐ Ⓑ Ⓒ Ⓓ Ⓔ	11 Ⓐ Ⓑ Ⓒ Ⓓ Ⓔ	21 Ⓐ Ⓑ Ⓒ Ⓓ Ⓔ	31 Ⓐ Ⓑ Ⓒ Ⓓ Ⓔ	41 Ⓐ Ⓑ Ⓒ Ⓓ Ⓔ	51 Ⓐ Ⓑ Ⓒ Ⓓ Ⓔ
2 Ⓕ Ⓖ Ⓗ Ⓙ Ⓚ	12 Ⓕ Ⓖ Ⓗ Ⓙ Ⓚ	22 Ⓕ Ⓖ Ⓗ Ⓙ Ⓚ	32 Ⓕ Ⓖ Ⓗ Ⓙ Ⓚ	42 Ⓕ Ⓖ Ⓗ Ⓙ Ⓚ	52 Ⓕ Ⓖ Ⓗ Ⓙ Ⓚ
3 Ⓐ Ⓑ Ⓒ Ⓓ Ⓔ	13 Ⓐ Ⓑ Ⓒ Ⓓ Ⓔ	23 Ⓐ Ⓑ Ⓒ Ⓓ Ⓔ	33 Ⓐ Ⓑ Ⓒ Ⓓ Ⓔ	43 Ⓐ Ⓑ Ⓒ Ⓓ Ⓔ	53 Ⓐ Ⓑ Ⓒ Ⓓ Ⓔ
4 Ⓕ Ⓖ Ⓗ Ⓙ Ⓚ	14 Ⓕ Ⓖ Ⓗ Ⓙ Ⓚ	24 Ⓕ Ⓖ Ⓗ Ⓙ Ⓚ	34 Ⓕ Ⓖ Ⓗ Ⓙ Ⓚ	44 Ⓕ Ⓖ Ⓗ Ⓙ Ⓚ	54 Ⓕ Ⓖ Ⓗ Ⓙ Ⓚ
5 Ⓐ Ⓑ Ⓒ Ⓓ Ⓔ	15 Ⓐ Ⓑ Ⓒ Ⓓ Ⓔ	25 Ⓐ Ⓑ Ⓒ Ⓓ Ⓔ	35 Ⓐ Ⓑ Ⓒ Ⓓ Ⓔ	45 Ⓐ Ⓑ Ⓒ Ⓓ Ⓔ	55 Ⓐ Ⓑ Ⓒ Ⓓ Ⓔ
6 Ⓕ Ⓖ Ⓗ Ⓙ Ⓚ	16 Ⓕ Ⓖ Ⓗ Ⓙ Ⓚ	26 Ⓕ Ⓖ Ⓗ Ⓙ Ⓚ	36 Ⓕ Ⓖ Ⓗ Ⓙ Ⓚ	46 Ⓕ Ⓖ Ⓗ Ⓙ Ⓚ	56 Ⓕ Ⓖ Ⓗ Ⓙ Ⓚ
7 Ⓐ Ⓑ Ⓒ Ⓓ Ⓔ	17 Ⓐ Ⓑ Ⓒ Ⓓ Ⓔ	27 Ⓐ Ⓑ Ⓒ Ⓓ Ⓔ	37 Ⓐ Ⓑ Ⓒ Ⓓ Ⓔ	47 Ⓐ Ⓑ Ⓒ Ⓓ Ⓔ	57 Ⓐ Ⓑ Ⓒ Ⓓ Ⓔ
8 Ⓕ Ⓖ Ⓗ Ⓙ Ⓚ	18 Ⓕ Ⓖ Ⓗ Ⓙ Ⓚ	28 Ⓕ Ⓖ Ⓗ Ⓙ Ⓚ	38 Ⓕ Ⓖ Ⓗ Ⓙ Ⓚ	48 Ⓕ Ⓖ Ⓗ Ⓙ Ⓚ	58 Ⓕ Ⓖ Ⓗ Ⓙ Ⓚ
9 Ⓐ Ⓑ Ⓒ Ⓓ Ⓔ	19 Ⓐ Ⓑ Ⓒ Ⓓ Ⓔ	29 Ⓐ Ⓑ Ⓒ Ⓓ Ⓔ	39 Ⓐ Ⓑ Ⓒ Ⓓ Ⓔ	49 Ⓐ Ⓑ Ⓒ Ⓓ Ⓔ	59 Ⓐ Ⓑ Ⓒ Ⓓ Ⓔ
10 Ⓕ Ⓖ Ⓗ Ⓙ Ⓚ	20 Ⓕ Ⓖ Ⓗ Ⓙ Ⓚ	30 Ⓕ Ⓖ Ⓗ Ⓙ Ⓚ	40 Ⓕ Ⓖ Ⓗ Ⓙ Ⓚ	50 Ⓕ Ⓖ Ⓗ Ⓙ Ⓚ	60 Ⓕ Ⓖ Ⓗ Ⓙ Ⓚ

TEST 3

1 Ⓐ Ⓑ Ⓒ Ⓓ	8 Ⓕ Ⓖ Ⓗ Ⓙ	15 Ⓐ Ⓑ Ⓒ Ⓓ	22 Ⓕ Ⓖ Ⓗ Ⓙ	29 Ⓐ Ⓑ Ⓒ Ⓓ	36 Ⓕ Ⓖ Ⓗ Ⓙ
2 Ⓕ Ⓖ Ⓗ Ⓙ	9 Ⓐ Ⓑ Ⓒ Ⓓ	16 Ⓕ Ⓖ Ⓗ Ⓙ	23 Ⓐ Ⓑ Ⓒ Ⓓ	30 Ⓕ Ⓖ Ⓗ Ⓙ	37 Ⓐ Ⓑ Ⓒ Ⓓ
3 Ⓐ Ⓑ Ⓒ Ⓓ	10 Ⓕ Ⓖ Ⓗ Ⓙ	17 Ⓐ Ⓑ Ⓒ Ⓓ	24 Ⓕ Ⓖ Ⓗ Ⓙ	31 Ⓐ Ⓑ Ⓒ Ⓓ	38 Ⓕ Ⓖ Ⓗ Ⓙ
4 Ⓕ Ⓖ Ⓗ Ⓙ	11 Ⓐ Ⓑ Ⓒ Ⓓ	18 Ⓕ Ⓖ Ⓗ Ⓙ	25 Ⓐ Ⓑ Ⓒ Ⓓ	32 Ⓕ Ⓖ Ⓗ Ⓙ	39 Ⓐ Ⓑ Ⓒ Ⓓ
5 Ⓐ Ⓑ Ⓒ Ⓓ	12 Ⓕ Ⓖ Ⓗ Ⓙ	19 Ⓐ Ⓑ Ⓒ Ⓓ	26 Ⓕ Ⓖ Ⓗ Ⓙ	33 Ⓐ Ⓑ Ⓒ Ⓓ	40 Ⓕ Ⓖ Ⓗ Ⓙ
6 Ⓕ Ⓖ Ⓗ Ⓙ	13 Ⓐ Ⓑ Ⓒ Ⓓ	20 Ⓕ Ⓖ Ⓗ Ⓙ	27 Ⓐ Ⓑ Ⓒ Ⓓ	34 Ⓕ Ⓖ Ⓗ Ⓙ	
7 Ⓐ Ⓑ Ⓒ Ⓓ	14 Ⓕ Ⓖ Ⓗ Ⓙ	21 Ⓐ Ⓑ Ⓒ Ⓓ	28 Ⓕ Ⓖ Ⓗ Ⓙ	35 Ⓐ Ⓑ Ⓒ Ⓓ	

TEST 4

1 Ⓐ Ⓑ Ⓒ Ⓓ	8 Ⓕ Ⓖ Ⓗ Ⓙ	15 Ⓐ Ⓑ Ⓒ Ⓓ	22 Ⓕ Ⓖ Ⓗ Ⓙ	29 Ⓐ Ⓑ Ⓒ Ⓓ	36 Ⓕ Ⓖ Ⓗ Ⓙ
2 Ⓕ Ⓖ Ⓗ Ⓙ	9 Ⓐ Ⓑ Ⓒ Ⓓ	16 Ⓕ Ⓖ Ⓗ Ⓙ	23 Ⓐ Ⓑ Ⓒ Ⓓ	30 Ⓕ Ⓖ Ⓗ Ⓙ	37 Ⓐ Ⓑ Ⓒ Ⓓ
3 Ⓐ Ⓑ Ⓒ Ⓓ	10 Ⓕ Ⓖ Ⓗ Ⓙ	17 Ⓐ Ⓑ Ⓒ Ⓓ	24 Ⓕ Ⓖ Ⓗ Ⓙ	31 Ⓐ Ⓑ Ⓒ Ⓓ	38 Ⓕ Ⓖ Ⓗ Ⓙ
4 Ⓕ Ⓖ Ⓗ Ⓙ	11 Ⓐ Ⓑ Ⓒ Ⓓ	18 Ⓕ Ⓖ Ⓗ Ⓙ	25 Ⓐ Ⓑ Ⓒ Ⓓ	32 Ⓕ Ⓖ Ⓗ Ⓙ	39 Ⓐ Ⓑ Ⓒ Ⓓ
5 Ⓐ Ⓑ Ⓒ Ⓓ	12 Ⓕ Ⓖ Ⓗ Ⓙ	19 Ⓐ Ⓑ Ⓒ Ⓓ	26 Ⓕ Ⓖ Ⓗ Ⓙ	33 Ⓐ Ⓑ Ⓒ Ⓓ	40 Ⓕ Ⓖ Ⓗ Ⓙ
6 Ⓕ Ⓖ Ⓗ Ⓙ	13 Ⓐ Ⓑ Ⓒ Ⓓ	20 Ⓕ Ⓖ Ⓗ Ⓙ	27 Ⓐ Ⓑ Ⓒ Ⓓ	34 Ⓕ Ⓖ Ⓗ Ⓙ	
7 Ⓐ Ⓑ Ⓒ Ⓓ	14 Ⓕ Ⓖ Ⓗ Ⓙ	21 Ⓐ Ⓑ Ⓒ Ⓓ	28 Ⓕ Ⓖ Ⓗ Ⓙ	35 Ⓐ Ⓑ Ⓒ Ⓓ	

Use a soft lead No. 2 pencil only. Do NOT use a mechanical pencil, ink, ballpoint, or felt-tip pens.

Begin WRITING TEST here.

If you need more space, please continue on the next page.

1

WRITING TEST

_____
_____
_____
_____
_____
_____
_____
_____
_____
_____
_____
_____
_____
_____
_____
_____
_____
_____
_____
_____
_____
_____
_____
_____
_____
_____
_____
_____

If you need more space, please continue on the back of this page.

2

WRITING TEST

_____

_____

_____

_____

_____

_____

_____

_____

_____

_____

_____

_____

_____

_____

_____

_____

_____

_____

_____

_____

_____

_____

_____

_____

_____

_____

_____

If you need more space, please continue on the next page.

WRITING TEST

_____

_____

_____

_____

_____

_____

_____

_____

_____

_____

_____

_____

_____

_____

_____

_____

_____

_____

_____

_____

_____

_____

_____

_____

_____

_____

_____

_____

_____

_____

_____

_____

_____

STOP!

English Test

45 Minutes—75 Questions

DIRECTIONS: In the five passages that follow, certain words and phrases are underlined and numbered. In the right-hand column, you will find alternatives for the underlined part. In most cases, you are to choose the one that best expresses the idea, makes the statement appropriate for standard written English, or is worded most consistently with the style and tone of the passage as a whole. If you think the original version is best, choose "NO CHANGE." In some cases, you will find in the right-hand column a question about the underlined part. You are to choose the best answer to the question.

You will also find questions about a section of the passage, or about the passage as a whole. These questions do not refer to an underlined portion of the passage, but rather are identified by a number or numbers in a box.

For each question, choose the alternative you consider best and fill in the corresponding circle on your answer document. Read each passage through once before you begin to answer the questions that accompany it. For many of the questions, you must read several sentences beyond the question to determine the answer. Be sure that you have read far enough ahead each time you choose an alternative.

Passage I

Milton's Style: A Critical Controversy

[1]

The English poet John Milton is best known for his biblical epic poem *Paradise Lost*—a work that has provoked centuries of debate about the suitability of its style. Although Milton differed, from his immediate peers by refusing to use rhyme, his most heated critics appeared

1. **A.** NO CHANGE
   B. Although Milton differed from
   C. Although, Milton differed from
   D. Although, Milton, differed from

later, and starting in the eighteenth century. Readers of

2. **F.** NO CHANGE
   G. and, starting
   H. and, started
   J. starting

Paradise Lost have most commonly objected to the poems' complicated sentence structure and unusual word choices.

3. **A.** NO CHANGE
   B. poems
   C. poem's
   D. poem

[2]

The critic Samuel Johnson, in a series of essays written in 1751, argued that Milton's poetic language was often too harsh and jarring. He claimed that Milton chose

GO ON TO THE NEXT PAGE.

and arranged words in ways that <u>fail</u> to create a
4

pleasant <u>effect and a musical effect.</u> However, Johnson did
5

very modestly admit that he still might "fall below the

illustrious writer" of *Paradise Lost*, suggesting his

continued high regard for Milton in other ways. Although

Johnson was an important tastemaker in his time, in spite of

an appearance marred by scars from a childhood illness, the

pendulum swung back strongly in Milton's favor in

subsequent decades. ▢6

[3]

In the nineteenth century, Milton's poetry received

acclaim from important figures like Mary Shelley, Percy

Bysse Shelley, Thomas Coleridge, and William <u>Blake and in</u>
7

<u>fact</u> many poets of the Romantic period in English literature
7

chose to write in a similar way—a high form of praise!

[4]

<u>However,</u> many readers in the twentieth century
8

once again found fault with Milton's style. T.S. Eliot, one of

the most famous poets <u>within</u> his generation, was among the
9

4. **F.** NO CHANGE
    G. fails
    H. failed
    J. had failed

5. **A.** NO CHANGE
    B. pleasant, musical effect.
    C. pleasant effect, and a musical one.
    D. pleasant effect which would be musical.

6. The writer is considering deleting the following clause from the preceding sentence:

    in spite of an appearance marred by scars from a childhood illness,

    Should the writer make this deletion?

    F. No, because the clause establishes Johnson's unusual authority as a tastemaker.
    G. No, because it prevents confusion with other eighteenth-century writers named Samuel Johnson.
    H. Yes, because it suggests that Johnson's unusual appearance was a hindrance rather than an asset.
    J. Yes, because it introduces material that is not immediately relevant.

7. **A.** NO CHANGE
    B. Blake and, in fact
    C. Blake. In fact,
    D. Blake, in fact

8. **F.** NO CHANGE
    G. Also,
    H. Meanwhile,
    J. Furthermore,

9. **A.** NO CHANGE
    B. at
    C. amongst
    D. of

GO ON TO THE NEXT PAGE.

Practice Tests

most greatest critical. In a 1946 essay, he called Milton both
<u>   </u>
10

a "great artist" and a "bad influence." According to Eliot,

Milton led other poets astray by encouraging them to focus

<u>rather than their meanings, on the sounds of words.</u> He cited
                     11

a number of examples in *Paradise Lost* where, he claimed,

the poem did not make any sense. Yet Milton continued to

have his defenders; Christopher Ricks, in his 1965 book

Milton's Grand Style, <u>implicated</u> Eliot of simply
                 12

misunderstanding the passages that he claims are nonsense.

[5]

Scholars of literature today have broadened their

<u>C.S. Lewis and William Empson, two additional critics,</u>
                     13
<u>were less concerned with the style of Milton's poem than</u>
                     13
<u>they were with its religious themes.</u>
               13

horizons and are <u>less likely to focus on style solely</u> when
                        14

they make claims about Milton. [15]

---

10. **F.** NO CHANGE
    G. most
    H. most great
    J. greater

11. **A.** NO CHANGE
    B. rather on their meanings, than the sounds of words.
    C. on the sounds of words rather than their meanings.
    D. on, rather their meanings, the sounds of words.

12. **F.** NO CHANGE
    G. implied
    H. prosecuted
    J. accused

13. Given that all of the following choices are true, which one would best maintain the focus of the preceding paragraph?

    A. NO CHANGE
    B. Ricks then went on to receive considerable praise and awards throughout his career, later becoming the president of the Association of Literary Scholars and Critics.
    C. Ricks' book remains well-regarded, and his opinions have helped to shape current thinking on Milton's work.
    D. Milton also wrote a great deal of nonfiction, including treatises on government, religion, and education.

14. **F.** NO CHANGE
    G. solely less likely to focus on style
    H. less solely likely to focus on style
    J. less likely to focus solely on style

15. Given that all of the following choices are true, which option provides the best concluding sentence for the passage as a whole?

    A. However, the critical history of Milton's work is still taught, and scholars continue to discuss and critique *Paradise Lost*.
    B. With its rich critical history, I can strongly recommend *Paradise Lost* to anyone who enjoys poetry.
    C. Samuel Johnson's essays, as public domain documents, can be read by all.
    D. *Paradise Lost* is still widely anthologized and translated.

GO ON TO THE NEXT PAGE.

Passage II

The Science of Chocolate Chip Cookie Perfection

Few things are more delicious than a perfect chocolate chip cookie. Of course, "perfect" means different things to different people: some prefer a chewy cookie, while some want their cookies crisp; and others find a cake-like texture is the best.

Though there is room for debate about the definition of "perfection," what cannot be argued is this: No matter one's personal chocolate chip ideal, however, achieving one's personal chocolate chip cookie ideal all comes down to science. More specifically, it all comes down to chemistry.

[1] Most recipes, for chocolate chip cookies, start with the same basic ingredients. [2] These ingredients include butter, sugar, vanilla, eggs, flour, salt, and some kind of chemical leavening agent such as baking soda, baking powder, or a combination of the two. [3] However, making cookies is about much more than combining a list of ingredients. [4] It's the ways these ingredients are handled during preparation and the techniques used to combine them that determine what type of chocolate chip cookie will be achieved. [5] Changing the way one ingredient is used can have a significant effect.

As a result, consider how butter is used. The first step in most recipes called for combined the butter with sugar. They are beaten together, and the moisture in the butter dissolves some of the sugar, which will leaven the

16. F. NO CHANGE
    G. some prefer a chewy cookie, while some want their cookies crisp, and
    H. some prefer a chewy cookie; while some want their cookies crisp, and
    J. some prefer a chewy cookie; while some want their cookies crisp; and

17. A. NO CHANGE
    B. achieved
    C. achieves
    D. to achieve

18. F. NO CHANGE
    G. recipes for chocolate chip cookies start
    H. recipes, for chocolate chip cookies start
    J. recipes for chocolate chip cookies, start

19. Which of the following true statements, if added here, would provide the most effective link between Sentences 2 and 4?
    A. NO CHANGE
    B. The quality of individual ingredients can vary, and each ingredient must be of the highest quality.
    C. Baking is a fine art, and the greatest bakers can dedicate their lives to learning it.
    D. That would be like saying that painting is just a matter of putting colors on canvas!

20. F. NO CHANGE
    G. Therefore
    H. For example
    J. In contrast

21. A. NO CHANGE
    B. called for combining
    C. calls for combines
    D. calls for combining

GO ON TO THE NEXT PAGE.

cookies as they bake or, in other words, make them rise.
_____
                      22

If you combines melted butter and sugar, however, the
   ‾‾
   23
result is a denser cookie. Browning butter, which evaporates

the water content of the butter so that it won't dissolve sugar,

makes even more of a difference. ☐24

Then there's the effect of butter on gluten, the web
                                    _____
                                            25
of interconnected proteins that sets up when something is
_____
                25
baked. Gluten makes cookies crispier, and butter affects its

formation. Butter inhibits gluten to produce a more tender
       _____
                           26
cookie, which cannot form in fat. As a result, more butter
_____
              26
makes for a chewier cookie.

Conversely, less water also equals less gluten
_____
     27

22. **F.** NO CHANGE
    G. or make them rise.
    H. in other words, make them rise.
    J. DELETE the underlined portion.

23. **A.** NO CHANGE
    B. one
    C. they
    D. we

24. At this point, the writer is considering adding the following true statement:

    > The browned milk solids can also be removed to create clarified butter, which is often used as a dipping sauce for crab and other delicacies.

    Should the writer make this addition here?

    F. Yes, because it provides important information about another form of butter.
    G. Yes, because it helps the reader better understand how to use different types of butter.
    H. No, because it distracts the reader from the main focus of the paragraph.
    J. No, because it is inconsistent with the style and tone of the essay.

25. **A.** NO CHANGE
    B. on gluten. The web of interconnected proteins
    C. on gluten; the web of interconnected proteins
    D. on gluten the web of interconnected proteins

26. **F.** NO CHANGE
    G. The butter, which cannot form in fat, inhibits gluten to produce a more tender cookie.
    H. The butter inhibits gluten, which cannot form in fat, to produce a more tender cookie.
    J. Unable to form in fat, butter inhibits gluten to produce a more tender cookie.

27. **A.** NO CHANGE
    B. Therefore,
    C. However,
    D. Furthermore,

GO ON TO THE NEXT PAGE.

development so a cookie made with browned butter will be
_____
28

softer and chewier than one made with creamed butter or

even melted butter.

 If different ways of dealing with the butter make

such an enormous difference, then it's clear that the role of
_____
29

each ingredient must be considered when thinking about

chocolate chip cookies.

28. **F.** NO CHANGE
 G. development, so
 H. development so,
 J. development, so,

29. **A.** NO CHANGE
 B. a jumbo
 C. an epic
 D. a very, very big

> Question 30 asks about the preceding passage as a whole.

30. Suppose the writer had chosen to write a brief essay comparing the health benefits of chocolate chip cookies made with sweet butter with those made with salted butter. Would this essay successfully fulfill the writer's goal?

 F. Yes, because the essay does explain how different forms of butter affect the final cookies.

 G. Yes, because the essay includes salt in the list of ingredients used in most recipes.

 H. No, because the essay presents theories that do not reflect the effect of salt in butter on health.

 J. No, because the essay focuses only on the chemical effects of various forms of the ingredient in a recipe.

Passage III

Crab Fishing on the Pier

[1]

 I grew up next to the Pacific Ocean, where, it was
_____
31

common to see people fishing for crabs on the pier. Even in

wet weather there would often be one or two dedicated

families standing at the railing in their raincoats, waiting to
_____
32

31. **A.** NO CHANGE
 B. Pacific Ocean, where it
 C. Pacific Ocean where, it
 D. Pacific Ocean where it

32. The best placement for the underlined phrase would be:
 F. where it is now.
 G. after the word *Even*.
 H. after the word *weather*.
 J. after the word *traps*.

GO ON TO THE NEXT PAGE.

haul up their traps. I can remembering my own
_____
33

family going crab fishing as a family just once, though.
_____
34

[2]

I was only about five years old at the time, and the

big, clumsy crab pot looked to me like some sort of weird
____
35

metal basket. I also thought it was funny that my dad

used, leftover chicken from lunch, as the bait. He tossed the
_____
36

trap over the edge of the pier, and then the boring part
_____
37 .

started, we waited.
____
37

Therefore, my dad let me hold the yellow nylon line that led
_____
38

down to the trap on the seabed, and I felt proud to have such

an important job.

[3]

After a few unsuccessful hauls with nothing in the

trap, we finally pulled up a load of crabs. This was quite an
__
39

exciting moment for me. [40] I'm not sure if I'd been to the

aquarium yet, but I had definitely gone to the pet store to

look at the fish, and I loved everything to do with the

33. **A.** NO CHANGE
   B. remembers
   C. remembered
   D. remember

34. **F.** NO CHANGE
   G. family going crab fishing just once, though.
   H. going crab fishing as a family just one time, though.
   J. family going crab fishing just once, though, as I recall.

35. **A.** NO CHANGE
   B. onerous
   C. gauche
   D. manageable

36. **F.** NO CHANGE
   G. used leftover chicken from lunch as the bait.
   H. used leftover chicken, from lunch as the bait.
   J. used leftover, chicken from lunch, as the bait.

37. **A.** NO CHANGE
   B. and then: the boring part started, we
   C. and then the boring part started: we
   D. and then the boring part started we

38. **F.** NO CHANGE
   G. Occasionally,
   H. Otherwise,
   J. Consequently,

39. **A.** NO CHANGE
   B. me
   C. us
   D. they

40. Given that all the following statements are true, which one provides the most relevant information at this point in the essay?
   F. It had been a long wait.
   G. I stifled a yawn as my father pulled the yellow nylon line.
   H. There were real crabs in the trap!
   J. I'd never experienced a successful haul up close before this.

GO ON TO THE NEXT PAGE.

undersea world. 41 The crabs waved their claws at us

through the metal basket, so I wondered if they'd enjoyed
                                          ___
                                          42
our chicken.

[4]

Oddly enough, I don't remember us eating the crabs

that we caught that day. They may simply have been too

small, but I have an even more likely theory. My dad is a

very tender-hearted man the sort that would never hurt a fly
                     _____
                                        43
and I'm not sure he could hurt a crab either. I imagine he let
___
43
them go back into the sea. That would also explain why we

never went crab fishing again.

41. The writer is considering deleting the preceding sentence from the paragraph. If the writer made this deletion, the paragraph would primarily lose:

   A. information that distracts from the main point of the paragraph.

   B. a detail that relates the narrator's previous experiences with crabs.

   C. a detail that helps explain why the narrator was excited to see the crabs in the pot.

   D. the repetition of a detail that is clearly stated elsewhere in the paragraph.

42. F. NO CHANGE
   G. and
   H. for
   J. yet

43. A. NO CHANGE
   B. man the sort that would—never—hurt a fly and
   C. man—the sort that would never hurt a fly—and
   D. man the sort that would never hurt a fly—and

Questions 44 and 45 ask about the preceding passage as a whole.

44. Upon reviewing the essay and realizing that some key information has been left out, the writer composes the following sentence incorporating that information:

   At other times, I amused myself by trying to read the signs that explained which crabs were too small to keep.

   The sentence would most logically be placed after the last sentence in Paragraph:

   F. 1
   G. 2
   H. 3
   J. 4

45. Suppose the writer's goal had been to write an essay focusing on the various ways in which people forage for wild foods. Would this essay fulfill this goal?

   A. Yes, because the essay explains that people who live near the Pacific Ocean regularly go crab fishing.

   B. Yes, because the essay focuses on the methods used to haul crabs from the ocean.

   C. No, because the essay focuses on the narrator's childhood fascination with all things aquatic.

   D. No, because the essay primarily focuses on a single event from the narrator's past.

GO ON TO THE NEXT PAGE.

Passage IV

Olmec Heads: A Marvel of Mesoamerican Sculpture

[1]

Three thousand years ago, the Olmec civilization

lived in the tropical forests of southeastern Mexico. We do

not know what the Olmec called themselves; "Olmec" was

a term used by their neighbors, and refers to the

numerically abundant supply of natural rubber in
_____
46

there homeland. While much else about the civilization
___
47

remain a mystery, archaeologists have uncovered a number
_____
48

of magnificent works of Olmec art. Perhaps, the most
_____
49

impressive of these artworks is seventeen colossal head
__
50

sculptures.

[2]

The heads. Which date to before 900 BCE, are carved
_____
51

out of huge blocks of basalt. These heads probably depict

important rulers even though the blocks weigh between six
_____
52

and fifty tons, the Olmec carried them over ninety miles in

swampy and uneven terrain to their final destination at

46. **F.** NO CHANGE
    G. abundant, numerically,
    H. abundant in number
    J. abundant

47. **A.** NO CHANGE
    B. their
    C. they're
    D. they are

48. **F.** NO CHANGE
    G. remains
    H. remained
    J. OMIT the underlined portion

49. **A.** NO CHANGE
    B. Perhaps:
    C. Perhaps
    D. Perhaps;

50. **F.** NO CHANGE
    G. was
    H. are
    J. is being

51. **A.** NO CHANGE
    B. The heads which
    C. The heads; which
    D. The heads, which

52. **F.** NO CHANGE
    G. rulers, even though
    H. rulers. Even though
    J. rulers. Even though,

GO ON TO THE NEXT PAGE.

multiple sites in the area. The Olmec did not have wheels or
                                        ___
                                        53
draft animals, and it is unclear how they accomplished such

a feat. [54]

[3]

The heads are very realistic, with a wide range of

detailed facial features and expressions. Each also depicts

headgear that, in life, will likely have been made of fabric.
                              ___
                              55
Based on pigments found on one of the heads, archaeologists

speculate that the pieces were originally painted.

[4]

[1] Therefore, the cultural purpose of the Olmec
    _____
                    56
heads is another topic of speculation. [2] Many were found

buried and show signs of alteration, and the anthropologist

David C. Grove offers a possible explanation in a chapter of

the 1981 book *The Olmec and Their Neighbours*. [3] Grove

notices that the marks on the sculptures are similar across

multiple sites, and implying a deliberate practice. [4]
_____
         57
However, some other scholars think they were simply

damaged during a conflict. [5] He suggests that the marking

and burial were part of a ceremony to record the passage of

53. At this point in the essay, the writer wants to provide specific information about the location of the colossal head sites. Given that all of the choices are true, which one best conveys that information?

  A. NO CHANGE
  B. present-day Veracruz and Tabasco.
  C. Southeastern Mexico.
  D. Mexico.

54. At this point, the writer is considering deleting the final sentence of the second paragraph. Should the writer make this deletion?

  F. Yes, because deleting the sentence preserves a captivating sense of mystery about the Olmec heads.
  G. Yes, because the sentence provides information that is already addressed more clearly in another paragraph.
  H. No, because the sentence anticipates questions the reader might have about how the Olmec transported the blocks.
  J. No, because the sentence shows how draft animals were important to the Olmec artistic process.

55. A. NO CHANGE
  B. would
  C. will have
  D. was

56. F. NO CHANGE
  G. However, the cultural purpose
  H. Alternately, the cultural purpose
  J. The cultural purpose

57. A. NO CHANGE
  B. sites and implying
  C. sites, and, implying
  D. sites, implying

GO ON TO THE NEXT PAGE.

time or acknowledge a change in ruling dynasties. 58

[5]

While the original purpose of the Olmec heads
_____
                    59
remains open to scholarly debate, it is clear that the great
_____
                    59

stone colossi have a new role in our time: they make
                                              _____
                                                  60
travelers and museum-goers worldwide say, "Wow!"
_____
                    60

58. For the sake of logic and coherence, sentence 4 should be placed:

  F. where it is now.
  G. after sentence 1.
  H. after sentence 2.
  J. after sentence 5.

59. Which of the following would be the LEAST logical alternative for the underlined portion?

  A. Though it remains unclear what needs Olmec heads fulfilled for ancient people,
  B. While it is unclear what role Olmec heads might play in present-day society,
  C. Although the ancient role of the Olmec heads remains a mystery,
  D. Even though we can't be totally certain about why the Olmec built their heads millennia ago,

60. F. NO CHANGE
  G. captivate the imaginations of travelers and museum-goers worldwide.
  H. are really, really impressive to tourists and travelers.
  J. are a super interesting tourist attraction, and are very appealing to people from around the world.

PASSAGE V

The Platypus: A Creature Full of Surprises

[1]

The platypus is an Australian mammal that lays eggs,
makes venom, and has a bill like a duck. This has long given
it a reputation as a very unusual animal. In a story told by
indigenous Australians, birds, water animals, and land
animals all invite the platypus to join them, but because it is
                                                _____
                                                    61
so independent-minded it rejects them all. Early scientists
also recognized the singularity of the platypus, and some

61. Which of the following alternatives to the underlined portion would be LEAST acceptable?

  A. but since
  B. but as
  C. and although
  D. yet because

GO ON TO THE NEXT PAGE.

even refuse to believe that such a creature could exist: when
<u>62</u>

the English zoologist George S'haw first saw a preserved

specimen in 1799, he thought that somebody was trying to

play <u>the prank</u> on him. No one doubts the platypus's
<u>63</u>

existence now, but its <u>sublime</u> abilities continue to surprise us.
<u>64</u>

[2]

Venomous <u>mammals, are</u> also very unusual. The only
<u>65</u>

other mammals to share this quality <u>are</u> certain shrews and
<u>66</u>

bats—venom is otherwise mostly found <u>in:</u> reptiles and fish.
<u>67</u>

The male platypus carries a powerful venom <u>amidst</u> the
<u>68</u>

hollow spurs on its hind legs.

[3]

Egg-laying mammals, known as "monotremes," are

very rare. This category includes, along with the platypus,

the echidna—a hedgehog-like animal also found in

62. F. NO CHANGE
G. refused
H. refuses
J. refusing

63. A. NO CHANGE
B. his prank
C. the pranks
D. a prank

64. F. NO CHANGE
G. remarkable
H. wicked
J. wonderful

65. A. NO CHANGE
B. mammals are
C. mammals, are,
D. mammals are,

66. F. NO CHANGE
G. is
H. as
J. was

67. A. NO CHANGE
B. in;
C. in
D. in,

68. F. NO CHANGE
G. among
H. within
J. about

GO ON TO THE NEXT PAGE.

Australia. Australia's biodiversity is among the greatest on
earth. Platypus eggs are soft, much like a reptile's. Once
⁶⁹

they hatch, likewise, baby platypuses drink their mother's
⁷⁰
milk like other mammals.

[4]

The snout of the platypus gives it the uncommon
sense of "electrolocation." It is covered with highly sensitive
electroreceptors. These sensors allow the platypus to sense
the electrical fields set off by the muscle movements of prey,
such as shrimp and larvae. Only a few other mammals
⁷¹
echidnae and dolphins share this sense. When the platypus
⁷¹
hunts underwater, it keeps its eyes, ears, and nose closed; its
electroreceptors are its only means of finding food.

[5]

The platypus is not the only mammal to lay eggs,
secrete venom, or use electrolocation, but it is the only one
to do all three. It can proudly take it's place as one of the
⁷²

most uniquest animals in the world.
⁷³

69. At this point, the writer is considering deleting the underlined sentence. Should the writer make this deletion?

   A. Yes, because the sentence does not relate to the subject of the paragraph at large.

   B. Yes, because it introduces a boastful tone that is inappropriate when writing about animals.

   C. No, because it relates logically to the previous sentence in the paragraph.

   D. No, because it helps to explain why the platypus evolved in Australia.

70. F. NO CHANGE
   G. however,
   H. too,
   J. similarly,

71. A. NO CHANGE
   B. mammals echidnae, and dolphins
   C. mammals—echidnae and dolphins—
   D. mammals: echidnae and dolphins

72. F. NO CHANGE
   G. its'
   H. it is
   J. its

73. A. NO CHANGE
   B. uniquer
   C. uniquest
   D. most unique

GO ON TO THE NEXT PAGE.

Questions 74 and 75 ask about the preceding passage as a whole.

74. Suppose the writer intends to produce a passage describing cultural responses to the platypus. Does the preceding passage fulfill that goal?

F. Yes, because it explains how indigenous Australians and 18th-century English scientists reacted to the platypus's famous duck-bill.

G. Yes, because it begins by discussing the historical role of the platypus in Australian pranks.

H. No, because the passage is much more closely focused on the platypus's physical features.

J. No, because the passage devotes most of its attention to the place of dolphins, birds, and echidnae in culture.

75. For the sake of logic and coherence, Paragraph 2 should be placed:

A. where it is now.

B. after paragraph 3.

C. after paragraph 4.

D. after paragraph 5.

END OF TEST 1.

STOP! DO NOT TURN THE PAGE UNTIL YOU ARE TOLD TO DO SO.

Mathematics Test

60 Minutes—60 Questions

DIRECTIONS: For each problem, solve for the correct answer, select your choice and fill in the corresponding bubble on your answer document.

Some problems may take a longer time to solve, but do not take too much time on any single problem. Solve the easier questions first, then return to the harder questions in the remaining time for this test.

A calculator is allowed on this test. While you may be able to solve some problems without a calculator, you are allowed to use a calculator for all of the problems on this test.

Note: Unless otherwise directed, all of the following statements are considered correct.

1. All drawn figures are NOT necessarily drawn to scale.
2. All geometric figures are in a plane.
3. The word *line*, when used, is the same as a straight line.
4. The word *average*, when used, is the same as arithmetic mean.

---

1. How many real solutions exist for the equation $0 = x^2 + x$?

   A. 0
   B. 1
   C. 2
   D. 3
   E. Infinitely many

2. $C + D - 2(C + D) = ?$

   F. $3C + 3D$
   G. $-C + 3D$
   H. $-C - D$
   J. $-C$
   K. $-D$

3. For all nonzero values of x, $\dfrac{4x^4 + 8x^3 + 16x^2}{4x^2} = ?$

   A. $x^2 + 2x$
   B. $x^2 + 2x + 4$
   C. $x^2 + 2x^{\frac{3}{2}} + 4$
   D. $4x^4 + 8x^3 + 12x^2$
   E. $4x + 12$

4. Gabriella purchases tickets to a baseball game on sale for $6.00 each. She spends $42.00 on her tickets, which is $56.00 less than if she had bought them at regular price. What was the regular ticket price?

   F. $ 8.00
   G. $10.00
   H. $12.00
   J. $14.00
   K. $16.00

5. What is the greatest common factor of 51, 68, and 119?

   A. 3
   B. 4
   C. 7
   D. 13
   E. 17

6. Henry wants to paint the 4 walls of his bedroom and has enough paint for 175 square feet. If the walls of the bedroom are each 9 feet high and 13 feet long, and Henry uses all of his paint, what is the area of his walls, in square feet, that will remain unpainted?

   F. 0
   G. 175
   H. 293
   J. 468
   K. 936

GO ON TO THE NEXT PAGE.

7. If $\dfrac{2}{x} + \dfrac{3}{x} = 40$, what is the value of x?

   A. $\dfrac{1}{2}$

   B. $\dfrac{1}{4}$

   C. $\dfrac{1}{6}$

   D. $\dfrac{1}{8}$

   E. $\dfrac{1}{40}$

8. In the diagram below, $\overline{AB}$ and $\overline{CD}$ are parallel. What is the value of q?

   F. 47
   G. 60
   H. 73
   J. 81
   K. 120

11. How many prime numbers are there between 80 and 100?

    A. 3
    B. 4
    C. 5
    D. 6
    E. 7

12. In the diagram below, lines $\overline{LM}$ and $\overline{NP}$ are parallel to each other. What is the value of c, in degrees?

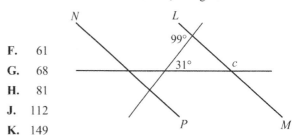

    F. 61
    G. 68
    H. 81
    J. 112
    K. 149

9. Alex works as an unpaid intern at an office for a month for college credit. She does the work that the company would otherwise pay an employee $12 per hour to do. If there are twenty 8-hour work days in this month, how much money does the company save by having Alex work instead of a paid employee?

   A. $ 336
   B. $ 836
   C. $1,920
   D. $2,420
   E. $2,920

13. Which of the following is equal to $20x + 8y - 80$?

    A. $3x + y - 10$
    B. $5x + 2y - 20$
    C. $4(5x + 2y - 20)$
    D. $4(5x + 2y - 40)$
    E. $4(5x + 8y - 20)$

10. In the standard (x,y) coordinate plane, point Q has coordinates $(1,4)$ and point R has coordinates $(5,a)$, where a is an unknown number. If the distance between Q and R is 4, which of the following is the value of a?

    F. 1
    G. 2
    H. 3
    J. 4
    K. 5

14. In the standard (x,y) coordinate plane, a line segment has its endpoints at $(-10,-4)$ and $(6,8)$. What are the coordinates of the midpoint of the line segment?

    F. $(-2,2)$
    G. $(-2,6)$
    H. $(2,2)$
    J. $(2,6)$
    K. $(8,6)$

GO ON TO THE NEXT PAGE.

15. The following chart shows the current enrollment in Grade 11 science classes offered by Centennial High School.

Grade 11	
Biology	55
Chemistry	41
Physics	28
Total	124

If there are only 84 Grade 11 students enrolled in science classes, what is the maximum number of Grade 11 students who are enrolled in more than one science class?

A. 28
B. 40
C. 55
D. 61
E. 84

16. A large triangle is composed of 16 equal smaller triangles, as shown below. What is the ratio of the shaded area to the area of the whole triangle?

F. 1:2
G. 1:3
H. 1:4
J. 1:5
K. 1:6

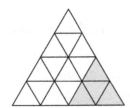

17. Herb is building a fence around his field. On the first day, he builds 15 fence-posts. He plans to build 5 more fence-posts on each successive day than he built the day before. If Herb will finish his fence on the first day he builds 60 fence-posts, how many fence-posts will he have built in total?

A. 60
B. 75
C. 375
D. 600
E. 750

18. In the standard (x,y) coordinate plane, shape A contains points that are all the same distance from its center. Which of the following figures is shape A?

F. Square
G. Line segment
H. Triangle
J. Circle
K. Plane

19. The expression $(3a^2 - 4b)(3a^2 + 4b)$ is equivalent to:

A. $9a^2 - 16b^2$
B. $9a^4 - 16b^2$
C. $9a^2 - 16b^4$
D. $6a^2 - 8b^2$
E. $9a^2 + 16b^2$

20. A salesman sells suits for $200 each. As a weekly promotion, he offers a shirt at a discount price of $20 to anyone who purchases a suit. If he sells a discount shirt with 10% of the suits he sells and makes a total of $8,080, how many suits does he sell?

F.   4
G.   20
H.   40
J. 202
K. 220

21. A kite is constructed by sewing together two triangular pieces of fabric. The two triangles share a base with a length of 20 inches. What is the length of h, to the nearest inch?

A. 22
B. 28
C. 30
D. 39
E. 41

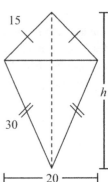

GO ON TO THE NEXT PAGE.

22. What 3 numbers could be placed in the blanks below so that the difference between consecutive numbers is the same?

$$\_\_ , 12, \_\_ , 22, \_\_$$

F. 2, 22, 32

G. 6, 16, 26

H. 7, 17, 27

J. 9, 19, 29

K. 10, 14, 24

23. Howard is baking a cake. He has half a bag of flour and 1 liter of milk. There are 14 cups in 1 bag of flour and 4 cups in 1 liter of milk. If Howard needs $1\frac{2}{3}$ cups of flour and $\frac{3}{4}$ cups of milk per cake, what is the maximum number of whole cakes he can bake?

A. 3

B. 4

C. 5

D. 6

E. 8

24. Martin and Robert share a pizza. If Martin eats $\frac{1}{3}$ of the pizza and Robert eats $\frac{2}{7}$ of the pizza, what is the ratio of Martin's share to Robert's share?

F. 7:6

G. 6:7

H. 3:7

J. 3:2

K. 3:1

25. A square is inscribed in a second square, as shown in the figure below. What must the value of x be, in degrees?

A. 45

B. 90

C. 110

D. 125

E. 135

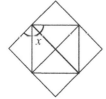

26. The table below shows the weekly crate production of a factory for month A and month B.

	Production (crates/week)	
	Month A	Month B
Week 1	2,000	2,000
Week 2	3,000	1,000
Week 3	2,000	3,000
Week 4	3,000	0

What is the percent decrease in average weekly crate production from month A to month B?

F. 25%

G. 39%

H. 40%

J. 50%

K. 66%

27. If x is a negative integer, which of the following expressions, if any, are equal for all possible values of x?

    I. $-x$

   II. $-|x|$

  III. $|-x|$

A. I and II

B. I and III

C. II and III

D. I, II, and III

E. None of the expressions are equal for all values of x.

28. What is the value of $\left(\dfrac{g^2}{g+1}\right) + \left(\dfrac{g+1}{g^2}\right)$ when $g = 4$?

F. 1

G. $\dfrac{271}{80}$

H. $\dfrac{281}{80}$

J. $\dfrac{153}{40}$

K. $\dfrac{281}{40}$

GO ON TO THE NEXT PAGE.

29. Last month, 200 people donated food items to the Downtown Food Bank as shown in the figure below.

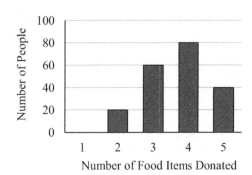

Number of People (y-axis)
Number of Food Items Donated (x-axis)

Which of the following statements is justifiable from the given information?

A. The mode is greater than the median.

B. The mean is greater than the median.

C. The median is greater than the mode.

D. The mode is equal to the median.

E. The mean is equal to the median.

30. If a and b are integers such that $a < 0$ and $b < 0$, then which of the following inequalities *must* be true?

F. $\dfrac{a}{b} > 1$

G. $ab > 2$

H. $a^2 > b^2$

J. $a^2b^3 > 0$

K. $a^2b^2 > 0$

31. Two horses—Cleo and Jordan—race against 8 other horses. The horses all have similar chances to win the race. If Cleo finishes first, what is the probability, to the nearest percent, that Jordan finishes second?

A. 1%

B. 10%

C. 11%

D. 20%

E. 47%

32. Joanne bounces a basketball as shown in the figure below. It bounces off the ground at time $t = 0$, and its height during its first bounce, h, at time t, in seconds, is given by $h = -t^2 + 4t$. After what time, in seconds, does the basketball hit the ground again?

F. 2

G. 4

H. 6

J. 8

K. 16

33. If $f(x) = x^2 + 2x$ and $g(x) = \sqrt{2x}$, what is the value of $f(g(8))$?

A. $32 + 16\sqrt{2}$

B. 32

C. 24

D. 16

E. $4\sqrt{2}$

34. The number line shown below represents which of the following systems of inequalities?

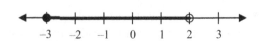

F. $x < -3$ and $x \leq 2$

G. $x > -3$ and $x \leq 2$

H. $x \geq -3$ and $x < 2$

J. $x \geq -3$ or $x < 2$

K. $x > -3$ or $x \leq 2$

GO ON TO THE NEXT PAGE.

35. The base of a cookie box is constructed by attaching two semicircles to the opposite sides of a square, as shown below. If one side of the square measures 6 centimeters and the box is 9 centimeters deep, what is the volume of the box, to the nearest cubic centimeter?

A.   149
B.   494
C.   578
D.   1,072
E.   1,342

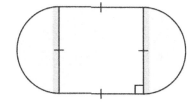

36. Which of the following expressions is equivalent to

$$\frac{\sqrt{x^2 + 6x + 9}}{x^2 - 9} ?$$

F. $(x + 3)(x - 3)$

G. $\dfrac{x + 3}{x - 3}$

H. $\dfrac{\sqrt{x + 3}}{x - 3}$

J. $\dfrac{\sqrt{x^2 + 6x + 9}}{x - 3}$

K. $\dfrac{1}{x - 3}$

37. Two parallel lines l and m are graphed in the standard (x,y) coordinate plane below. If these lines extend infinitely in both directions, which of the following statements is FALSE?

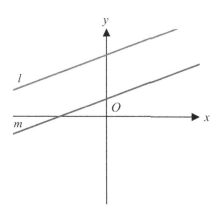

A.   Line l and line m never intersect.
B.   The y-intercept of line m is positive.
C.   Line l does not intersect the x-axis.
D.   Line l and line m may both contain positive and negative y-coordinates.
E.   Line l and line m have the same slope.

Use the following information to answer questions 38–40.

The exponential growth of bacterial populations is modeled by the following function, where A, f, and r are constants, and P and t are variables:

$$P(t) = A\,(f)^{rt}$$

P is the population size at time t, in hours. A is the initial size of the population when $t = 0$, f is the factor by which the population is multiplied in every growth interval, and r is the number of growth intervals per hour.

38. One strain of bacteria grows according to the equation $P(t) = 20(10)^t$. What would be the size of this bacterial population after 3 hours of growth?

F.   200
G.   500
H.   6,000
J.   10,000
K.   20,000

39. If a strain of bacteria doubles during every half-hour and began with an initial population of 50 bacteria, which of the following equations would accurately express the growth of the strain per hour?

A. $P = 50(2)^{2t}$
B. $P = 50(2)^{0.5t}$
C. $P = 50(2)^2$
D. $P = 2(50)^{2t}$
E. $50 = A(2)^{2t}$

40. Another type of bacteria grows by a factor of 5 during each growth interval. If a population of 1000 of these bacteria grew from an initial population of 40 over a period of 5 hours, how many growth intervals did the bacteria undergo per hour?

F. $\dfrac{1}{5}$

G. $\dfrac{2}{5}$

H.   1

J.   2

K.   5

GO ON TO THE NEXT PAGE.

41. A square with one side measuring 3 units is inscribed in a circle, as shown below. What is the area of the circle, in square units?

A. $\dfrac{19\pi}{4}$

B. $\dfrac{\sqrt{18}}{2}\pi$

C. $\sqrt{18}\pi$

D. $\dfrac{9\pi}{2}$

E. 18π

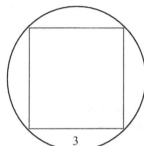

42. Four identical overlapping rectangles are drawn, as shown in the figure below. Each rectangle is 10 inches long and 3 inches wide. What is the sum, in inches, of the inner and outer perimeters formed by these rectangles?

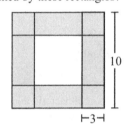

F. 28
G. 40
H. 44
J. 56
K. 64

43. For 2 consecutive integers, the result of adding twice the smaller integer and half the larger integer is 33. What are the 2 integers?

A. 10, 11
B. 11, 12
C. 12, 13
D. 13, 14
E. 14, 15

44. Which of the following is the equation of a line perpendicular to the line $y = 5x - 3$ and passing through the point $(-4,4)$ in the standard (x,y) coordinate plane?

F. $y = \dfrac{1}{5}x + \dfrac{16}{5}$

G. $y = \dfrac{1}{5}x - \dfrac{24}{5}$

H. $y = -\dfrac{1}{5}x + \dfrac{24}{5}$

J. $y = -\dfrac{1}{5}x + \dfrac{16}{5}$

K. $y = -5x$

45. Matrix A, $\begin{bmatrix} 7 & -2 \\ -1 & 8 \end{bmatrix}$, can be multiplied by a constant, k, to yield matrix B, $\begin{bmatrix} -21 & 6 \\ 3 & -24 \end{bmatrix}$. What is the value of k?

A. 3
B. -3
C. 2
D. -2
E. 5

46. Triangle BFG with vertices B, F, and G is shown in the standard (x,y) coordinate plane below.

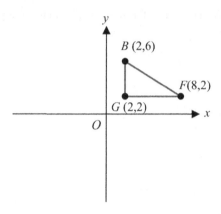

Triangle BFG is reflected across the y-axis and translated 4 units to the right. Which of the following graphs shows the result of these transformations?

F.
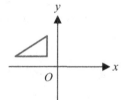

J.
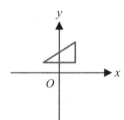

G.
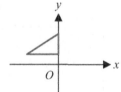

K.
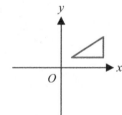

H.
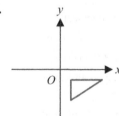

GO ON TO THE NEXT PAGE.

47. An exam room seats a maximum of 9 students. Which of the following expressions gives the number of permutations for 120 students who are taking a test in this exam room?

A. $120(9)$

B. $9!$

C. $\dfrac{120!}{9!}$

D. $\dfrac{120!}{(120-9)!}$

E. $\dfrac{120!}{(9!)(120-9)!}$

48. Which of the following is the graph of the equation $y = \dfrac{x^2 - 7x - 8}{x + 1}$ in the standard (x,y) coordinate plane?

F.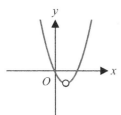

J.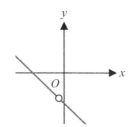

G.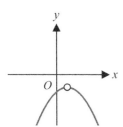

K.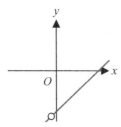

H.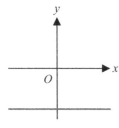

49. If $\log_2 x = a$ and $\log_2 y = b$, then $\log_2 xy = ?$

A. ab

B. $\dfrac{a}{b}$

C. $a - b$

D. $a + b$

E. $2ab$

50. Bricks with uniform dimensions of 18 inches by 7 inches are laid to form a wall such that the edge of the brick on top of the row below it lies at the midpoint of the brick directly beneath it, as shown in the figure below. A brick is cut in half if it is too long for the edge of the wall, and its other half is used on the other side of the wall. How many bricks need to be used to make a wall that is 42 inches tall by 126 inches long?

F. 40
G. 41
H. 42
J. 43
K. 44

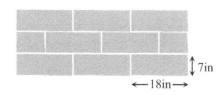

51. When graphed in the standard (x,y) coordinate plane, the lines $x = \dfrac{2y - 7}{5}$ and $y = 6 - x$ intersect at what point?

A. $\left(\dfrac{2}{5}, -1 \right)$

B. $\left(\dfrac{37}{7}, \dfrac{5}{7} \right)$

C. $\left(\dfrac{5}{7}, \dfrac{37}{7} \right)$

D. $(\ 0,\ 6)$

E. $\left(-\dfrac{37}{7}, \dfrac{5}{7} \right)$

GO ON TO THE NEXT PAGE.

52. A triangular prism is placed in a box, which measures 14 inches by 14 inches by 6 inches, as shown in the diagram below.

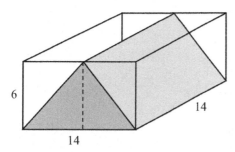

After the prism is placed in the box, how much empty space remains in the box, in inches cubed?

F. 84

G. 588

H. 980

J. 1,092

K. 1,176

53. A rectangle is graphed such that each of its vertices are located in a different quadrant of the standard (x,y) coordinate plane below. The rectangle is then rotated 180 degrees and reflected across the x-axis.

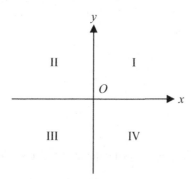

Quadrants of the Standard
(x,y) Coordinate plane

If vertex A of the rectangle was originally located in quadrant I, in which quadrant is it located after the rectangle's rotation and reflection?

A. I

B. II

C. III

D. IV

E. The quadrant cannot be determined.

54. Xiao the lumberjack leans a ladder against a vertical tree, as shown in the figure below. If the ladder reaches a height of 12 feet up the tree trunk and makes an angle of 25° with the ground, which of the following expressions represents the length of the ladder?

F. 12sin(25)

G. 12sin(65)

H. $\dfrac{12}{\sin(25)}$

J. $\dfrac{12}{\cos(25)}$

K. 12tan(25)

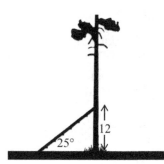

55. In the circle shown below in the standard (x,y) coordinate plane, the center lies at (4,–2) and the point (7,–1) lies on the circle. Which of the following points must also lie on the circle?

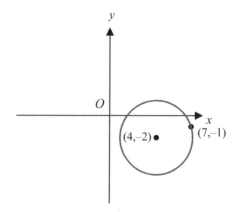

A. (4,–3)

B. (1,–4)

C. (1,–3)

D. (1,–2)

E. (–1,–3)

GO ON TO THE NEXT PAGE.

56. Triangle ABC is shown below. The length of a is 16 and $\cos(B) = \dfrac{4}{5}$. What is the length of c?

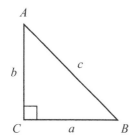

F. 4
G. 5
H. 16
J. 18
K. 20

θ is such that $0 < \theta < \dfrac{\pi}{2}$.

57. Which of the following statements must be true?

    I. $\sin\theta < 0$
   II. $\cos\theta < 0$
  III. $\tan\theta > 0$

A. I only
B. II only
C. III only
D. I and II
E. I, II, and III

58. The expression $\dfrac{2(\sin^2(\theta) + \cos^2(\theta))}{4}$ is equivalent to:

F. 0

G. $\dfrac{1}{2}$

H. 1

J. $\sin x$

K. $\tan x$

59. A rectangle has 2 diagonals, a pentagon has 5 diagonals, and a hexagon, with 6 sides, has 9 diagonals. If a nonagon has 9 sides, how many diagonals does it have?

A. 9
B. 12
C. 17
D. 27
E. 35

60. The volume for a pyramid with a square base is calculated with the equation $v = \dfrac{l^2 h}{3}$, where v is volume, l is the length of one side of the base, and h is the pyramid's height from the center of the base to its top. Measurements of the square-based pyramid below are given in meters. What is the volume, in cubic meters, of the pyramid?

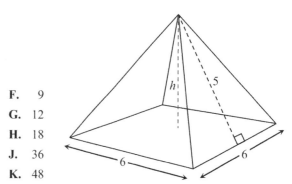

F. 9
G. 12
H. 18
J. 36
K. 48

END OF TEST 2.

STOP! DO NOT TURN THE PAGE UNTIL YOU ARE TOLD TO DO SO.

DO NOT RETURN TO THE PREVIOUS TEST.

Reading Test

35 Minutes—40 Questions

DIRECTIONS: There are multiple passages in this test. Each one is accompanied by several questions. After reading a passage, choose the best answer to every question and fill in the matching circle on your scoring sheet. You can refer back to the passages as often as necessary.

Passage I

Prose Fiction: This passage is adapted from the short story "Arrangement" by Rob Morris (©2003 by Rob Morris).

After they moved the fold-out sofa into the den and the old bed into the guest room, the men from the furniture store carried two new beds into the bedroom and arranged them side by side, leaving a corridor the
5 width of the night table between them. She tipped the men and sent them away, and now it seemed to her that their heavy steps had stirred up a layer of dust.

She was sure the house needed cleaning, and she set to work with a rag and a can of furniture polish.

10 She felt industrious, the way she felt on the first mild day in April. In fact it was January. Snow had drifted into their driveway. Window panes made tiny cracking noises. She bent over the dining room table, wiping firmly in small circles. Even from a low angle,
15 even with the sallow afternoon light illuminating the table's surface, she had to admit that the table—and every other surface in the room—was remarkably clean.

And yet this fact made her work seem all the more necessary. The silver picture frame on the side table
20 cried out to be held and buffed and set down at a jaunty angle. Her hands begged to wipe the candlesticks. The weight of the sugar bowl, the crust around its rim, the curve of the rocking chair's legs—the house gathered itself up and called to her, and she responded, moving
25 with a sure step from room to room.

In the den she discovered that her husband's files were poorly kept, and she applied herself to the task of straightening them. But as she opened first one folder and then another, their contents seemed alien and brittle.
30 There were ancient carbons the color of bad teeth, knickknacks and gifts from students and secretaries. A frog made from green felt dropped from a folder and into her lap. The frog had bubble eyes with black discs for pupils, and they made a weak rattle. The weight of his

35 life at the school pressed down on her shoulders. She had pulled out a file drawer, and now she saw it stretch before her like tracks laid across a prairie—all that distance covered with files, all those files filled with material that she could not improve. She tried to shut the door as she
40 stood, and in her hurry she caught the tip of a finger in the drawer's path.

She considered the benefit of yelling. It might release the hot thumping pulse in her finger, which she now held to her side.

45 She yelled. It was an orderly yell, and it offered no relief. Her finger still pulsed. She convinced herself that any swelling or injury would be less important than finishing the project she had started, so she picked up her rag and began again.

50 Now evening hung outside—the drifts were the color of light from television—and she went upstairs to start in on their bedroom. She imagined a traveler passing the house on foot and noticing the square of yellow light—their bedroom window—set against the dusk. He
55 would gaze at her industry as if it were a fire.

She stood and squared herself to look at the beds. She gave them the face she would give an errant child. The mattresses had the sheen and smell of satin. The beds needed sheets, so she went to the hall linen closet to find
60 them.

The closet needed straightening too, and she set it to rights while looking for single sheets. She refolded towels and stacked them neatly on one shelf. Washcloths were folded into squares and set on top of pillowcases,
65 which looked as smooth and fine as party gloves. Sheets were held out and examined, then folded and set in separate stacks—one for top sheets, one for bottom sheets. All of the sheets were made for king-size beds.

"Well," she said, shutting the closet door and
70 holding two sets of sheets against her chest, "I guess we'll just have to look a little baggy."

GO ON TO THE NEXT PAGE.

As she readied herself to spread out the first bottom sheet, a door clicked shut downstairs.

She set the sheets down on one bed, still folded.

75   Her husband wore soft-soled shoes, so she could hardly hear him come up the stairs. But she knew his pace well enough to count it off; she knew the exact moment when his head would poke around the corner of the stairwell. And there it was. And there, too, was the
80   sigh he let out as he pulled himself to the top step, exaggerating the effort.

"Oh, the banker's wife, the banker's wife," he said. "You could have been the banker's wife." He said this facing the bathroom door, so she saw him in profile, like
85   a president on a coin. Now he turned to her and said, "Instead, you got me. How does it feel? How does it feel to be the principal's wife?"

He looked into the room. "Ah hah," he said. He pressed past her and slid into the room.

90   "Now this is something new."

1.   The passage focuses mainly on:

A.   the protagonist's last-minute efforts to prepare the spare room for the arrival of an unexpected guest.

B.   the conflicted feelings the protagonist experiences when her husband changes careers.

C.   the protagonist's tenseness and consequent desire to clean and rearrange her house.

D.   the protagonist's anguish about the cold and foreboding winter weather.

2.   As used in line 45, the word "orderly" most nearly means:

F.   commanding.

G.   clinical.

H.   neat.

J.   restrained.

3.   The passage implies that there are only king-sized sheets in the closet because:

A.   the protagonist and her husband cannot afford other sizes of sheets.

B.   before the time of the story, there were only ever king-sized beds in the house.

C.   the family who lives in the house is forgetful and a little disorganized.

D.   the furniture store made a mistake and sent the wrong size of sheets.

4.   Compared with the way she felt while cleaning the rest of the house, when the protagonist tries to clean up her husband's files, she feels:

F.   more welcome.

G.   less comfortable.

H.   more confident.

J.   less rushed.

5.   In the context of the passage, lines 34-35 most likely indicate that the protagonist:

A.   resents how often she had to help her husband finish his schoolwork when he was younger.

B.   is fatigued after spending so much time arranging her husband's files.

C.   feels dejected that she is unable to engage with her husband's work life.

D.   has sympathy for the student who gave her husband the frog as a gift.

6.   Based on the passage, the protagonist would most likely describe her husband as:

F.   genial and disorganized.

G.   unsentimental and distant.

H.   stately and dignified.

J.   world-weary and hopeless.

7.   The third paragraph (lines 10-17) primarily serves to:

A.   depict the desolate weather, which suggests the coldness of the characters.

B.   clarify that the protagonist's wish to clean is because of her inner emotional state, not the house's untidiness.

C.   describe the protagonist's superior technique, which reveals an important aspect of her personality.

D.   establish a timetable of events that foreshadows a later tragedy.

8.   Which of the following questions is NOT answered by information in the passage?

F.   How long have the husband and protagonist been married?

G.   What is the protagonist's husband's occupation?

H.   Does the husband expect to see the new single beds?

J.   Does the protagonist stop cleaning after she hurts her finger?

9.   As used in the passage in line 55, the word "industry" most nearly means:

A.   machinery.

B.   business.

C.   skilled trade.

D.   work.

GO ON TO THE NEXT PAGE.

10. The protagonist would most likely agree with which of the following statements?

F. Cleaning is a tedious necessity, best avoided for as long as possible.

G. Through life's changes, it can be reassuring to have control over something like cleanliness.

H. There's no point trying to clean your house when it is already tidy.

J. Receiving new furniture can cause a mess, so it is a good idea to clean up after a delivery.

Passage II

Social Science: This passage is adapted from the article "In Our Wi-Fi World, the Internet Still Depends on Undersea Cables" by Nicole Starosielski (©2015 by Nicole Starosielski).

Not many people realize that undersea cables transport nearly 100% of transoceanic data traffic. These lines are laid on the very bottom of the ocean floor. They're about as thick as a garden hose and carry the [5] world's internet, phone calls, and even TV transmissions between continents at the speed of light. A single cable can carry tens of terabits of information per second. While researching my book *The Undersea Network*, I realized that the cables we all rely on to send everything [10] from email to banking information across the seas remain largely unregulated and undefended. Although they are laid by only a few companies and often funneled along narrow paths, the ocean's vastness has often provided them protection.

[15] The fact that we route internet traffic through the ocean—amidst deep sea creatures and hydrothermal vents—runs counter to most people's imaginings of the internet. Didn't we develop satellites and Wi-Fi to transmit signals through the air? Haven't we moved to [20] the cloud? Undersea cable systems sound like a thing of the past. The reality is that the cloud is actually under the ocean. Even though they might seem behind the times, fiber-optic cables are actually state-of-the-art global communications technologies. Since they use light to [25] encode information and remain unfettered by weather, cables carry data more quickly and cheaply than satellites can. They crisscross the continents too—a message from New York to California also travels by fiber-optic cable. These systems are not going to be [30] replaced by aerial communications anytime soon.

The biggest problem with cable systems is not technological—it's human. Because they run underground, underwater, and between telephone poles,
cable systems populate the same spaces we do. As a result, [35] we accidentally break them all the time. Local construction projects dig up terrestrial lines. Boaters drop anchors on cables. And submarines can disturb systems under the sea. Are global communications networks at risk of disruption? What would happen if these cables were cut? The answer [40] to this is not black and white. Any individual cable is always at risk, but likely far more so from boaters and fishermen than any saboteur. Over history, the single largest cause of disruption has been people unintentionally dropping anchors and nets.

[45] The International Cable Protection Committee has been working for years to prevent such breaks. As a result, cables today are covered in steel armor and buried beneath the seafloor at their shore-ends, where the human threat is most concentrated. This provides some level of [50] protection. In the deep sea, the ocean's inaccessibility largely safeguards cables—they need only to be covered with a thin polyethelene sheath. It's not that it's much more difficult to sever cables in the deep ocean, it's just that the primary forms of interference are less likely to [55] happen. The sea is so big and the cables are so narrow, the probability isn't that high that you'd run across one.

Sabotage has actually been rare in the history of undersea cables. There have been occurrences, but these are disproportionately publicized. The World War I [60] German raid of the Fanning Island cable station in the Pacific Ocean gets a lot of attention. And there was speculation about sabotage in the cable disruptions outside Alexandria, Egypt, in 2008, which cut off 70% of the country's internet, affecting millions. Yet we hear [65] little about the regular faults that occur, on average, about 200 times each year. The fact is it's incredibly difficult to monitor these lines. Cable companies have been trying to do so for more than a century, since the first telegraph lines were laid in the 1800s. But the ocean is too vast and [70] the lines simply too long. It would be impossible to stop every vessel that came anywhere near critical communications cables. We'd need to create extremely long "no-go" zones across the ocean, which itself would profoundly disrupt the economy.

[75] Fewer than 300 cable systems transport almost all transoceanic traffic around the world. And these often run through narrow pressure points where small disruptions can have massive impacts. Since each cable can carry an extraordinary amount of information, it's [80] not uncommon for an entire country to rely on only a handful of systems. In many places, it would take only a few cable cuts to take out large swathes of the internet. If the right cables were disrupted at the right time, it could

GO ON TO THE NEXT PAGE.

disrupt global internet traffic for weeks or even months. The thing that protects global information traffic is the fact that there's some redundancy built into the system. Since there is more cable capacity than there is traffic, when there is a break, information is automatically rerouted along other cables. Because there are many systems linking to the United States, and a lot of internet infrastructure is located here, a single cable outage is unlikely to cause any noticeable effect for Americans.

Any single cable line has been and will continue to be susceptible to disruption. And the only way around this is to build a more diverse system. But as things are, even though individual companies each look out for their own network, there is no economic incentive or supervisory body to ensure the global system as a whole is resilient. If there's a vulnerability to worry about, this is it.

11. The passage suggests that a single cable outage would cause:

  A. significant disruptions for Americans, but limited disruptions elsewhere.

  B. significant disruptions for both Americans and people elsewhere.

  C. moderate disruptions for both Americans and people elsewhere.

  D. negligible disruptions for Americans, but potentially significant disruptions elsewhere.

12. As used in the third paragraph, the word "populate" (line 34) most closely means:

  F. popularize.

  G. produce.

  H. occupy.

  J. exit.

13. The author's tone can be described as:

  A. sarcastic.

  B. informative.

  C. surprised.

  D. excited.

14. The main point of the second paragraph (lines 15–30) is that:

  F. oceanic cables are mostly a thing of the past.

  G. satellites are the fastest and cheapest way to send signals.

  H. deep-sea creatures cause excessive traffic in the ocean.

  J. undersea cables are still the best way to carry data.

15. The passage states that, compared to the risk of accidental damage, the risk of deliberate sabotage of undersea cables is:

  A. slightly higher.

  B. about the same.

  C. slightly lower.

  D. significantly lower.

16. According to the passage, undersea cables are buried and surrounded by steel armor as a result of:

  F. the International Cable Protection Committee's struggles to protect cables from deliberate cutting.

  G. efforts by the International Cable Protection Committee to protect cables from nets and anchors.

  H. a cable company's special initiative to stop seawater from eroding cables.

  J. British attempts to deter German raids on Fanning Island during World War I.

17. As used in the fifth paragraph, the word "critical" (line 71) most nearly means:

  A. perilous.

  B. important.

  C. disparaging.

  D. broken.

18. The purpose of the final paragraph is to show that:

  F. the largest potential weakness of the world's undersea cable networks is a lack of global cooperation.

  G. the world's undersea cable system is more resilient, as a whole, than its individual parts.

  H. cable lines remain vulnerable to snipping, crushing, and corrosion.

  J. a more diverse system must incorporate satellites and cloud computing to improve transmission speeds.

19. The passage states that outages affecting 70% of a nation's internet access occurred in:

  A. Egypt in 2008.

  B. Germany during World War I.

  C. France in 2011.

  D. The United States in 1999.

GO ON TO THE NEXT PAGE.

20. Based on the fifth paragraph (lines 57–74), which of the following statements would the author most likely agree with regarding the protection of undersea cables from damage?

 F. Governments must cooperate to stop ships from sailing too close to communications cables.

 G. The media has not done enough to warn citizens to be vigilant about the sabotage of cables.

 H. It would be a waste of time and money to focus efforts on preventing damage from ships.

 J. Emulating telegraph companies of the 1800s would allow for more efficient monitoring of cables.

Passage III

Humanities: Passage A is adapted from the article "When it Comes to Comics, Let's Put Literary Criticism Back on the Shelf" by David Sweeney (©2014 by David Sweeney). Passage B is adapted from "Teaching Graphic Novels as Literature: *The Complete Maus* Enters the Curriculum" by Catherine Beavis (©2013 by Catherine Beavis).

Passage A by David Sweeney

The absorption of comic books into a culturally highbrow setting should not go unquestioned. Some believe that a "high-quality" text can only be enjoyed by a similarly sophisticated audience, and something
5 similar often happens when comics are discussed as "graphic novels."

I have always disliked the term "graphic novel." I have found that it is often used in an attempt to elevate certain comics, and their readers, to a more legitimate
10 social position. Deploying the notion of the novel in this way demonstrates an ignorance of its cultural history. After all, the novel as we know it today only achieved preeminence relatively recently, beginning in the 18th century. Hitherto it was considered inferior to poetry and
15 drama, and was seen to be a form of entertainment for the lower classes, rather than "serious" literature. The novel rose to its current status in parallel with the rise of the bourgeoisie, for whom it became their original literary form.

20 Alan Moore, one of the best-known and most highly regarded writers in the comics field, has remarked that growing up in Britain in the 1950s and 1960s, comics were "just something you have, like rickets." In this comment, the association of a lowly textual form with a
25 lowly social class—rickets being a condition associated in Britain with the working class—is explicit. Moore is credited with bringing depth and maturity to comics with his "revisionist" superhero series *Watchmen*, illustrated by Dave Gibbons, which attempted to present a realist
30 view of the superhero genre.

Several other British writers, most notably Neil Gaiman, offered radical reinterpretations of existing comic book characters, which challenged and ultimately redefined the superhero genre. Gaiman in particular was
35 marketed as a novelist who just so happened to be working in the comic book field; Gaiman's image as a "serious" writer was further emphasized by the forewords and endorsements from prose novelists which accompanied the collected editions of his work,
40 including Norman Mailer's description of his *Sandman* series as "a comic strip for intellectuals."

But the success of comics has also increased the number of "readers" who seek to identify some intellectual merit in comic books. This is particularly true
45 in academia, where comparative literature programs place comics alongside works of literary and popular prose fiction. On the surface this appears to be a progressive step, but I wonder whether this inclusion, and seeming elevation, of comic books is not in fact a
50 reduction.

In being absorbed into highbrow literary discourse, the comic book form is often treated, at best, as a version of the prose novel. I am not saying that comic books aren't worthy of academic inquiry, but they should be
55 taken on their own terms and not those of established literary criticism. They require no elevation.

Passage B by Catherine Beavis

As a literary and artistic form, graphic novels combine the visual with text to create rich and complex narratives. But they also require a different kind of
60 "reading" than the school texts students might be used to. The recent move to include graphic novels in the curriculum invites a new examination of kinds of literacy and their demands on teachers, students, and examiners.

The Victorian Curriculum and Assessment
65 Authority (VCAA) provides a list of approved texts for study as part of English and English as an Additional Language. The text list includes a selection of texts in a range of categories—novels, short stories, poetry or songs, plays, nonfiction texts and, from 2014,
70 "multimodal," formerly the "film" category.

The move to expand the category "film" to "multimodal," and to provide teachers and students with the opportunity to study a graphic novel, is significant. For some time now, teachers and education bodies have

GO ON TO THE NEXT PAGE.

75 been conscious of the changing nature of literacy, and the need for students to be confident and competent users of both traditional and more contemporary forms.

The decision suggests two significant shifts in thinking. First, the graphic narrative now stands
80 alongside plays, poetry, and novels as a sophisticated and complex text form worthy of study and close analysis, meeting the common criteria for all texts on the list. Second, graphic novels are recognized as unique forms in their own right, with their own types of logic
85 and organization which differ significantly from both print-based genres and from film. This means that teachers and students will have the opportunity to explore and analyze the text, but also to recognize the importance of the visual elements of the story.

90 Pages in graphic novels and graphic narratives are made up of words, images, and panels. To read them effectively, and to understand their complex and subtle meanings, requires attention to the ways in which both images and words work independently and together.
95 Each has its own logic and way of organizing meaning.

In writing, one thing usually follows another. Theorist Gunther Kress describes the "logic" of writing as about time and sequence. With images, on the other hand, lots of information is presented at once. The
100 "logic" of the image is of "space and simultaneity".

Graphic narratives are quintessentially multimodal, and require new ways of reading that call on both visual and verbal modes. As the field has matured, a canon of sophisticated, multilayered graphic novels and
105 narratives has developed. They are worthy of study in senior secondary English classes alongside other forms of literature in more familiar print and multimedia genres.

Questions 21-25 ask about Passage A.

21. One of the main arguments the author is trying to make in Passage A is that:

A. all forms of writing, from novels to comic books, are worthy of academic study.

B. comic books do not need to be elevated to "serious literature" in order to have merit.

C. critics should spend more time analyzing a comic book's form rather than its narrative.

D. comic books should be taught alongside novels and other prose fiction in schools.

---

22. The author of Passage A indicates that he feels that the term "graphic novel" is:

F. unnecessary and misleading.

G. confusing and esoteric.

H. suitable and practical.

J. clear and explanatory.

23. In Passage A, the repetition of words like *lowly* and *lower* (lines 16–25) is most likely intended by the author to convey:

A. the historical association of popular forms of literature with the lower classes.

B. the relative inexpensiveness of comics as compared to other forms of literature.

C. the general critical classification of comics based on length and subject matter.

D. the place of literature in comparison to other forms of art, such as painting and music.

24. As it is used in line 36, the word *image* most nearly means:

F. appearance.

G. copy.

H. portrait.

J. reputation.

25. The author states that the elevation of comic books may actually be a "reduction" (line 50) because:

A. academic analysis tends to lump comic books in with other prose fiction.

B. critics have historically viewed comic books as a lowbrow form of fiction.

C. academics rarely treat comic books with the same rigor as novels and short stories.

D. most critics tend to forget about comic books in their literary analyses.

Questions 26-28 ask about Passage B.

26. Passage B best supports which of the following conclusions about graphic novels?

F. Graphic novels have replaced videos as the most popular multimodal form of storytelling.

G. Graphic novels have their own form of presentation that relies heavily on visual elements.

H. Graphic novels are a simpler form of storytelling than novels and film.

J. Graphic novels are now included in major curricula because of their strong moral themes.

GO ON TO THE NEXT PAGE.

27. Within Passage B, the author brings up the theorist Gunther Kress in lines 96–100 in order to:

    A. offer evidence of the usefulness of academic conversation about graphic novels.

    B. argue that graphic novels represent a less serious form of literature.

    C. contrast the logic of writing with the logic of images.

    D. suggest that the logic of comic books is less clear than the logic of novels.

28. The second paragraph of Passage B states that one of the changes instituted by the VCAA was that:

    F. schools were mandated to include at least three different forms of literature in each class.

    G. comic books were banned from inclusion in high school courses.

    H. graphic novels replaced prose fiction in most school curricula.

    J. the "film" category was transformed into the "multimodal" category.

Questions 29 and 30 ask about both passages.

29. The authors of both passages would likely agree with which of the following statements?

    A. Comic books have yet to become a serious form of literature.

    B. Critics should give more attention to comics.

    C. Comic books have literary qualities unique to their form.

    D. More authors than ever are now experimenting with graphic novels.

30. Unlike Passage A, Passage B views the inclusion of comic books in academic curricula as:

    F. praiseworthy.

    G. foolish.

    H. ambitious.

    J. detrimental.

GO ON TO THE NEXT PAGE.

Passage IV

Natural Science: This passage is adapted from the article "The ultimate in stealth, puff adders employ camouflage at every level" by Ashadee Kay Miller and Graham Alexander (©2016 Ashadee Kay Miller and Graham Alexander).

The puff adder (*Bitis arietans*) is one of the most widespread and venomous snakes in Africa. It is responsible for more deaths on the continent than any other snake. It is an extreme ambush forager, often lying
5 motionless for days at a time, waiting for prey to pass within striking range.

Unlike other snakes, puff adders spend most of their lives above ground, seldom seeking refuge beneath rocks or down burrows. During these long bouts in
10 ambush, an easily detectable puff adder would be a sitting duck to any predator, its ability to flee limited by its squat body. Instead, puff adders must rely on their ability to hide in plain sight using their astonishingly good camouflage.

15 The puff adder's risk of being eaten is remarkably high. It has as many as 42 documented species of predators, and in some years, annualized mortality rates can approach 50% of the adult population. In a system like this, the selective pressures acting on a species are
20 great, and may result in an evolutionary arms race between predator and prey. The puff adder's impressive visual camouflage is testament to this; its cryptic coloration and patterning are highly effective.

The puff adder has an additional survival
25 mechanism that, until now, has been little known: it doesn't carry a scent. This makes it undetectable to even the most keenly nosed predators. Not all of the puff adder's predators rely on vision to locate their prey. As many as 15, including dogs, meerkats, and mongooses,
30 rely on their keen sense of smell to find their food. This hunting style simply bypasses the effectiveness of the puff adder's visual camouflage.

Yet, from our observations in the field, it is clear that in response to an approach by predators, resting and
35 ambushing puff adders choose to remain motionless. In fact, they are so committed to this that we have observed dogs and mongooses walking directly over puff adders with no response from the snakes.

These observations led us to a very intriguing
40 question. Are puff adders evading their scent-orientated predators by hiding or reducing their scent? To answer this question, our research team implemented a novel approach. We enlisted a team of scent-matching dogs and meerkats. These puff adder predators were trained to
45 test whether they could locate puff adders using smell alone.

The use of detection dogs as research tools is growing in popularity within the field of ecology. They are now routinely used to locate rare, elusive, or invasive
50 species. Dogs are trained onto a specific target scent, which they must reliably and repeatedly indicate to gain reward.

But in this case the research team needed their dogs and meerkats to do much more. You can't train a dog or
55 meerkat onto a species' target scent if the species is scentless. So, the dogs and meerkats were required to match pairs of new scents to each other among a line-up of scent options. This is much more challenging, and it took the dogs and meerkats months to learn this skill. But
60 once they had, the researchers were able to test how smelly some snake species were to these sniffer extraordinaires.

It turned out that of the six snake species tested, one stood out as being undetectable. In 100 scent-matching
65 trials, puff adders stumped both the dog and meerkat teams every time. These teams failed to correctly match the puff adder scent pairs to each other at rates greater than chance.

The results from the other snake species were very
70 different. Both dogs and meerkats were able to match pairs of these smelly snake scents around 90% of the time. This makes the puff adder the first terrestrial vertebrate species for which chemical crypsis—the art of being scentless—has been demonstrated.

75 Although these findings are a world first, we believe that this phenomenon is likely to be common in the animal world. Ambushing animals that experience high mortality rates as a result of predation, and animals that remain in an exposed locality, such as incubating,
80 ground-nesting birds and newly born fawns, are likely to derive great benefit from being scentless or being able to mask their odor in some way.

Chemical crypsis has probably not been shown before simply due to research focus being biased toward
85 our own primary sense—vision. We hope that the findings act as a springboard for research on chemical crypsis in other systems. For now, we are focused on figuring out how puff adders are doing it.

GO ON TO THE NEXT PAGE.

31. The authors' purpose in writing this passage is most likely to:

    A. describe the discovery of a new species of snake.

    B. argue for increased research on chemical crypsis.

    C. detail the unusual camouflage abilities of puff adders.

    D. summarize recent research conducted on dogs and meerkats.

32. It can reasonably be inferred from the passage that puff adders' natural defenses:

    F. have weakened over time in response to decreased predation.

    G. are based mainly on their poisonous bodies.

    H. include fierce attacks on predators that discover them.

    J. still do not protect them from substantial population losses.

33. What does the passage offer as evidence that puff adders and their predators are engaged in an "evolutionary arms race" (line 20)?

    A. Annualized mortality rates of puff adders can reach 50%.

    B. Chemical crypsis may actually be more common than once believed.

    C. Over 42 different species have been known to prey upon puff adders.

    D. Puff adders have developed camouflaged coloring and patterning.

34. According to the passage, the use of detection dogs to locate species is:

    F. unprecedented.

    G. unpopular.

    H. revered.

    J. customary.

35. As it is used in line 11, the phrase *sitting duck* most nearly refers to the fact that puff adders would be:

    A. helpless in evading detection from skilled predators.

    B. easy prey without their camouflage defenses.

    C. less effective hunters if they carried a scent.

    D. mostly harmless if not for their chemical defenses.

36. The main purpose of the study described in the passage was to determine:

    F. the biological mechanisms behind the puff adders' chemical crypsis defense.

    G. whether puff adders were using chemical crypsis to avoid predators.

    H. how predators like dogs and meerkats hunted puff adders.

    J. whether puff adders could be trained to use chemical rather than camouflage defenses.

37. The passage suggests that unlike other snakes, the puff adder is unusual in that it:

    A. makes use of camouflage to avoid predators.

    B. can defend itself against dogs and meerkats.

    C. uses stealth to capture its prey.

    D. can avoid detection through chemical crypsis.

38. Within the passage, the statement in lines 77–82 serves mainly to:

    F. list some of the key results from the study discussed in the passage.

    G. provide support for the theory that chemical crypsis is common among animals.

    H. show that scentless animals are actually much rarer than once thought.

    J. offer evidence that puff adders prey upon a wide variety of creatures.

39. It can most reasonably be inferred that the word *stumped* in line 65 refers to puff adders' ability to:

    A. baffle their natural predators.

    B. confuse the researchers.

    C. engineer defenses against dogs and meerkats.

    D. flee from dangerous threats.

40. The authors indicate that research into chemical crypsis has sometimes been overlooked due to:

    F. a lack of available research funds.

    G. a bias towards researching visual camouflage.

    H. a focus on more common defenses.

    J. ignorance of the science behind it.

END OF TEST 3.

STOP! DO NOT TURN THE PAGE UNTIL YOU ARE TOLD TO DO SO.

DO NOT RETURN TO THE PREVIOUS TEST.

Science Test

35 Minutes—40 Questions

DIRECTIONS: There are several passages in this test, and each is accompanied by several questions. After reading a passage, choose the best answer to each question and fill in the corresponding oval on your answer document. You may refer to the passages as often as necessary.

You are NOT permitted to use a calculator on this test.

Passage I

Paper chromatography is a laboratory technique used to study mixtures. This technique uses a solvent to carry compounds through the fibers of a piece of paper. Different compounds will travel different distances through the paper according to their affinity for the solvent. Compounds with a higher affinity will travel farther, relative to the distance traveled by the solvent.

Students performed two experiments to determine the chemical composition of an unknown mixture, Mixture Z.

Study 1

The students collected 8 pure compounds (Compounds 1–8) from around the laboratory. They placed one drop of each compound near the bottom edge of a rectangular sheet of filter paper, as shown in Diagram 1. The bottom edge of the filter paper was placed in a beaker of acetone. As the acetone moved up the filter paper, it carried the samples of Compounds 1–8 with it. When the acetone neared the top of the filter paper, the students removed the filter paper from the acetone bath. The final positions reached by the acetone and by Compounds 1–8 are shown in Figure 1.

For each compound, the students measured the distance traveled and calculated a *retention factor* (R_f) value, which describes how far the compound traveled relative to the acetone solvent. The R_f values were calculated using the following formula:

$$R_f = \frac{\text{distance traveled by compound}}{\text{distance traveled by solvent}}$$

All results are shown in Table 1.

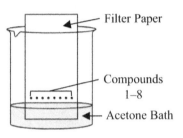

Diagram 1

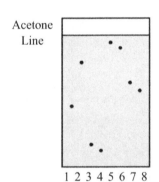

Figure 1

Table 1		
Compound	Distance traveled (cm)	R_f
Acetone	9.8	n/a
Compound 1	3.4	0.347
Compound 2	7.6	0.776
Compound 3	1.1	0.114
Compound 4	0.8	0.082
Compound 5	9.3	0.949
Compound 6	8.8	0.898
Compound 7	5.1	0.520
Compound 8	4.7	0.480

GO ON TO THE NEXT PAGE.

Study 2

The students repeated Study 1 using Mixture Z. Unlike the pure compounds from Study 1, Mixture Z separated into three spots (Z_1, Z_2, and Z_3) as it traveled through the filter paper. The final positions reached by the acetone and by the various components of Mixture Z are shown in Figure 2. The students measured the distances traveled and calculated the R_f values for Z_1, Z_2, and Z_3. The results are shown in Table 2.

Figure 2

Table 2		
Compound	Distance traveled (cm)	R_f
Acetone	9.7	n/a
Z_1	5.1	0.525
Z_2	0.7	0.076
Z_3	3.3	0.351

1. When attempting to replicate Studies 1 and 2, one of the students decides to use water, instead of acetone, as her solvent. Will she be able to compare her results to the results of Studies 1 and 2?

   A. No; the affinity of the compounds for water and acetone are the same.
   B. No; the affinity of the compounds for water and acetone may not be the same.
   C. Yes; the affinity of the compounds for water and acetone are the same.
   D. Yes; the affinity of the compounds for water and acetone may not be the same.

2. Based on the results of Study 1, which of the following compounds had the highest affinity for acetone?

   F. Compound 3
   G. Compound 4
   H. Compound 5
   J. Compound 6

3. One of the students finds another pure substance, Compound 9, in the lab. Compound 9 is known to have a higher affinity for acetone than Compound 2 and a lower affinity than Compound 6. The R_f value of Compound 9 is most likely:

   A. less than 0.520.
   B. between 0.520 and 0.776.
   C. between 0.776 and 0.898.
   D. greater than 0.898.

4. In both Studies 1 and 2, if the acetone had traveled farther up the filter paper, the distances traveled by Compounds 1–8 and Mixture Z would most likely have:

   F. decreased only.
   G. stayed the same.
   H. increased only.
   J. changed with no apparent trend.

5. A student makes a mixture of Compound 1, Compound 2, and Compound 3. In order to most effectively separate the components of this mixture, he should use:

   A. a solvent for which the three compounds have very different affinities.
   B. a solvent for which the compounds have very similar, but not identical, affinities.
   C. a solvent for which the compounds have identical affinities.
   D. a solvent for which the compounds have unknown affinities.

6. According to Table 2, Mixture Z is most likely composed of which of following sets of compounds?

   F. Compound 1, Compound 4, Compound 7
   G. Compound 1, Compound 4, Compound 8
   H. Compound 1, Compound 2, Compound 7
   J. Compound 6, Compound 7, Compound 8

7. The students most likely calculated R_f in addition to measuring the distances traveled by the compounds in order to:

   A. ensure that the distances traveled by the acetone were identical in both Study 1 and Study 2.
   B. compare the results of Study 1 and Study 2, even though the distances traveled by the acetone were not identical.
   C. calculate the density of acetone.
   D. determine the order in which Z_1, Z_2, and Z_3 were mixed to produce Compound Z.

GO ON TO THE NEXT PAGE.

Passage II

Biological aging involves a decrease in *metabolism*, the processes of chemical breakdown and synthesis necessary for life. It also involves a decrease in reproductive capability and in the ability to maintain *homeostasis*, a state in which cell and organ systems function at optimal capacity. Aging eventually leads to cell and organismal death. Four scientists discuss the causes of aging.

Scientist 1

Genes are composed of nucleic acids and instruct cells to produce proteins. When genes are active, their proteins are produced; when they are inhibited, their proteins are not produced. Regulatory genes, which are responsible for the activation and inhibition of other genes, are programmed to increasingly suppress metabolism, reproduction, and homeostasis genes over time. This process results in a gradual decrease in protein production, and eventual cell and organismal death.

Scientist 2

Free radicals are reactive oxygen-based chemicals that cause damage to important cellular components and to nucleic acids, and this damage accumulates over time. Eventually, this damage renders cellular components functionless and mutates nucleic acids, which means cells are no longer able to produce proteins involved in metabolism, reproduction, and homeostasis. Free radicals are produced as a byproduct of metabolic processes and can also be absorbed from the environment.

Scientist 3

Telomeres are nucleic acid structures that do not instruct cells to produce proteins. Instead, they are found at the end of protein-producing nucleic acids and protect them from damage. Every time a cell divides, its telomeres get shorter. When a telomere is too short, it can no longer protect protein-producing nucleic acids from damage. Over time, these nucleic acids are damaged and mutated, which means they are no longer able to produce proteins involved in metabolism, reproduction, and homeostasis.

Scientist 4

Hormones are chemical signals that circulate through an organism and initiate protein production in specific cells and tissues. Hormones are produced by endocrine glands, which gradually stop producing most hormones over time. Without hormones to initiate metabolic, reproductive, and homeostatic protein production, these processes cease. Other hormones signal these processes to slow and gradually stop.

8. Which scientist asserts that aging is caused by the shortening of nucleic acids?
   F. Scientist 1
   G. Scientist 2
   H. Scientist 3
   J. Scientist 4

9. Which scientist(s) claim(s) that decreased protein production is a part of the cause of aging?
   A. Scientist 1 only
   B. Scientist 3 only
   C. Scientists 1 and 2
   D. Scientists 1, 2, 3, and 4

10. *Antioxidants* are chemicals that inhibit the activity of reactive oxygen. Which scientist would agree with the claim that antioxidants slow the aging process?
   F. Scientist 1
   G. Scientist 2
   H. Scientist 3
   J. Scientist 4

11. Which of the following experimental discoveries is consistent with Scientist 1's viewpoint?
   A. The inhibition of the *Indy* regulatory gene allows fruit flies to live twice as long.
   B. The absence of the *IGF-1* hormone allows roundworms to live twice as long.
   C. Shortening telomeres with x-ray radiation causes yeast to live half as long.
   D. Damage to endocrine glands causes lab mice to live half as long.

12. There are two classes of aging hypothesis. The *Program Hypothesis* states that aging is triggered by internal biological mechanisms, like a self-destruct timer. The *Error Hypothesis* states that aging is caused by damage accumulated over time, like a tool wearing out from use. Which scientist(s) would agree with the *Error hypothesis*?
   F. Scientist 2 only
   G. Scientist 3 only
   H. Scientists 2 and 3
   J. Scientists 2, 3, and 4

GO ON TO THE NEXT PAGE.

Practice Tests

13. Another scientist claims that aging is caused by the loss of immune system function over time. The immune system protects organisms from disease and damage. How would Scientist 4 respond to this claim?

A. Immune system function is regulated by genes. When these genes inhibit the immune system, it ceases to function.

B. Immune system function is impaired by telomere shortening. When telomeres are too short, the immune system ceases to function.

C. Immune system function is triggered by hormones. When hormones are no longer produced, the immune system ceases to function.

D. Hormones are damaged by the loss of immune function. When the immune system ceases to function, hormones are no longer produced.

14. Metabolism produces molecules that store energy in an easily usable form. Which of the following molecules is produced during metabolism?

F. DNA

G. RNA

H. ATP

J. Chlorophyll

GO ON TO THE NEXT PAGE.

Passage III

Global warming has increased vegetation cover across northern *tundra*—regions with frozen subsoil, shrubs, and no trees. From the year 1880 to the present, the Alaskan moose (*Alces alces gigas*) has extended its range from *boreal* regions, which are heavily forested, across the *treeline* and into the northern tundra.

Moose bones were recovered from eroding *permafrost*, which is a subsurface layer of earth that remains frozen year-round. The bones were dated using carbon isotopes and were found to be from between 1880 and 1950. After 1940, a moose tracking program was established in Alaska. Figure 1 shows the locations of moose bones and sightings and the extent of moose habitats.

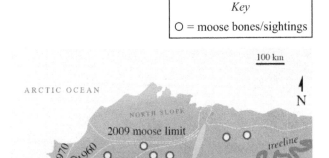

Figure 1

Moose require shrubs protruding above the snow in late winter for their habitat and food. The trend line in Figure 2 shows the mean shrub height, and Figure 3 shows the mean July temperature in Alaska since 1860. Figure 4 shows the average foliage mass of *A. gigas's* preferred shrubs, *Salix alaxensis* and *Salix richardsonii*.

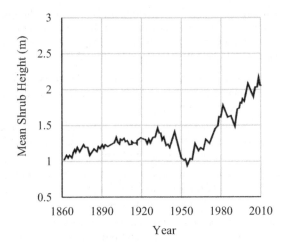

Figure 2

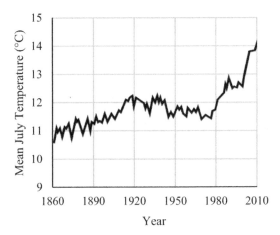

Figure 3

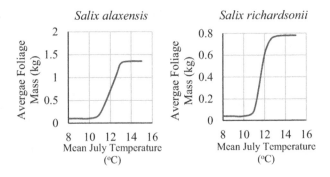

Figure 4

All figures adapted from Ken D. Tape et al., "Range Expansion of Moose in Arctic Alaska Linked to Warming and Increased Shrub Habitat." ©2016 by PloS One. 10.1371/journal.pone.0152636.

GO ON TO THE NEXT PAGE.

15. According to Figure 3, the greatest increase in mean July temperature observed in Alaska was between the years:

    A. 1890 and 1920.

    B. 1920 and 1950.

    C. 1950 and 1980.

    D. 1980 and 2010.

16. According to Figure 2, the greatest mean shrub height observed between the years 1860 and 1980 was:

    F. less than 1.5 m.

    G. between 1.5 m and 2.0 m.

    H. between 2.0 m and 2.5 m.

    J. greater than 2.5 m.

17. Which of the following figures best depicts the location of the treeline?

    A.
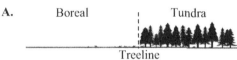

    B.
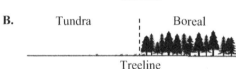

    C.

    D.

18. If the trend observed in Figure 3 continues, then the habitat of *A. gigas* will:

    F. extend into the North Slope.

    G. extend into the Seward Peninsula.

    H. contract into the Brooks Range.

    J. contract south of the treeline.

19. Suppose that the mean July temperature in 2016 was approximately the same as the mean July temperature in 2010. What will be the average foliage mass of *S. richardsonii* in 2016?

    A. 1.50 kg

    B. 1.25 kg

    C. 0.78 kg

    D. 0.65 kg

20. According to Figure 4, which of the shrubs preferred by *A. gigas* exhibited a greater increase in average foliage mass when the mean July temperature increased?

    F. *S. alaxensis* exhibited the greater increase in average foliage mass.

    G. *S. richardsonii* exhibited the greater increase in average foliage mass.

    H. Both *S. alaxensis* and *S. richardsonii* exhibited the same increase in average foliage mass.

    J. Neither *S. alaxensis* nor *S. richardsonii* exhibited an increase in average foliage mass.

GO ON TO THE NEXT PAGE.

Passage IV

Students studied *surface tension*, which is caused by the attraction of the particles in the surface of a solution to the bulk of the solution. The higher the surface tension, the more force will be required to break the surface of the solution.

Activity 1

Four beakers (Beakers 1–4) at 25°C were filled with 200 mL of distilled water, 200 mL of salt water, 200 mL of glycerol, and 200 mL of acetone, respectively. The students used a single-beam balance with an 8 cm-long needle suspended horizontally from its beam end. The length of the string holding the needle was adjusted so that the needle rested on the surface of the substance. Masses, in mg, were added to the tray of the balance until the needle was pulled from the surface of the substance, as shown in Diagram 1. The results are recorded in Table 1.

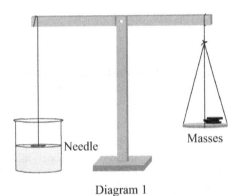

Diagram 1

Table 1	
Beaker	Mass required to remove needle (mg)
1	1175
2	1210
3	1145
4	1015

Activity 2

Each beaker was placed on a hot plate with a thermometer. Activity 1 was repeated and the mass required to remove the needle was measured at 4 temperatures, as shown in Figure 1.

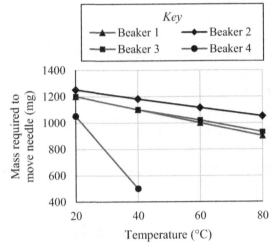

Figure 1

Activity 3

The surface tensions, s, of the substances at 25°C were calculated using the formula $s = \frac{2d}{F}$, where d is the length of the needle and F is the force required to remove the needle from the surface of the substance. The results are recorded in Table 2.

Table 2	
Beaker	Surface tension (dyn/cm)
1	71.97
2	74.09
3	70.18
4	62.32

Note: dyn = 1 g·cm/s^2

GO ON TO THE NEXT PAGE.

21. According to Activity 1, which of the following substances had the greatest surface tension?

   A. Distilled water

   B. Salt water

   C. Glycerol

   D. Acetone

22. The students predicted that increasing the temperature of a substance would decrease its surface tension. Are the results of Activity 2 consistent with this prediction?

   F. No; for each substance tested, the mass required to remove the needle was greater at a higher temperature.

   G. No; for each substance tested, the mass required to remove the needle was lower at a higher temperature.

   H. Yes; for each substance tested, the mass required to remove the needle was greater at a higher temperature.

   J. Yes; for each substance tested, the mass required to remove the needle was lower at a higher temperature.

23. In Activity 3, force (F) equals $m \times g$, where m is the mass required to pull the needle from the surface of the solution, and g is the acceleration due to gravity. Which of the following equations allows the students to correctly calculate surface tension?

   A. $s = 2dmg$

   B. $s = \dfrac{2d}{mg}$

   C. $s = \dfrac{mg}{2d}$

   D. $s = \dfrac{dm}{2g}$

24. Activity 1 differed from Activity 2 in which of the following ways?

   F. Only different substances were tested in Activity 1, whereas different temperatures were also tested in Activity 2.

   G. Only different temperatures were tested in Activity 1, whereas different substances were also tested in Activity 2.

   H. Surface tension was calculated in Activity 1 and not in Activity 2.

   J. Surface tension was calculated in Activity 2 and not in Activity 1.

25. Suppose that during Activity 1, the students forgot to rinse and dry the needle between Beaker 3 and Beaker 4. Compared to the *measured* mass required to pull the needle from the surface of the substance in Beaker 4, the *actual* mass would be:

   A. significantly greater.

   B. slightly greater.

   C. slightly less.

   D. exactly the same.

26. Of the following facts about acetone, which best explains the lack of data points at 60°C and 80°C for Beaker 4 in Figure 1?

   F. Acetone boils at 56°C.

   G. Acetone has a 10-day half-life.

   H. Acetone is an organic solvent.

   J. Acetone's chemical formula is C_3H_6O.

27. Suppose the students tested acetic acid using the same procedure as in Activity 1. They then calculated the surface tension using the formula in Activity 3, and found it to be 64.52 dyn/cm. What is the order of the substances, from the substance with the lowest surface tension to the substance with the highest?

   A. Salt water, distilled water, glycerol, acetone, acetic acid

   B. Salt water, distilled water, glycerol, acetic acid, acetone

   C. Acetone, acetic acid, glycerol, distilled water, salt water

   D. Acetic acid, acetone, glycerol, distilled water, salt water

GO ON TO THE NEXT PAGE.

Passage V

Researchers studied how the Saharan silver ant, *Cataglyphis bombycina*, tolerates high temperatures using small hairs that cover its body. The hairs reflect light and emit heat, which allows *C. bombycina* to survive in a temperature range uninhabitable by many other species of ants.

Study 1

Researchers collected 200 Saharan silver ants from sand dunes in Morocco and anesthetized the ants through exposure to carbon dioxide (CO_2), a non-toxic gas. Next, they removed the hairs on 100 of the ants' abdomens using a scalpel, and divided the ants into two groups: one of 100 shaved ants, and one of 100 unshaved ants. Each group of ants was placed in a gray *well plate* (a plate containing a matrix of round depressions), one ant per well. Each ant was then illuminated by 9 wavelengths of light for 90 seconds using a fitted bulb. The *reflectance*—percent of light reflected—of each ant at each wavelength was measured using a spectrophotometer, and the results for the two groups were averaged. Researchers recorded these results in Table 1.

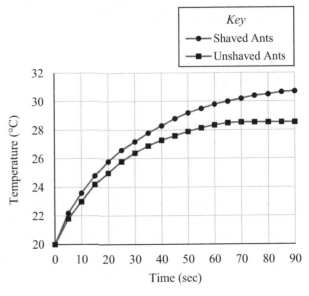

Figure 1

Table and figures adapted from Quentin Willot et al., "Total Internal Reflection Accounts for the Bright Color of the Saharan Silver Ant." ©2016 by PLOS One. 10.1371/journal.pone.0152325.

Table 1

Wavelength (nm)	Reflectance of Shaved Ants	Reflectance of Unshaved Ants
400	2.2%	5.9%
450	2.6%	5.5%
500	2.9%	5.5%
550	3.3%	5.5%
600	3.4%	5.3%
650	3.6%	5.1%
700	3.8%	5.0%
750	3.9%	5.0%
800	4.0%	4.9%

Study 2

Using the same gray well plates, researchers exposed the abdomens of both the 100 shaved Saharan silver ants and the 100 unshaved ants from Study 1 to light from a solar simulator for 90 seconds, and measured the ants' internal temperature using a digital thermometer. The internal temperatures of each group were averaged and recorded in Figure 2.

28. Based on Table 1, which of the following groups has the highest reflectance?

   F. Shaved ants exposed to light of 500 nm
   G. Shaved ants exposed to light of 750 nm
   H. Unshaved ants exposed to light of 500 nm
   J. Unshaved ants exposed to light of 750 nm

29. What was the dependent variable in Study 1?

   A. Heat emission
   B. Amount of hair
   C. Wavelength
   D. Reflectance

30. Suppose that an additional trial in Study 1 had been performed using a wavelength of 350 nm. The reflectance of shaved ants would most likely be:

   F. less than 1.7%.
   G. between 1.7 and 2.2%.
   H. between 2.2 and 2.7%.
   J. greater than 2.7%.

GO ON TO THE NEXT PAGE.

31. The researchers had predicted that shaving ants' hair would make them more likely to be affected by a temperature increase. Are the results of Study 2 consistent with this prediction?

  A. No; the internal temperature of shaved ants rose more rapidly than the internal temperature of unshaved ants.

  B. No; the internal temperature of unshaved ants rose more rapidly than the internal temperature of shaved ants.

  C. Yes; the internal temperature of shaved ants rose more rapidly than the internal temperature of unshaved ants.

  D. Yes; the internal temperature of unshaved ants rose more rapidly than the internal temperature of shaved ants.

32. One way Study 1 differed from Study 2 was that in Study 1:

  F. ants with only one type of hair were measured under different conditions, while in Study 2, ants with different types of hair were measured.

  G. ants with different types of hair were measured, while in Study 2, ants with only one type of hair were measured under different conditions.

  H. ants' internal temperature was measured, while in Study 2, ants' reflectance was measured.

  J. ants' reflectance was measured, while in Study 2, ants' internal temperature was measured.

33. A researcher discovers that Saharan silver ants perish when their internal temperature reaches 30°C. Based on the results of Study 2, which of the following groups would not survive?

  A. Shaved ants after 70 seconds of exposure

  B. Shaved ants after 50 seconds of exposure

  C. Unshaved ants after 70 seconds of exposure

  D. Unshaved ants after 50 seconds of exposure

34. One group of ants reached an internal temperature of 30°C after 65 seconds of exposure to light from a solar simulator. At 450 nm, what would the reflectance of these ants most likely be?

  F. 2.6%

  G. 4.0%

  H. 5.5%

  J. It is impossible to determine from the given information.

GO ON TO THE NEXT PAGE.

Passage VI

The *Coriolis effect* is the deflection of a moving object from its original path due to the inertial force caused by the counterclockwise rotation of the Earth. Figure 1 shows that an object is deflected to the east of its original path in the Northern Hemisphere and to the west of its original path in the Southern Hemisphere. Figure 2 shows the change in the rate of Earth's rotation from the Equator (0°N) to the North Pole (90°N). Figure 3 shows the strength of the inertial force that causes the Coriolis effect when the mass and velocity of the affected object varies.

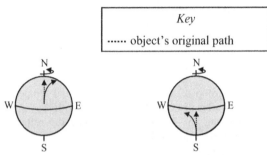

Figure 1

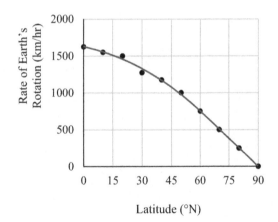

Figure 2

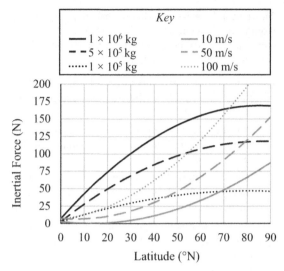

Figure 3

Note: An object with a mass of 5×10^5 kg was measured at different velocities, and objects of different masses were measured at 50 m/s.

35. If an object travels south in a straight line from Point A in the Northern Hemisphere then, due to the Coriolis effect, which point will the object most likely reach?

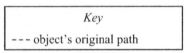

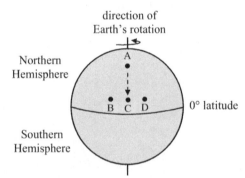

A. Point A

B. Point B

C. Point C

D. Point D

GO ON TO THE NEXT PAGE.

36. According to Figure 2, as latitude increases from the Equator to the North Pole, the rate of Earth's rotation:

F. increases only.

G. decreases only.

H. remains constant, then decreases.

J. remains constant, then increases.

37. According to Figure 3, the inertial force acting on an object with a mass of 7.5×10^5 kg traveling at 50 m/s at 90°N latitude would be:

A. less than 50 N.

B. between 50 and 100 N.

C. between 100 and 150 N.

D. greater than 150 N.

38. According to Figures 2 and 3, for an object of uniform mass and velocity, as the rate of the Earth's rotation increases, the Coriolis effect:

F. increases only.

G. decreases only.

H. increases, then decreases.

J. varies, but with no clear trend.

39. Which of the following properties of a moving object changes due to the Coriolis effect?

A. Velocity

B. Weight

C. Mass

D. Density

40. Which of the following objects would be most significantly affected by the Coriolis effect?

F. An object with a mass of 1×10^6 kg, traveling at 50 m/s at 0°N latitude.

G. An object with a mass of 1×10^6 kg, traveling at 100 m/s at 0°N latitude.

H. An object with a mass of 1×10^6 kg, traveling at 50 m/s at 60°N latitude.

J. An object with a mass of 1×10^6 kg, traveling at 100 m/s at 60°N latitude.

END OF TEST 4.

STOP! DO NOT TURN THE PAGE UNTIL YOU ARE TOLD TO DO SO.

DO NOT RETURN TO THE PREVIOUS TEST.

Writing Test
40 Minutes—1 Prompt

Directions: This is a test of your writing ability. You'll have 40 minutes to read the prompt, plan your response, and write your essay. Before you begin, read all of the material in this test section carefully and make sure you understand what is being asked of you.

You should write your essay on the lined pages included in your answer sheet. Only your writing on those pages will be scored. Your work on these pages will not be scored.

Your essay will be graded based on the evidence it provides and your ability to:

- analyze and evaluate different perspectives on complicated issues
- express and develop your own perspective on the issue
- explain and support your arguments with logical reasoning and detailed examples
- clearly and logically organize your ideas in an essay
- effectively communicate your point of view in English

Stop writing and put down your pencil as soon as time is called.

DO NOT BEGIN THE WRITING TEST UNTIL YOU ARE TOLD TO DO SO.

Repatriation of Museum Artifacts

Visitors to museums don't often stop to think about how artifacts from distant places make their way into collections. Yet archaeologists sometimes acquire pieces through dishonest or illegal means. Consider the Elgin Marbles: originally part of the Parthenon in Greece, they were removed by a Scottish aristocrat without permission. They remain in the British Museum despite two centuries of controversy. Those who support the "repatriation," or return, of stolen artifacts to their points of origin argue that to keep them would be unjust. They also emphasize the educational value of encountering artifacts in their original settings. Critics of the return of artifacts like the Elgin Marbles worry that it would set a precedent for the return of all museum holdings. Additionally, they cite the convenience of concentrating many of the world's artifacts in one place. Should museums return artifacts to their places of origin if they were acquired unethically, or should they keep them?

Read and carefully consider these perspectives. Each suggests a particular way of thinking about the repatriation of museum artifacts.

Perspective 1	Perspective 2	Perspective 3
If we looked closely at the collections of most museums, we would probably find that a great many of their pieces were acquired unethically. It would be impractical to return them all, and an inconvenience for museum-goers.	Returning a dishonestly acquired artifact to its home country or indigenous community rights a historical wrong, and allows the piece to be appreciated in its original context.	In cases where a museum considers it too impractical to return a stolen artifact, they should be compelled to make, at their own expense, a high-quality replica for the country of origin as compensation.

Essay Task

Write a unified, coherent essay in which you evaluate multiple perspectives on the return of unethically acquired artifacts in museums. In your essay, be sure to:

- analyze and evaluate the perspectives given
- state and develop your own perspective on the issue
- explain the relationship between your perspective and those given

Your perspective may be in full agreement with any of the others, in partial agreement, or wholly different. Whatever the case, support your ideas with logical reasoning and detailed, persuasive examples.

Planning Your Essay

Your work on these prewriting pages will not be scored.

Use the space below and on the back cover to generate ideas and plan your essay. You may wish to consider the following as you think critically about the task:

Strengths and weaknesses of the three given perspectives

- What insights do they offer, and what do they fail to consider?
- Why might they be persuasive to others, or why might they fail to persuade?

Your own knowledge, experience, and values

- What is your perspective on this issue, and what are its strengths and weaknesses?
- How will you support your perspective in your essay?

Note

- Your practice Writing Test includes scratch paper and four lined sheets for your essay.
- Your official ACT exam will include a test booklet with space for planning and four lined sheets to write your essay.
- Review Answers and Scoring for instructions on how to grade your exam.

Practice Test 4

The ACT

This practice test contains tests in English, Math, Reading, and Science. These tests measure skills and abilities related to high school course work and college preparedness. **You can use a calculator on the math test only.**

The questions in each test are numbered, and the suggested answers for each question are lettered. On the answer sheet, the rows are numbered to match the questions, and the circles in each row are lettered to correspond to the suggested answers.

For each question, choose the best answer and fill in the corresponding circle on your answer document. Use a soft lead pencil and make your marks heavy and black. **Do not use a ballpoint pen.**

Fill in only one answer to each question. If you change your mind about an answer, completely erase your first mark before filling in your new answer. For each question, make certain that you mark in the row of ovals with the same number as the question.

Only responses marked on your answer sheet will be scored. Your score on each test will be based only on the number of questions you answer correctly during the time allowed for that test. You will NOT be penalized for guessing. **Even if you are unsure about an answer, you should make a guess.**

You may work on each test ONLY when your proctor tells you to do so. If you complete a test before the end of your allotted time, use the extra minutes to check your work on that section only. Do NOT use the time to work on another section. Doing this will disqualify your scores.

Put down your pencil immediately when time is called at the end of each test. You are not allowed to continue answering questions after the allotted time has run out. This includes marking answers on your answer sheet that you previously noted in your test booklet.

You are not allowed to fold or tear the pages of your test booklet.

Do Not Open This Booklet Until You Are Told to Do So.

Marking Directions: Mark only **one** oval for each question. Fill in response completely. Erase errors cleanly without smudging.

Correct mark: ○ ● ○ ○

Do NOT use these *incorrect* **or** *bad* **marks.**

Incorrect marks: ⊘ ⊗ ○ ○
Overlapping mark: ○ ○ ◖○
Cross-out mark: ○ ◉ ○ ○ ○
Smudged erasure: ○ ◉ ◑ ○
Mark is too light: ◑ ○ ○ ○

NAME: _____

DATE: _____

TEST 1

1 Ⓐ Ⓑ Ⓒ Ⓓ	14 Ⓕ Ⓖ Ⓗ Ⓙ	27 Ⓐ Ⓑ Ⓒ Ⓓ	40 Ⓕ Ⓖ Ⓗ Ⓙ	53 Ⓐ Ⓑ Ⓒ Ⓓ	66 Ⓕ Ⓖ Ⓗ Ⓙ
2 Ⓕ Ⓖ Ⓗ Ⓙ	15 Ⓐ Ⓑ Ⓒ Ⓓ	28 Ⓕ Ⓖ Ⓗ Ⓙ	41 Ⓐ Ⓑ Ⓒ Ⓓ	54 Ⓕ Ⓖ Ⓗ Ⓙ	67 Ⓐ Ⓑ Ⓒ Ⓓ
3 Ⓐ Ⓑ Ⓒ Ⓓ	16 Ⓕ Ⓖ Ⓗ Ⓙ	29 Ⓐ Ⓑ Ⓒ Ⓓ	42 Ⓕ Ⓖ Ⓗ Ⓙ	55 Ⓐ Ⓑ Ⓒ Ⓓ	68 Ⓕ Ⓖ Ⓗ Ⓙ
4 Ⓕ Ⓖ Ⓗ Ⓙ	17 Ⓐ Ⓑ Ⓒ Ⓓ	30 Ⓕ Ⓖ Ⓗ Ⓙ	43 Ⓐ Ⓑ Ⓒ Ⓓ	56 Ⓕ Ⓖ Ⓗ Ⓙ	69 Ⓐ Ⓑ Ⓒ Ⓓ
5 Ⓐ Ⓑ Ⓒ Ⓓ	18 Ⓕ Ⓖ Ⓗ Ⓙ	31 Ⓐ Ⓑ Ⓒ Ⓓ	44 Ⓕ Ⓖ Ⓗ Ⓙ	57 Ⓐ Ⓑ Ⓒ Ⓓ	70 Ⓕ Ⓖ Ⓗ Ⓙ
6 Ⓕ Ⓖ Ⓗ Ⓙ	19 Ⓐ Ⓑ Ⓒ Ⓓ	32 Ⓕ Ⓖ Ⓗ Ⓙ	45 Ⓐ Ⓑ Ⓒ Ⓓ	58 Ⓕ Ⓖ Ⓗ Ⓙ	71 Ⓐ Ⓑ Ⓒ Ⓓ
7 Ⓐ Ⓑ Ⓒ Ⓓ	20 Ⓕ Ⓖ Ⓗ Ⓙ	33 Ⓐ Ⓑ Ⓒ Ⓓ	46 Ⓕ Ⓖ Ⓗ Ⓙ	59 Ⓐ Ⓑ Ⓒ Ⓓ	72 Ⓕ Ⓖ Ⓗ Ⓙ
8 Ⓕ Ⓖ Ⓗ Ⓙ	21 Ⓐ Ⓑ Ⓒ Ⓓ	34 Ⓕ Ⓖ Ⓗ Ⓙ	47 Ⓐ Ⓑ Ⓒ Ⓓ	60 Ⓕ Ⓖ Ⓗ Ⓙ	73 Ⓐ Ⓑ Ⓒ Ⓓ
9 Ⓐ Ⓑ Ⓒ Ⓓ	22 Ⓕ Ⓖ Ⓗ Ⓙ	35 Ⓐ Ⓑ Ⓒ Ⓓ	48 Ⓕ Ⓖ Ⓗ Ⓙ	61 Ⓐ Ⓑ Ⓒ Ⓓ	74 Ⓕ Ⓖ Ⓗ Ⓙ
10 Ⓕ Ⓖ Ⓗ Ⓙ	23 Ⓐ Ⓑ Ⓒ Ⓓ	36 Ⓕ Ⓖ Ⓗ Ⓙ	49 Ⓐ Ⓑ Ⓒ Ⓓ	62 Ⓕ Ⓖ Ⓗ Ⓙ	75 Ⓐ Ⓑ Ⓒ Ⓓ
11 Ⓐ Ⓑ Ⓒ Ⓓ	24 Ⓕ Ⓖ Ⓗ Ⓙ	37 Ⓐ Ⓑ Ⓒ Ⓓ	50 Ⓕ Ⓖ Ⓗ Ⓙ	63 Ⓐ Ⓑ Ⓒ Ⓓ	
12 Ⓕ Ⓖ Ⓗ Ⓙ	25 Ⓐ Ⓑ Ⓒ Ⓓ	38 Ⓕ Ⓖ Ⓗ Ⓙ	51 Ⓐ Ⓑ Ⓒ Ⓓ	64 Ⓕ Ⓖ Ⓗ Ⓙ	
13 Ⓐ Ⓑ Ⓒ Ⓓ	26 Ⓕ Ⓖ Ⓗ Ⓙ	39 Ⓐ Ⓑ Ⓒ Ⓓ	52 Ⓕ Ⓖ Ⓗ Ⓙ	65 Ⓐ Ⓑ Ⓒ Ⓓ	

TEST 2

1 Ⓐ Ⓑ Ⓒ Ⓓ Ⓔ	11 Ⓐ Ⓑ Ⓒ Ⓓ Ⓔ	21 Ⓐ Ⓑ Ⓒ Ⓓ Ⓔ	31 Ⓐ Ⓑ Ⓒ Ⓓ Ⓔ	41 Ⓐ Ⓑ Ⓒ Ⓓ Ⓔ	51 Ⓐ Ⓑ Ⓒ Ⓓ Ⓔ
2 Ⓕ Ⓖ Ⓗ Ⓙ Ⓚ	12 Ⓕ Ⓖ Ⓗ Ⓙ Ⓚ	22 Ⓕ Ⓖ Ⓗ Ⓙ Ⓚ	32 Ⓕ Ⓖ Ⓗ Ⓙ Ⓚ	42 Ⓕ Ⓖ Ⓗ Ⓙ Ⓚ	52 Ⓕ Ⓖ Ⓗ Ⓙ Ⓚ
3 Ⓐ Ⓑ Ⓒ Ⓓ Ⓔ	13 Ⓐ Ⓑ Ⓒ Ⓓ Ⓔ	23 Ⓐ Ⓑ Ⓒ Ⓓ Ⓔ	33 Ⓐ Ⓑ Ⓒ Ⓓ Ⓔ	43 Ⓐ Ⓑ Ⓒ Ⓓ Ⓔ	53 Ⓐ Ⓑ Ⓒ Ⓓ Ⓔ
4 Ⓕ Ⓖ Ⓗ Ⓙ Ⓚ	14 Ⓕ Ⓖ Ⓗ Ⓙ Ⓚ	24 Ⓕ Ⓖ Ⓗ Ⓙ Ⓚ	34 Ⓐ Ⓑ Ⓒ Ⓓ Ⓔ	44 Ⓕ Ⓖ Ⓗ Ⓙ Ⓚ	54 Ⓕ Ⓖ Ⓗ Ⓙ Ⓚ
5 Ⓐ Ⓑ Ⓒ Ⓓ Ⓔ	15 Ⓐ Ⓑ Ⓒ Ⓓ Ⓔ	25 Ⓐ Ⓑ Ⓒ Ⓓ Ⓔ	35 Ⓐ Ⓑ Ⓒ Ⓓ Ⓔ	45 Ⓐ Ⓑ Ⓒ Ⓓ Ⓔ	55 Ⓐ Ⓑ Ⓒ Ⓓ Ⓔ
6 Ⓕ Ⓖ Ⓗ Ⓙ Ⓚ	16 Ⓕ Ⓖ Ⓗ Ⓙ Ⓚ	26 Ⓕ Ⓖ Ⓗ Ⓙ Ⓚ	36 Ⓕ Ⓖ Ⓗ Ⓙ Ⓚ	46 Ⓕ Ⓖ Ⓗ Ⓙ Ⓚ	56 Ⓕ Ⓖ Ⓗ Ⓙ Ⓚ
7 Ⓐ Ⓑ Ⓒ Ⓓ Ⓔ	17 Ⓐ Ⓑ Ⓒ Ⓓ Ⓔ	27 Ⓐ Ⓑ Ⓒ Ⓓ Ⓔ	37 Ⓐ Ⓑ Ⓒ Ⓓ Ⓔ	47 Ⓐ Ⓑ Ⓒ Ⓓ Ⓔ	57 Ⓐ Ⓑ Ⓒ Ⓓ Ⓔ
8 Ⓕ Ⓖ Ⓗ Ⓙ Ⓚ	18 Ⓕ Ⓖ Ⓗ Ⓙ Ⓚ	28 Ⓕ Ⓖ Ⓗ Ⓙ Ⓚ	38 Ⓕ Ⓖ Ⓗ Ⓙ Ⓚ	48 Ⓕ Ⓖ Ⓗ Ⓙ Ⓚ	58 Ⓕ Ⓖ Ⓗ Ⓙ Ⓚ
9 Ⓐ Ⓑ Ⓒ Ⓓ Ⓔ	19 Ⓐ Ⓑ Ⓒ Ⓓ Ⓔ	29 Ⓐ Ⓑ Ⓒ Ⓓ Ⓔ	39 Ⓐ Ⓑ Ⓒ Ⓓ Ⓔ	49 Ⓐ Ⓑ Ⓒ Ⓓ Ⓔ	59 Ⓐ Ⓑ Ⓒ Ⓓ Ⓔ
10 Ⓕ Ⓖ Ⓗ Ⓙ Ⓚ	20 Ⓕ Ⓖ Ⓗ Ⓙ Ⓚ	30 Ⓕ Ⓖ Ⓗ Ⓙ Ⓚ	40 Ⓕ Ⓖ Ⓗ Ⓙ Ⓚ	50 Ⓕ Ⓖ Ⓗ Ⓙ Ⓚ	60 Ⓕ Ⓖ Ⓗ Ⓙ Ⓚ

TEST 3

1 Ⓐ Ⓑ Ⓒ Ⓓ	8 Ⓕ Ⓖ Ⓗ Ⓙ	15 Ⓐ Ⓑ Ⓒ Ⓓ	22 Ⓕ Ⓖ Ⓗ Ⓙ	29 Ⓐ Ⓑ Ⓒ Ⓓ	36 Ⓕ Ⓖ Ⓗ Ⓙ
2 Ⓕ Ⓖ Ⓗ Ⓙ	9 Ⓐ Ⓑ Ⓒ Ⓓ	16 Ⓕ Ⓖ Ⓗ Ⓙ	23 Ⓐ Ⓑ Ⓒ Ⓓ	30 Ⓕ Ⓖ Ⓗ Ⓙ	37 Ⓐ Ⓑ Ⓒ Ⓓ
3 Ⓐ Ⓑ Ⓒ Ⓓ	10 Ⓕ Ⓖ Ⓗ Ⓙ	17 Ⓐ Ⓑ Ⓒ Ⓓ	24 Ⓕ Ⓖ Ⓗ Ⓙ	31 Ⓐ Ⓑ Ⓒ Ⓓ	38 Ⓕ Ⓖ Ⓗ Ⓙ
4 Ⓕ Ⓖ Ⓗ Ⓙ	11 Ⓐ Ⓑ Ⓒ Ⓓ	18 Ⓕ Ⓖ Ⓗ Ⓙ	25 Ⓐ Ⓑ Ⓒ Ⓓ	32 Ⓕ Ⓖ Ⓗ Ⓙ	39 Ⓐ Ⓑ Ⓒ Ⓓ
5 Ⓐ Ⓑ Ⓒ Ⓓ	12 Ⓕ Ⓖ Ⓗ Ⓙ	19 Ⓐ Ⓑ Ⓒ Ⓓ	26 Ⓕ Ⓖ Ⓗ Ⓙ	33 Ⓐ Ⓑ Ⓒ Ⓓ	40 Ⓕ Ⓖ Ⓗ Ⓙ
6 Ⓕ Ⓖ Ⓗ Ⓙ	13 Ⓐ Ⓑ Ⓒ Ⓓ	20 Ⓕ Ⓖ Ⓗ Ⓙ	27 Ⓐ Ⓑ Ⓒ Ⓓ	34 Ⓕ Ⓖ Ⓗ Ⓙ	
7 Ⓐ Ⓑ Ⓒ Ⓓ	14 Ⓕ Ⓖ Ⓗ Ⓙ	21 Ⓐ Ⓑ Ⓒ Ⓓ	28 Ⓕ Ⓖ Ⓗ Ⓙ	35 Ⓐ Ⓑ Ⓒ Ⓓ	

TEST 4

1 Ⓐ Ⓑ Ⓒ Ⓓ	8 Ⓕ Ⓖ Ⓗ Ⓙ	15 Ⓐ Ⓑ Ⓒ Ⓓ	22 Ⓕ Ⓖ Ⓗ Ⓙ	29 Ⓐ Ⓑ Ⓒ Ⓓ	36 Ⓕ Ⓖ Ⓗ Ⓙ
2 Ⓕ Ⓖ Ⓗ Ⓙ	9 Ⓐ Ⓑ Ⓒ Ⓓ	16 Ⓕ Ⓖ Ⓗ Ⓙ	23 Ⓐ Ⓑ Ⓒ Ⓓ	30 Ⓕ Ⓖ Ⓗ Ⓙ	37 Ⓐ Ⓑ Ⓒ Ⓓ
3 Ⓐ Ⓑ Ⓒ Ⓓ	10 Ⓕ Ⓖ Ⓗ Ⓙ	17 Ⓐ Ⓑ Ⓒ Ⓓ	24 Ⓕ Ⓖ Ⓗ Ⓙ	31 Ⓐ Ⓑ Ⓒ Ⓓ	38 Ⓕ Ⓖ Ⓗ Ⓙ
4 Ⓕ Ⓖ Ⓗ Ⓙ	11 Ⓐ Ⓑ Ⓒ Ⓓ	18 Ⓕ Ⓖ Ⓗ Ⓙ	25 Ⓐ Ⓑ Ⓒ Ⓓ	32 Ⓕ Ⓖ Ⓗ Ⓙ	39 Ⓐ Ⓑ Ⓒ Ⓓ
5 Ⓐ Ⓑ Ⓒ Ⓓ	12 Ⓕ Ⓖ Ⓗ Ⓙ	19 Ⓐ Ⓑ Ⓒ Ⓓ	26 Ⓕ Ⓖ Ⓗ Ⓙ	33 Ⓐ Ⓑ Ⓒ Ⓓ	40 Ⓕ Ⓖ Ⓗ Ⓙ
6 Ⓕ Ⓖ Ⓗ Ⓙ	13 Ⓐ Ⓑ Ⓒ Ⓓ	20 Ⓕ Ⓖ Ⓗ Ⓙ	27 Ⓐ Ⓑ Ⓒ Ⓓ	34 Ⓕ Ⓖ Ⓗ Ⓙ	
7 Ⓐ Ⓑ Ⓒ Ⓓ	14 Ⓕ Ⓖ Ⓗ Ⓙ	21 Ⓐ Ⓑ Ⓒ Ⓓ	28 Ⓕ Ⓖ Ⓗ Ⓙ	35 Ⓐ Ⓑ Ⓒ Ⓓ	

Use a soft lead No. 2 pencil only. Do NOT use a mechanical pencil, ink, ballpoint, or felt-tip pens.

Begin WRITING TEST here.

If you need more space, please continue on the next page.

WRITING TEST

If you need more space, please continue on the back of this page.

WRITING TEST

_____

_____

_____

_____

_____

_____

_____

_____

_____

_____

_____

_____

_____

_____

_____

_____

_____

_____

_____

_____

_____

_____

_____

_____

_____

_____

_____

_____

If you need more space, please continue on the next page.

3

WRITING TEST

_____

_____

_____

_____

_____

_____

_____

_____

_____

_____

_____

_____

_____

_____

_____

_____

_____

_____

_____

_____

_____

_____

_____

_____

_____

STOP!

4

English Test

45 Minutes—75 Questions

DIRECTIONS: In the five passages that follow, certain words and phrases are underlined and numbered. In the right-hand column, you will find alternatives for the underlined part. In most cases, you are to choose the one that best expresses the idea, makes the statement appropriate for standard written English, or is worded most consistently with the style and tone of the passage as a whole. If you think the original version is best, choose "NO CHANGE." In some cases, you will find in the right-hand column a question about the underlined part. You are to choose the best answer to the question.

You will also find questions about a section of the passage, or about the passage as a whole. These questions do not refer to an underlined portion of the passage, but rather are identified by a number or numbers in a box.

For each question, choose the alternative you consider best and fill in the corresponding circle on your answer document. Read each passage through once before you begin to answer the questions that accompany it. For many of the questions, you must read several sentences beyond the question to determine the answer. Be sure that you have read far enough ahead each time you choose an alternative.

Passage I

A Long-Term Commitment

Asparagus is a popular, vegetable, but it can be
$\underline{}$
                    1
expensive in the market, so many gardeners consider

growing their own at home. Anyone thinking about growing

asparagus, as a result, should know that it takes years of
            $\underline{}$
                  2
hard work and dedication before a gardener gets to harvest

even a single stalk. For this hard work, the payoff is that a
                                    $\underline{}$
                                        3
well-tended bed of asparagus will produce for as long as

twenty years.

Choose a spot with full sun and well-draining soil

for an asparagus bed. This bed should be about four feet

wide, because asparagus spreads, and the soil should be

prepared by removed any weeds and roots before adding
            $\underline{}$
                4
aged manure or compost to the soil. It's possible to grow

asparagus from seeds, but it is more efficient to start with

one-year-old "crowns," or seedlings. Plant the crowns six

1. A. NO CHANGE
    B. popular vegetable but it can be,
    C. popular vegetable, but it can be
    D. popular vegetable, but it, can be

2. F. NO CHANGE
    G. however
    H. therefore
    J. meanwhile

3. A. NO CHANGE
    B. reckoning
    C. bribe
    D. calculation

4. F. NO CHANGE
    G. removing
    H. remove
    J. removes

Go On to the Next Page.

inches deep and about two feet apart in a single foot-wide

trench in the center of the prepared bed, and then top <u>them</u>

₅

with about three inches of soil. Every two weeks add another

inch or two of soil <u>until slight mounds like manmade anthills</u>

₆

<u>that mound up over the crowns develop</u> along the trench.

₆

<u>Also must weed.</u>

₇

[1] While watering, check for asparagus beetles and

asparagus miners, pests that can destroy the crop before it

even begins to produce. [2] <u>For the first two years regularly,</u>

₈

<u>the asparagus bed needs to be watered and fertilized in the</u>

₈

<u>spring and fall.</u> [3] Remember to not harvest any wispy,

₈

fern-like <u>asparagus' spears'</u> that appear during the first two

₉

years because the plants need to devote their energy to

building deep roots. [4] When getting ready for winter, cover

the bed with straw and any lingering <u>foliage, just remember</u>

₁₀

to destroy the fern-like foliage before the new

growth appears in the spring. [11]

5. **A.** NO CHANGE
   B. themselves
   C. they
   D. itself

6. **F.** NO CHANGE
   G. until slight mounds like miniature, rounded versions of the great pyramids develop
   H. until rolling mounds, reminiscent of low hills or mountains made entirely of dirt, begin to develop
   J. until slight, rounded mounds develop

7. **A.** NO CHANGE
   B. Weed the asparagus bed as needed.
   C. Must weed as needed.
   D. Also, must weed the asparagus bed as needed.

8. **F.** NO CHANGE
   G. For the first two years, the asparagus bed needs to be watered regularly and fertilized in the spring and fall.
   H. Regularly, for the first two years, the asparagus bed needs to be watered and fertilized in the spring and fall.
   J. For the first two years, regularly, in the spring and the fall, the asparagus bed needs to be watered and fertilized.

9. **A.** NO CHANGE
   B. asparagus spears'
   C. asparagus' spears
   D. asparagus spears

10. **F.** NO CHANGE
    G. foliage just remember
    H. foliage; just remember
    J. foliage just remember;

11. For the sake of logic and coherence, Sentence 1 should be placed:
    A. where it is now.
    B. after Sentence 2.
    C. before Sentence 4.
    D. after Sentence 4.

Go On to the Next Page.

In the third season, the asparagus is finally ready to be harvested. [12] In the fourth year, the asparagus grows

more robustly, and the harvest period lasted for eight weeks.
                                              ‾‾‾‾‾‾
                                               13

Eventually, over many years it may be necessary to pick
‾‾
                         14
asparagus as much as twice a day to keep up.
‾‾
                   14

12. At this point the writer is considering adding the following sentence:

> Harvest the spears during a four-week period by cutting them with a sharp knife at or just below the ground level.

Should the writer make this addition?

- **F.** Yes, because the focus of the paragraph is harvesting asparagus.
- **G.** Yes, because if readers understand how to pick asparagus they will want to plant some.
- **H.** No, because the paragraph focuses on how many times per day asparagus must be picked.
- **J.** No, because the paragraph doesn't say anything about why asparagus must be cut at or below ground level.

13. A. NO CHANGE
  - **B.** would have lasted
  - **C.** would last
  - **D.** lasts

14. F. NO CHANGE
  - **G.** Eventually, it may be necessary to pick asparagus as often as twice a day to keep up.
  - **H.** After the fourth year, it may eventually be necessary to harvest the asparagus spears as often as twice each day to keep up with the production.
  - **J.** After many years it may eventually become necessary to pick asparagus as much as twice a day to keep up.

Question 15 asks about the preceding passage as a whole.

---

15. Suppose the writer had chosen to write an essay that indicates that growing asparagus is an economically viable business for a new farm. Would this essay successfully fulfill the writer's goal?

- **A.** Yes, because the essay explains how much asparagus costs to grow, and what it sells for.
- **B.** Yes, because the essay details the amount of asparagus that must be planted in order to earn a profit.
- **C.** No, because the essay does not explain how to establish and care for an asparagus patch.
- **D.** No, because the essay is limited to describing how to establish and care for an asparagus patch.

Go On to the Next Page.

Passage II

The Stranger and the Palm Reader

[1]

I grew up by the shore at the heart of

Miami Beach where there were always more vacationers
                    16

than there were locals. Mom ran a guesthouse, so there were

always strangers around. I never spoke with them—Mom

was somewhat dead-set on this rule—except that I
                    17

would usually say "hello" and most of the guests were kind
                                    18

enough to return the greeting.

[2]

Even if I had wanted to become friendly

with, our guests, they rarely stayed for more than a few
                    19

days; after all, there was only so much one could do in

Miami Beach. Most would reserve one day for the beach,

another for shopping, both nights for either a show or a

nightclub, and maybe a third day for a visit to downtown

Miami—but that was about it. 20

16. **F.** NO CHANGE
    G. Miami Beach, there
    H. Miami Beach, where there
    J. Miami Beach. Where there

17. **A.** NO CHANGE
    B. strict about
    C. fiercely stern about
    D. utterly fixed on

18. **F.** NO CHANGE
    G. "hello," and most
    H. "hello," most
    J. "hello" most

19. **A.** NO CHANGE
    B. with our guests they rarely stayed
    C. with our guests, they rarely stayed
    D. with our guests, they rarely stayed,

20. The writer is considering deleting the following phrase from the preceding sentence:

    —but that was about it

    If the writer were to make this deletion, would the meaning of the sentence change?

    F. Yes, because the phrase adds a new item to the list of activities that tourists enjoyed in Miami Beach.

    G. Yes, because the phrase emphasizes the point that there was a limited selection of activities available in Miami Beach.

    H. No, because the phrase repeats information provided earlier in the sentence.

    J. No, because the sentence already implies that there are other activities available in Miami Beach.

Go On to the Next Page.

[3]

One summer, though, a man booked a room at the
                        ___
                        21
guesthouse for a whole month. He didn't have much luggage

with him, and I remember Mom, bemused and perhaps

slightly suspicious, double- and triple-checking the booking.

She let him in, but only after some hesitation. He didn't

seem suspicious to me: maybe a little downcast, but

harmless.

[4]

During his time with us, he made frequently visits
                                    _____
                                        22

to one of the palm readers who roamed the shore while he
                             _____
                                        23
was staying with us. That was strange: it didn't
_____
       23

happened very often that a clairvoyant would see the same
_____
   24
tourist more than once, as most tourists just saw a session as

an afternoon's entertainment. But the two seemed to really

connect; the palm-reader would even have visited the house
                                       _____
                                            25
in the afternoons, and they would talk for hours at a time.

After about two weeks of this, the man left—they didn't
                                               ____
                                                26
even check out, he was just gone.

21. A. NO CHANGE
    B. bloke
    C. gent
    D. dude

22. F. NO CHANGE
    G. frequent
    H. frequented
    J. frequency

23. A. NO CHANGE
    B. who roamed the shore
    C. whom he visited while she roamed the shore
    D. who, while he was with us, roamed the shore

24. F. NO CHANGE
    G. happening
    H. happen
    J. happens

25. A. NO CHANGE
    B. visit
    C. have been visiting
    D. be visiting

26. F. NO CHANGE
    G. those
    H. him
    J. he

Go On to the Next Page.

[5]

I never speak to our guests. I don't even remember
27

most of them, but I've never stopped wondering about that
28

man and the palm-reader.

27. At this point, the writer wants to repeat an idea expressed earlier in the passage in order to create a dramatic contrast with her continuing curiosity about the man who saw the fortune teller. Which of the following sentences best accomplishes this?

    A. NO CHANGE

    B. There wasn't much to do in Miami Beach.

    C. Most of our guests would spend a day shopping.

    D. There were palm readers on the beach.

28. **F.** NO CHANGE

    G. them, and

    H. them, as

    J. them; in fact,

Questions 29 and 30 ask about the preceding passage as a whole.

---

29. The writer has decided to add the following sentence:

    I never understood why it was such a popular vacation spot.

What would be the best place to add this sentence?

    A. After the last sentence of Paragraph 1.

    B. After the last sentence of Paragraph 2.

    C. Before the first sentence of Paragraph 4.

    D. Before the first sentence of Paragraph 5.

30. Suppose the writer's primary purpose had been to relate a story from the narrator's childhood that illustrated why the narrator does not trust strangers. Would this essay accomplish that goal?

    F. Yes, because the stranger that the story focuses on is clearly described as "suspicious" and "downcast."

    G. Yes, because the story focuses mainly on how the narrator rarely interacted with strangers.

    H. No, because the story ends by emphasizing the narrator's abiding love of strangers.

    J. No, because while the narrator's mother is suspicious of the stranger, the narrator is curious about the stranger.

Passage III

The "Wind Walls" of Japan

[1]

The Japanese screens known as byōbu were first
31
used to block drafts, introduced to Japan by the Chinese
31
during the eighth century. In fact, byōbu means "wind
31
wall," and the earliest single-panel screens were purely

31. **A.** NO CHANGE

    B. Introduced to Japan by the Chinese during the eighth century, the Japanese screens known as byōbu were first used to block drafts.

    C. Introduced to Japan by the Chinese during the eighth century, the Japanese screens were first used to block drafts, known as byōbu.

    D. Known as byōbu, the Japanese screens were first used to block drafts, introduced to Japan by the Chinese during the eighth century.

Go On to the Next Page.

Practice Test 4

feasible additions to open-layout homes of that period.
32

When byōbu were adopted by members of the imperial

court, however, the screens became most ornate than
33

the first screens. Simple rice paper panels were enhanced

with sumptuous materials and elegant calligraphy or

paintings, by the 17th century byōbu became an art form
34

that was highly valued as a status symbol.

[2]

Yet the structure of byōbu remained relatively basic
35

it starts with a lattice bamboo structure held together with
35

bamboo nails that serves as the skeleton for each panel.
35

Layers of washi, Japanese paper made from the fibers of

the mulberry tree, are fastened to the structure with glue

made from rice to create a firm base for the next layers that

transform this humble screen into an art form.

[3]

Although the washi used to make the "canvas" was a
36

traditional hand-crafted paper, it was often actually stronger
36

than modern wood-pulp paper is. That "canvas" was then
36

covered with a layer of silk or gold leaf, which served as the

background for most traditional byōbu. The most famous

screens from the 17th century featured pen-and-ink

calligraphy, monochromatic landscapes, and nature-themed

32. **F.** NO CHANGE
   G. practical
   H. down-to-earth
   J. applied

33. **A.** NO CHANGE
   B. mostly ornate
   C. more ornate
   D. ornate

34. **F.** NO CHANGE
   G. paintings, and by
   H. paintings by
   J. paintings; and by

35. **A.** NO CHANGE
   B. Yet the structure of byōbu remained relatively basic, it starts with a lattice bamboo structure held together with bamboo nails that serves as the skeleton for each panel.
   C. Yet the structure of byōbu remained relatively basic. It starts with a lattice bamboo structure held together with bamboo nails serves as the skeleton for each panel.
   D. Yet the structure of byōbu remained relatively basic. A lattice bamboo structure held together with bamboo nails serves as the skeleton for each panel.

36. Given that all of the following sentences are true, which one provides the most effective transition from paragraph 2 to paragraph 3?
   F. NO CHANGE
   G. Modern byōbu panels are joined by paper hinges, which are light enough for the portable frames but strong enough to endure regular use.
   H. Once the individual screens are assembled, they could be joined together with paper hinges to create a "canvas" as wide as the artist desires.
   J. Canvas is actually a form of cloth made from plant fibers or yarn, but the word "canvas" is often used metaphorically to refer to any surface suitable for painting—including byōbu.

Go On to the Next Page.

scenes, while later byōbu can be bought online even
                                                        37

today. 38
37

[4]

Once a screen was painted, a layer of silk brocade

was added to create a frame for the piece. Although the
                  39

byōbu are sturdy, their surfaces are quite fragile, a
                                              40

misplaced finger can easily poked a hole.
                           41

Therefore, lacquered wooden frames were often applied to
42

37. Given that all the choices are true, which one provides the most relevant information with regard to how byōbu evolved over time?

  A. NO CHANGE
  B. depicted everything from mythical dragons to scenes of daily life
  C. could be made in factories instead of by hand
  D. became even more popular when they were made of wood

38. The writer is considering adding the following sentence:

   The byōbu were decorated with both calligraphy and painting.

   Should the writer make this addition here?

  F. Yes, because it explains the evolution of the art depicted on the byōbu.
  G. Yes, because it provides a significant detail about how byōbu became more popular.
  H. No, because it repeats information that has already been expressed in the passage.
  J. No, because it deviates from the paragraph's focus on the construction of byōbu.

39. A. NO CHANGE
  B. added, to create a frame for the piece
  C. added to create a frame, for the piece
  D. added, to create a frame, for the piece

40. F. NO CHANGE
  G. fragile, a:
  H. fragile a
  J. fragile: a

41. A. NO CHANGE
  B. poke
  C. pokes
  D. poking

42. F. NO CHANGE
  G. Otherwise,
  H. In contrast,
  J. Yet,

Go On to the Next Page.

Practice Test 4

protect the edges of the screen. Such precautions proved
<u>vital because, although the byōbu were considered an art</u>
<u>form, they were also considered portable, and they were</u>
<u>often stored between uses.</u>
₄₃

43. **A.** NO CHANGE

B. Although byōbu were considered an art form, they were considered a portable art form, and they had to be stored between uses, so such precautions proved vital.

C. Such precautions proved vital, even after byōbu became an art form, because they were an art form that was portable, and they were stored between uses.

D. Such precautions proved vital, because byōbu were portable art pieces that were stored between uses.

Questions 44 and 45 ask about the preceding passage as a whole.

---

44. For the sake of the logic and coherence of the essay, Paragraph 4 should be placed

F. where it is now.

G. before Paragraph 1.

H. before Paragraph 2.

J. before Paragraph 3.

45. Suppose the writer's goal had been to provide a general overview of a specific Japanese art form. Would this essay accomplish that goal?

A. Yes, because it provides an overview of the history, style, and construction of one form of Japanese art.

B. Yes, because it describes the general forms and style of Japanese art using a specific art form as an example.

C. No, because it focuses on Japanese art in general rather than a specific art form.

D. No, because it provides specific details about multiple art forms rather than a general overview of one art form.

Passage IV

A Writer's Struggles

[1]

Louisa May Alcott is <u>most best</u> known for *Little*
₄₆
Women, but her own life was just as fascinating as the story
of the four March sisters. She grew up surrounded by liberal
<u>thinkers of the day, they included the most</u> famous writers in
₄₇
American literature. Educated primarily by her
schoolteacher father Bronson, Louisa also received lessons
from his closest friends, Ralph Waldo Emerson and Henry
David Thoreau.

46. **F.** NO CHANGE

G. more best

H. more better

J. best

47. **A.** NO CHANGE

B. the day. The most

C. the day; the most

D. the day, including the most

---

[48] Margaret Fuller and Nathaniel Hawthorne helped Louisa learn how to write stories and poems.

[2]

[1] After this impoverished childhood, Louisa dreamed of becoming a rich and famous actress to

support her parents' and her three sisters'. [2] However,
                    49
because of Bronson's idealism, the family struggled financially. [3] When Louisa was eleven, Bronson moved the family to a utopian agrarian commune that collapsed in just seven months [51]
                 50

[4] The Alcotts moved back to Concord, where Emerson
                                    52
helped them buy a new home, almost completely bankrupt.
                                    52
[5] By the age of fifteen, though, she was forced to

48. At this point the writer wants to add a sentence that would further describe Louisa's educational experiences. Which of the following sentences would best accomplish this?

   F. Thoreau was well-known for writing *Walden: or Life in the Woods.*
   G. Emerson was a poet, essayist, and philosopher.
   H. Louisa spent hours with Emerson in his library, and Thoreau taught her science at Walden Pond.
   J. Both of the men had studied at Harvard, a private school in Cambridge, Massachusetts.

49. A. NO CHANGE
   B. her parents' and her three sisters.
   C. her parents and her three sister's.
   D. her parents and her three sisters.

50. F. NO CHANGE
   G. months?
   H. months.
   J. months,

51. For the sake of the logic and coherence of Paragraph 2, Sentence 1 should be:
   A. placed where it is now.
   B. placed after Sentence 2.
   C. placed after Sentence 4.
   D. OMITTED, because the paragraph focuses only on Louisa's experiences.

52. F. NO CHANGE
   G. Almost completely bankrupt, the Alcotts moved back to Concord, where Emerson helped them buy a new home.
   H. The Alcotts moved back to Concord where, almost completely bankrupt, Emerson helped them buy a new home.
   J. The Alcotts moved back to Concord where Emerson, almost completely bankrupt, helped them buy a new home.

Go On to the Next Page.

going to work. [6] The future novelist toiled as a governess,
53

teacher, seamstress, laundress, and live-in household

servant.

[3]

In conclusion, Louisa began to achieve some success
54

as a writer of short stories, and poetry. In 1862, she began
55

writing melodramatic novellas using the pen name A. M.

Barnard. On her thirtieth birthday, Louisa volunteered to

nurse soldiers, those of whom were wounded in the
56

American Civil War. This experience inspired her first

serious book, *Hospital Sketches*, a collection of fictionalized

accounts based on her letters home. Louisa, however, still

had to supplement her earnings by taking in sewing until one

of her publishers asked her to write a novel for young girls

based on her family's life, and the rest was historical.
5

[4]

It took her just a few weeks to write *Little Women*, a

book she disdained as a trivial morality tale for children, but
58

53. **A.** NO CHANGE
    B. gone
    C. went
    D. go

54. **F.** NO CHANGE
    G. In contrast,
    H. Therefore,
    J. Eventually,

55. **A.** NO CHANGE
    B. short stories and poetry.
    C. short, stories and of poetry.
    D. short stories, and, poetry.

56. **F.** NO CHANGE
    G. soldiers, those of whom had been wounded
    H. soldiers wounded
    J. soldiers, those that were wounded

57. **A.** NO CHANGE
    B. and the rest is history.
    C. the rest of which is historical.
    D. with the rest of it being history.

58. **F.** NO CHANGE
    G. adored
    H. promoted
    J. deranged

Go On to the Next Page.

the book brought Louisa the fame she had always desired.

59

59. Which of the following true sentences, if inserted here, would best conclude the essay as well as maintain the tone established earlier in the essay?

   A. What's really amazing is that Louisa took so long to write a best-seller; after all, she had studied with the greats of American literature.

   B. Imagine her relief at finally being able to support the family that had suffered so many financial hardships in their life.

   C. More important to Louisa than the fame, however, the financial success of *Little Women* made it possible for her to finally support her family.

   D. By writing *Little Women*, Louisa May Alcott won the kind of fame that lives on long after the author has passed away.

Question 60 asks about the preceding passage as a whole.

---

60. Suppose the writer's purpose had been to write an essay summarizing the participation of women authors in 19th century literature. Would this essay accomplish that purpose?

   F. Yes, because it uses a specific author's life as a general example of the lives of most female authors.

   G. Yes, because it discusses how 19th century female authors often also had to do other forms of work.

   H. No, because it focuses instead on an author who did not live and work in the 19th century.

   J. No, because it focuses instead on the life and work of a single female author.

Passage V

The Common Law? Not in the Federal Courts.

The popular view of how laws are made <u>are</u> informed
61

by our understanding of <u>the Constitution's separation of</u>
62

<u>powers</u>. The power to create law is reserved for the
62

legislative branch, and other branches may only enforce it.

61. **A.** NO CHANGE
    B. is
    C. were
    D. have been

62. **F.** NO CHANGE
    G. the Constitutions separation of power's
    H. the Constitution's separation of power's
    J. the Constitutions separation of powers

There is another kind of law, though. The "common law"
that emerges from the history of court decisions stretching
back to 15th century Europe. It can guide judges in
cracking the written law, or even give them the authority to
treat an act as a crime without a written law because the act

is custom treated as a crime. Because common law is based
on a tradition of court decisions, it is created by the courts—
not by the legislature. Moreover, it's still recognized in
many U.S. states today.

[F] There is, one area though in which common
law has been very narrowly limited: federal criminal law.
Ironically, the limitations come not from the legislature, but
rather from a Supreme Court decision. However, in the
case of *United States v. Hudson and Goodwin*, two men
were indicted for seditious libel, the crime of making
false, damaging statements about a state authority, after
they accused President Thomas Jefferson of conspiring to
bribe Napoléon Bonaparte. [G] There was no federal libel
law, but there was a history of punishing libel, so they
were indicted under the common law. After lower courts

failed to resolve there case, it went to the Supreme
Court. [H] At trial, no arguments were offered by the
attorney for the government, and no attorney even

63. **A.** NO CHANGE
   B. kind of law, though: the "common law"
   C. kind of law, though the "common law"
   D. kind of law. "Common law"

64. **F.** NO CHANGE
   G. disengaging
   H. opening up
   J. interpreting

65. **A.** NO CHANGE
   B. customary
   C. accustomed
   D. customarily

66. **F.** NO CHANGE
   G. There is one area though in which
   H. There is, one area though, in which
   J. There is one area, though, in which

67. **A.** NO CHANGE
   B. Likewise,
   C. For example,
   D. DELETE the underlined portion and capitalize the first letter of the next word.

68. Given that all of the choices are true, which one is the most relevant to the focus of the paragraph?
   F. NO CHANGE
   G. Napoléon agreed to the Treaty of Amiens with Spain
   H. Jefferson imposed an unpopular embargo on European nations
   J. the Supreme Court was defined in the constitution and lower courts were created later

69. **A.** NO CHANGE
   B. their
   C. they're
   D. theirs

Go On to the Next Page.

Practice Test 4

appears for the defense. [71] Thus, the Court was left to
_____
70
decide a case that could dramatically limit the scope of

70. F. NO CHANGE
    G. appeared
    H. will appear
    J. would appear

71. The writer is considering deleting the previous sentence. If the writer were to delete this sentence, would the overall meaning of the passage change?

    F. Yes, because the sentence sets up the information that follows.

    G. Yes, because the sentence explains the process by which the supreme court reaches decisions.

    H. No, because the sentence serves only to repeat an earlier point.

    J. No, because the additional narrative details provided in this sentence don't directly address the main point of the passage.

federal authority <u>without any of that stuff.</u>
                          72

72. A. NO CHANGE
    B. on pretty much nothing
    C. with basically nothing to even decide on
    D. without hearing any arguments

[J] Because there was no federal law against libel and no

specific constitutional authority for the federal courts to

prosecute common <u>law crimes, the Supreme Court</u> ruled that
                          73

federal courts had no right to prosecute libel—or any

other common law crime. Instead, they declared that the

legislature must pass a law making an act a crime in order

for federal courts to prosecute it as a crime. [74]

73. A. NO CHANGE
    B. law crimes: the Supreme Court ruled
    C. law crimes, and the Supreme Court ruled
    D. law crimes. The Supreme Court ruled

74. The writer is planning to split the information in this paragraph into one paragraph that describes events leading up to the trial, and another that describes the trial and subsequent decision. The best point to divide the paragraph in order to achieve that goal would be:

    F. F.
    G. G.
    H. H.
    J. J.

Go On to the Next Page.

Practice Test 4

> Question 75 asks about the preceding passage as a whole.

75. Suppose the writer's primary purpose had been to tell the story of a change in the powers of federal courts. Would this essay accomplish that purpose?

    A. Yes, because it discusses how the Supreme Court limited the powers of federal courts.

    B. Yes, because it explains how the Supreme Court transferred the powers of state courts to federal courts.

    C. No, because it is irrelevant whether federal courts can prosecute for common law crimes if state courts can do so.

    D. No, because the passage focuses mainly on a specific case, rather than on legal matters in general.

End of Test 1.

Stop! Do not turn the page until you are told to do so.

Do not return to the previous test.

Mathematics Test

60 Minutes—60 Questions

DIRECTIONS: For each problem, solve for the correct answer and fill in the corresponding circle on your answer document.

Some problems may take a longer time to solve, but do not take too much time on any single problem. Solve the easier questions first, then return to the harder questions in the remaining time for this test.

A calculator is allowed on this test. While you may be able to solve some problems without a calculator, you are allowed to use a calculator for all of the problems on this test.

Note: Unless otherwise directed, all of the following statements are considered correct.

/, All drawn figures are NOT necessarily drawn to scale.

0, All geometric figures are in a plane.

1, The word *line*, when used, is the same as a straight line.

2, The word *average*, when used, is the same as arithmetic mean.

1. Danielle, Arthur, and Carlos are responsible for bringing marshmallows to a party. Danielle has $1\frac{3}{4}$ bags, Arthur has $4\frac{2}{3}$ and Carlos has $3\frac{1}{2}$. How many bags of marshmallows do they have in total?

    A. $8\frac{2}{3}$

    B. $8\frac{11}{12}$

    C. $9\frac{1}{2}$

    D. $9\frac{11}{12}$

    E. 10

2. Fourteen boards cost \$26. How many boards can be purchased for \$6?

    F. 2
    G. 3
    H. 4
    J. 5
    K. 6

3. Which of the following values is smallest?

    A. $\frac{26}{51}$

    B. $\frac{1}{2}$

    C. $\frac{6}{12}$

    D. $\frac{3}{8}$

    E. $\frac{51}{100}$

4. In the standard (x, y) coordinate plane, which of the following lines is parallel to the line defined by the equation $4y = 8x + 4$?

    F. $-y = \frac{x+3}{2}$

    G. $y = \frac{-5x-8}{10}$

    H. $y = \frac{1-x}{2}$

    J. $y = 2x + 4$

    K. $y = -\frac{1}{2}x$

5. If $y = 2$, then $-3y(1-5) = ?$

    A. -36
    B. -24
    C. -6
    D. 12
    E. 24

6. All 100 students at City High School are enrolled in either calculus, statistics, or both. If 75 of these students are taking calculus and 50 of these students are taking statistics, what is the probability that this student is enrolled in both calculus and statistics?

    F. $\frac{1}{8}$

    G. $\frac{3}{16}$

    H. $\frac{1}{4}$

    J. $\frac{1}{2}$

    K. Cannot be determined from the information given

Go On to the Next Page.

7. Point *P* is 6 units east of point *M* on a line, and point *Q* lies 9 units east of point *N* on the same line. If point *N* is 2 units east of point *M*, how many units are between point *P* and point *Q*?

    A. 5
    B. 6
    C. 7
    D. 8
    E. 9

8. Otto is a traveling beach salesman. He sells beach balls for $17 and bags of cotton candy for $4. Every day, he travels along the same beach, and a fisherman gives him a $2 tip. Which of the following expressions represents Otto's daily profit, in dollars, if he sells *b* beach balls and *c* bags of cotton candy?

    F. $17b + 4c$
    G. $17c + 4b$
    H. $17c + 4b - 2$
    J. $17b + 4c + 2$
    K. $17c + 4b + 2$

9. How many solutions are there for the system of linear equations shown in the graph below?

    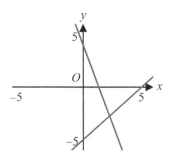

    A. 0
    B. 1
    C. 2
    D. 3
    E. Infinite

10. What is the smallest number that, when divided by 4 and 5, will yield a remainder of 2?

    F. 12
    G. 20
    H. 22
    J. 42
    K. 84

11. Which of the following is equivalent to $(3ab)^3 \cdot (2b)^2 \cdot (-a)^3$?

    A. $-108a^6b^5$
    B. $-108a^9b^6$
    C. $-36a^6b^7$
    D. $108a^6b^5$
    E. $108a^9b^6$

12. Sausages are sold in drums of 660 and buns are sold in crates of 1,122. Nathan wants to buy the same number of sausages as buns. What is the minimum total number of drums and crates that Nathan must buy?

    F. 11
    G. 22
    H. 27
    J. 80
    K. 121

13. In the figure below, lines *l* and *m* are parallel. What is the measure of $\angle ABC$?

    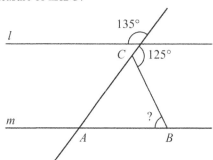

    A. 45°
    B. 55°
    C. 60°
    D. 80°
    E. 85°

14. Jose's wage of $19 per hour is directly proportional to the wage of his manager, who is paid $28 per hour. If Jose's manager's wage increases to $33 per hour, what is Jose's new wage to the nearest cent?

    F. $20.86
    G. $22.39
    H. $23.53
    J. $24.00
    K. $24.11

Go On to the Next Page.

15. At what point (x, y) does line l cross the x-axis?

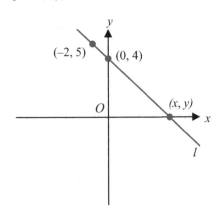

- **A.** $(0, 4)$
- **B.** $(2, 0)$
- **C.** $(4, 0)$
- **D.** $(0, 8)$
- **E.** $(8, 0)$

16. Kyle has determined that it will cost him $90 to paint the 4 walls of his square bedroom. The walls measure six feet in height and the area of his room's floor is 225 square feet. What is the cost of the paint, per square foot?

- **F.** $0.20
- **G.** $0.25
- **H.** $0.30
- **J.** $0.35
- **K.** $0.40

17. Which of the following number lines represents the inequality $\left| 2(x - 3) \right| \geq 10$?

A.

B.

C.

D.

E.

18. Mitch purchased a bottle of mustard on sale for $4.50, and Craig purchased a smaller bottle at full price for $3.20. Mitch noticed that the costs per unit of volume of mustard were the same. If Craig's bottle contained 500 mL of mustard and Mitch's contained x mL of mustard, which of the following equations does NOT express the relationship between the volume and cost of Craig's mustard and Mitch's mustard?

- **F.** $\dfrac{3.2}{500} = \dfrac{4.5}{x}$
- **G.** $\dfrac{3.2}{4.5} = \dfrac{500}{x}$
- **H.** $\dfrac{4.5}{3.2} = \dfrac{x}{500}$
- **J.** $\dfrac{500}{3.2} = \dfrac{x}{4.5}$
- **K.** $\dfrac{4.5}{500} = \dfrac{3.2}{x}$

19. What is the sum of the 2 roots of the equation $x^2 - 7x - 60 = 0$?

- **A.** -19
- **B.** -7
- **C.** 7
- **D.** 17
- **E.** 19

20. Ella is making a princess costume which includes a tiara, a gown, a pair of gloves, and a pair of shoes. If she chooses from 7 tiaras, 9 gowns, 4 pairs of gloves, and 3 pairs of shoes, how many possible different costumes could she make?

- **F.** 8
- **G.** 16
- **H.** 28
- **J.** 40
- **K.** 756

Go On to the Next Page.

Practice Test 4

21. The hypotenuse of the right triangle $\triangle BLT$ shown below is 25 meters. The tangent of $\angle T$ is $\frac{4}{3}$. How many meters long is $\overline{BL}$?

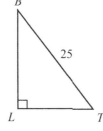

A. 3
B. 4
C. 9
D. 16
E. 20

22. In the standard (x, y) coordinate plane below, 3 of the 4 vertices of a square are shown. Which of the following coordinates is the fourth vertex of the square?

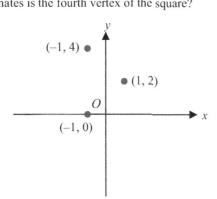

F. $(-3, 2)$
G. $(-3, 3)$
H. $(-3, 1)$
J. $(-2, 2)$
K. $(-2, 1)$

23. If $2^x \cdot 8^2 = 16^2$, then $x = ?$

A. 0

B. 1

C. $\frac{4}{3}$

D. 2

E. 3

24. Which of the following statements is FALSE?

F. The sum of any 2 odd numbers is even.

G. The sum of any 2 even numbers is even.

H. The sum of any odd number and any even number is odd.

J. The product of any odd number and any even number is even.

K. The product of any 2 odd numbers is even.

25. Alex has noticed that the price of a dozen apples has been increasing steadily. Alex's data is shown in the table below.

Year	2010	2011	2012	2013	2014
Price of a dozen apples ($)	6.75	6.84	6.93	7.02	7.11

If the price of a dozen apples over time can be expressed in the form $y = mx + b$ where y is the price of apples and x is the year, what is the value of m?

A. 0.09

B. 0.13

C. 0.18

D. 0.27

E. 0.32

26. Which of the following is equivalent to the inequality $2x + 5 > x - 11$?

F. $x > -16$

G. $x < -16$

H. $x > 16$

J. $x > -8$

K. $x < 8$

27. When $\frac{(x^2 - 1)}{(x + 1)}$ is written in the form $y = mx + b$, where m and b are integers, what is the value of $m + b$?

A. -2

B. -1

C. 0

D. 1

E. 2

Go On to the Next Page.

28. The graph below shows the number of motorcycles sold by Grant's Bikes from 2013 to 2016. By what percent did the number of motorcycles sold change from 2013 to 2016?

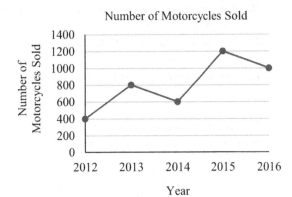

Number of Motorcycles Sold

F. 150%

G. 100%

H. 67%

J. 25%

K. 20%

29. Which of the following systems of inequalities is represented by the shaded region of the graph below?

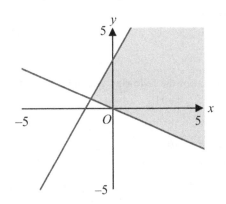

A. $y \le 2x + 3$ and $y \ge -\frac{1}{2}x$

B. $y \le 2x + 3$ or $y \ge -\frac{1}{2}x$

C. $y \ge 2x + 3$ and $y \ge -\frac{1}{2}x$

D. $y \ge 2x + 3$ or $y \ge -\frac{1}{2}x$

E. $y \le 2x + 3$ and $y \le -\frac{1}{2}x$

30. What is the sum of the first 12 terms of the arithmetic sequence 19, 13, 7, 1…?

F. 40

G. −162

H. −168

J. −204

K. −240

31. The median of a set of data containing 5 numbers is known. Two numbers were added to the set. One of these numbers was greater than the original median, and 1 was less than the original median. Which of the following statements *must* be true about the median of the new data set?

A. It is less than the original median.

B. It is greater than the original median.

C. It is the same as the original median.

D. It is equal to the mean of the 2 new values.

E. None of the above statements are true.

32. In the figure below, isosceles triangle $\triangle BEF$ is located between two parallel lines, $\overline{AC}$ and $\overline{DG}$. Lines $\overline{BE}$ and $\overline{BF}$ are congruent. If $\angle ABE$ is equal to $2x - 10°$ and $\angle BFE$ is equal to $x + 30°$, what is the value of $\angle EBF$?

F. 20°

G. 30°

H. 40°

J. 70°

K. 100°

33. x is a positive integer greater than 1. If $x^{\frac{a}{b}} < 1$, which of the following relations *must* be true?

A. $a < b$

B. $a > b$

C. $\frac{a}{b} < 0$

D. $\frac{a}{b} > 0$

E. $\frac{a}{b} = 0$

Go On to the Next Page.

34. Miriam plans to build a rectangular gate made of iron bars attached to a base at the end of her driveway, as shown below. Each iron bar is 2 inches wide, and Miriam plans to affix them vertically to the base, with exactly 2 inches of space between each bar. How many bars will Miriam need to build her gate? (Note: 1 ft = 12 in)

F.   11
G.   31
H.   60
J.   61
K.   120

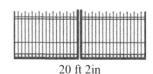

20 ft 2in

35. The graph shown below in the standard (x, y) coordinate plane is rotated 180° clockwise about the origin. Which of the following graphs shows the result of this rotation?

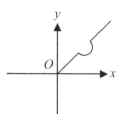

A.
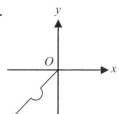

B.
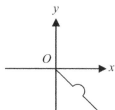

C.
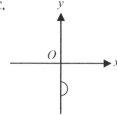

D.
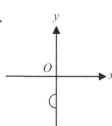

E.
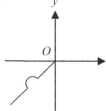

36. What is the matrix product $[5 \quad 1 \quad 4]\begin{bmatrix} 3 \\ 8 \\ 2 \end{bmatrix}$?

F. $[15 \quad 8 \quad 8]$

G. $\begin{bmatrix} 15 \\ 8 \\ 8 \end{bmatrix}$

H. $[31]$

J. $\begin{bmatrix} 15 & 3 & 12 \\ 40 & 8 & 32 \\ 10 & 2 & 8 \end{bmatrix}$

K. $\begin{bmatrix} 15 & 40 & 12 \\ 3 & 8 & 32 \\ 12 & 32 & 8 \end{bmatrix}$

37. A circle has a radius of 6 units and its center is at $(3, 2)$. What is the equation of the circle?

A. $(x - 3)^2 + (y - 2)^2 = 6$
B. $(x + 3)^2 + (y + 2)^2 = 6$
C. $(x - 3)^2 + (y - 2)^2 = 36$
D. $(x - 3)^2 + (y + 2)^2 = 36$
E. $(x + 3)^2 + (y + 2)^2 = 36$

38. In order for seedless watermelons to grow, $\frac{1}{3}$ of all plants in the field must be pollinators, and $\frac{2}{3}$ must be fruit-bearing. If a farmer plants 3,111 watermelons per acre on a field that is 26 acres, how many plants will be pollinators?

F.   20,221
G.   26,962
H.   35,472
J.   53,924
K.   80,886

Go On to the Next Page.

39. In the figure below, lines m and n are parallel, and transversals q and s intersect to form the equilateral triangle $\triangle BCD$. If $\angle E$ is equal to $\angle C$, what is the value of x?

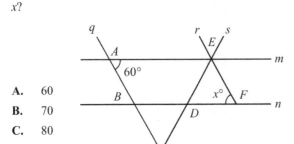

    A.   60

    B.   70

    C.   80

    D.   100

    E.   120

Use the following information to answer questions 40-41.

Event planners are setting up tables for their event. Each table holds a maximum of 5 people and the room holds 15 tables. Since the event is for charity, some donors are allowed 2 free tickets each, and other tickets are sold in advance.

40. If the planners sell 60% of their tickets and 20% of the remaining tickets are given to donors, how many tickets are left over?

    F.   15

    G.   21

    H.   24

    J.   45

    K.   60

41. A minimum of 2 people must sit at each table. If 60 people come to the event and NO tables are empty, what is the maximum possible number of full tables?

    A.   8

    B.   9

    C.   10

    D.   11

    E.   12

42. For the right triangle shown below, which of the following statements is FALSE?

    F. $\cot(C) = \dfrac{6}{8}$

    G. $\csc(C) = \dfrac{10}{8}$

    H. $\tan(C) = \dfrac{6}{8}$

    J. $\sin(C) = \dfrac{8}{10}$

    K. $\cos(C) = \dfrac{6}{10}$

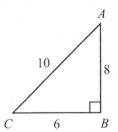

43. The point $(3, -5)$ is reflected across the x-axis and translated 4 units down and 5 units left. What quadrant was the point originally in, and what quadrant is it located in now?

    A.   Quadrant I, now Quadrant II

    B.   Quadrant II, now Quadrant IV

    C.   Quadrant IV, now Quadrant I

    D.   Quadrant IV, now Quadrant II

    E.   Quadrant IV, now Quadrant IV

44. A tightrope walker is stringing 2 ropes, r and s, between the roofs of 2 parallel buildings of the same height, A and B. He fastens them so that they form straight lines between the buildings. Rope r is attached to building A, with an interior angle of 75°. Rope s is attached to building A so that it intersects rope r at rope r's midpoint, forming a 15° angle with rope r. What is a possible angle used to attach rope s to building A?

    F.   15°

    G.   30°

    H.   45°

    J.   80°

    K.   90°

45. Two perpendicular lines intersect at the point $(-3, 1)$ in (x, y) coordinate plane. If one of the lines crosses through the point $(0, 2)$, where does the other line intersect with the y-axis?

    A. $(-4, \ 0)$

    B. $(-2, \ 0)$

    C. $(\ 0, -2)$

    D. $(\ 0, -4)$

    E. $(\ 0, -8)$

Go On to the Next Page.

Practice Test 4

46. The equation of a parabola is $-(x-1)^2 + 3 = y$. A line with an x-intercept of $(-1, 0)$ intersects with the parabola at its vertex in the standard (x, y) coordinate plane, as shown in the graph below. What is the slope of the line that intersects with the parabola?

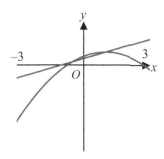

What is the slope of the line that intersects the parabola?

F. -2

G. $-\dfrac{3}{2}$

H. $-\dfrac{1}{2}$

J. 1

K. $\dfrac{3}{2}$

47. A 3-inch-by-7-inch rectangle is inscribed in a circle, as shown below. What is the radius of this circle, in inches?

A. $\dfrac{7}{2}$

B. $\dfrac{\sqrt{58}}{2}$

C. $\dfrac{\sqrt{85}}{2}$

D. $\sqrt{58}$

E. 85

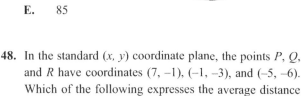

48. In the standard (x, y) coordinate plane, the points P, Q, and R have coordinates $(7, -1)$, $(-1, -3)$, and $(-5, -6)$. Which of the following expresses the average distance from P to R and Q to R?

F. 6

G. 7

H. 8

J. 9

K. 10

49. If $\log_x a = p - q$ and $\log_x b = -q$, then $\log_x(ab) = ?$

A. p

B. $p + q$

C. $p - q$

D. $p + 2q$

E. $p - 2q$

50. Julie slides down the longest slide at the waterpark, as shown below. How long is the lower, less steep portion of the slide (x), to the nearest foot?

(Note: You may use the following values, which are accurate to 2 decimal points: sin 20° = 0.34; cos 20° = 0.94; sin 40° = 0.64; cos 40° = 0.77; tan 40° = 0.84)

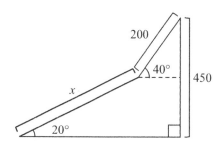

F. 322

G. 343

H. 376

J. 947

K. 1324

51. A formula used to compute the future value of a savings account is $A = P(1 + r)^n$, where A is the future value, P is the initial amount deposited, r is the interest rate for one compounding period, expressed as a decimal, and n is the number of years. Mrs. Skye decides to deposit a principal of \$400 into her savings account when the interest rate is 0.5%. If Mrs. Skye takes out her investment after 3.5 years, which of the following is closest to the value of her savings account at that time?

A. \$ 407.00

B. \$ 407.04

C. \$ 412.20

D. \$ 474.49

E. \$1,407.00

Go On to the Next Page.

52. If $f(x) = x^2 + 3$ and $g(x) = \dfrac{\sqrt{x}}{2}$, what is the value of $f(g(9))$?

F. $\dfrac{9}{2}$

G. $\dfrac{15}{4}$

H. $\dfrac{21}{4}$

J. 3

K. 6

53. To the nearest percent, what percent of the area of the triangle below, graphed in the standard (x,y) coordinate plane, is located in the second quadrant?

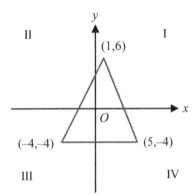

A. 5%

B. 9%

C. 15%

D. 27%

E. 40%

54. Line $\overline{AB}$ has endpoints at $(2, 3)$ and $(-7, -19)$. What are the coordinates of the midpoint of line $\overline{AB}$?

F. $\left(-\dfrac{5}{2}, -8\right)$

G. $(-5, -16)$

H. $(-9, -8)$

J. $(-9, 8)$

K. $\left(-\dfrac{9}{2}, -8\right)$

55. The force of gravity (F_G) between 2 objects is related to the product of their masses (m_1 and m_2) and to the distance that separates their centers (r) according to the following equation $F_G = \dfrac{Gm_1m_2}{r^2}$, where G is a constant. If the distance between the 2 objects is tripled and the mass of the first object is halved, the force of gravity between the two objects changes by what factor?

A. $\dfrac{1}{18}$

B. $\dfrac{1}{6}$

C. 2

D. 3

E. 9

56. A triangle is drawn in a circle on an (x, y) coordinate plane, as shown below.

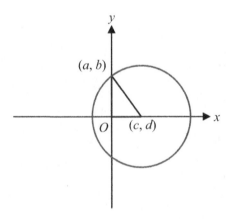

If the circle with center (c, d) intersects the x-axis at points $(-2, 0)$ and $(8, 0)$, and the y-axis at (a, b). what is the sum of the values of a, b, c, and d?

F. 9

G. 8

H. 7

J. 6

K. 5

Go On to the Next Page.

Practice Test 4

57. The function $f(x) = x^3 + 3$ is modified to create $g(x)$. If $g(-x) = -g(x)$ for all values of x, how is $f(x)$ modified to create $g(x)$?

A. $f(x)$ is reflected across the x-axis

B. $f(x)$ is reflected across the y-axis

C. $f(x)$ is translated 3 units right

D. $f(x)$ is translated 3 units down

E. $f(x)$ is rotated about the point $(0, 0)$

58. Two cylinders are shown below, with height and radius indicated. What is the relationship between the volume of Cylinder 1 (V_1) and the volume of Cylinder 2 (V_2)?

(Note: The formula for the volume of a cylinder is $V = \pi r^2 h$, where r is radius and h is height.)

Cylinder 2

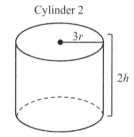

Cylinder 1

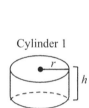

F. $V_2 = V_1$

G. $V_2 = 3V_1$

H. $V_2 = 6V_1$

J. $V_2 = 9V_1$

K. $V_2 = 18V_1$

59. What is the value of i^{1023}? (Note: $i = \sqrt{-1}$)

A. $-i$

B. -1

C. i

D. 1

E. $\sqrt{i}$

60. A trigonometric function with equation $f(x) = a\sin(bx)$, where a, b, and x are real numbers, is graphed in the standard (x, y) coordinate plane below. The *period* (ω) of the function $f(x)$ is the smallest positive number p such that $f(x + p) = f(x)$ for every real number x. Which of the following is the period of this function?

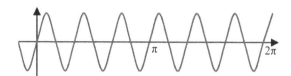

F. $\dfrac{\pi}{3}$

G. $\dfrac{\pi}{2}$

H. $\dfrac{2\pi}{3}$

J. π

K. $\dfrac{3\pi}{2}$

End of Test 2.

Stop! Do not turn the page until you are told to do so.

Do not return to the previous test.

Reading Test

35 Minutes—40 Questions

DIRECTIONS: There are multiple passages on this test. Each passage is accompanied by several questions. After reading a passage, choose the best answer to each question and fill in the corresponding circle on your answer document. You may refer to the passages as often as necessary.

Passage I

Prose Fiction: This passage is adapted from the story "Expiation," by Edith Wharton. Originally published in 1903, the story is set in the early 1900s in New York City, and follows a period in the career of the young Paula Fetherel.

Mrs. Fetherel was the kind of woman whose emotions never communicate themselves to her clothes—and the conventional background of the New York drawing-room, with its pervading implication of an
5 imminent tea-tray and of an atmosphere in which the social functions have become purely reflex, lent to her declaration a relief not unnoticed by her cousin Mrs. Clinch.

"The newspaper clippings," Mrs. Fetherel
10 whispered.

Mrs. Clinch smiled. "Well," she said, "I suppose you were prepared for the consequences of authorship?"

Mrs. Fetherel blushed brightly. "It isn't their coming," she owned—"it's their coming *now*."

15 "Now?"

"The Bishop's in town."

"Well—weren't you prepared for the Bishop?"

"Not now—at least, I hadn't thought of his seeing the clippings."

20 "And why should he see them?"

"Bella—*won't* you understand? It's John. He has taken the most unexpected tone—one might almost say out of perversity."

"Oh, perversity—" Mrs. Clinch murmured,
25 observing her cousin between lids wrinkled by amusement. "What tone has John taken?"

Mrs. Fetherel threw out her answer with the desperate gesture of a woman held by a marital grasp. "The tone of being proud of my book."

30 Mrs. Clinch laughed.

"Oh, you may laugh," Mrs. Fetherel insisted, "but it's no joke to me. In the first place, John's liking the book is so—so—false—it puts me in such a ridiculous position; and then it has set him watching for the
35 reviews—who would ever have suspected John of knowing that books were *reviewed?* Why, he's actually found out about the Clipping Bureau, and whenever the postman rings I hear John rush out of the library to see if there are any yellow envelopes. Of course, when they *do*
40 come he'll bring them into the drawing-room and read them aloud to everybody who happens to be here—and the Bishop is sure to happen to be here!"

Mrs. Clinch repressed her amusement. "The picture you draw is a lurid one," she conceded, "but your
45 modesty strikes me as abnormal, especially in an author. The chances are that some of the clippings will be rather pleasant reading. The critics are not all union men."

Mrs. Fetherel stared. "Union men?"

"Well, I mean they don't all belong to the well-known
50 Society-for-the-Persecution-of-Rising-Authors. Some of them have even been known to defy its regulations and say a good word for a new writer."

"Oh, I dare say," said Mrs. Fetherel, with the laugh her cousin's remark warranted. "But you don't quite see
55 my point. I'm not at all nervous about the success of my book—my publisher tells me I have no need to be—but I *am* afraid of its being a succes de scandale."

"Mercy!" said Mrs. Clinch, sitting up.

The butler and footman at this moment appeared
60 with the tea-tray, and when they had withdrawn, Mrs. Fetherel, bending her brightly rippled head above the kettle, confided, "I suppose to experienced authors there's always something absurd in the nervousness of a new writer, but in my case so much is at stake; I've put

Go On to the Next Page.

Practice Test 4

65 so much of myself into this book and I'm so afraid of
being misunderstood... of being, as it were, in advance
of my time... like poor Flaubert... I *know* you'll think me
ridiculous... and if only my own reputation were at stake,
I should never give it a thought... but the idea of dragging
70 John's name through the mud..."

Mrs. Clinch, who had risen and gathered her cloak
about her, stood surveying from her genial height her
cousin's agitated expression.

"Why did you use John's name, then?"

75   "That's another of my difficulties! I *had* to. There
would have been no merit in publishing such a book
under an assumed name; it would have been an act of
moral cowardice. A writer who dares to show up the
hollowness of social conventions must have the courage
80 of her convictions and be willing to accept the
consequences of defying society. Can you imagine Ibsen
or Tolstoy writing under a false name?" Mrs. Fetherel
lifted a tragic eye to her cousin. "You don't know, Bella,
how often I've envied you since I began to write. I used
85 to wonder sometimes—you won't mind my saying
so?—why, with all your cleverness, you hadn't taken up
some more exciting subject than natural history; but I see
now how wise you were. Whatever happens, you will
never be denounced by the press!"

90   "Is that what you're afraid of?" asked Mrs. Clinch,
as she clutched her umbrella.

Mrs. Fetherel lifted an undaunted brow. "I'm not
afraid," she proclaimed; and at the same instant she
dropped her spoon with a clatter and shrank back into
95 her seat. "There's the bell," she exclaimed, "and I know
it's the Bishop!"

1. At the time of the events of the story, Mrs. Fetherel is:

    A. a successful and established novelist.

    B. a newly published author.

    C. an expert natural historicist.

    D. a homemaker and aspiring writer.

2. It can reasonably be inferred from the passage that John
    is Mrs. Fetherel's:

    F. son.

    G. husband.

    H. brother.

    J. father.

3. The statement that John's interest in the reviews of Mrs.
    Fetherel's book is "out of perversity" (line 31) is meant
    to suggest that Mrs. Fetherel feels that:

    A. John has been using this interest to make
        unwelcome advances toward Mrs. Fetherel.

    B. John is incensed by Mrs. Fetherel's depiction of
        him in the book.

    C. John's interest in book reviews is extreme and
        embarrassing.

    D. John is a devoted fan of literature almost to the
        point of obsession.

4. The passage states that Mrs. Fetherel is apprehensive
    about the reviews of her book for all of the following
    reasons EXCEPT that she:

    F. believes the reviews will cause a scandal.

    G. worries what the Bishop will think of the reviews.

    H. is afraid the reviews will prevent the success of her
        book.

    J. is anxious about potentially damaging John's
        reputation.

5. Details in the passage suggest that the relationship
    between Mrs. Fetherel and Mrs. Clinch is:

    A. suspicious and distant.

    B. insincere and forced.

    C. businesslike and formal.

    D. candid and close.

6. The passage suggests that Mrs. Clinch reacts to Mrs.
    Fetherel's worry about the reviews of her book with:

    F. hostility.

    G. amusement.

    H. skepticism.

    J. concern.

Go On to the Next Page.

7. Why does Mrs. Fetherel say she is "like poor Flaubert" (line 75)?

    A. To illustrate the extent of her literary ambition

    B. To compare Flaubert's nervousness about reviews to her own

    C. To demonstrate her concern that, like Flaubert, she will not be understood

    D. To acknowledge that Flaubert would find her apprehension uncalled for

8. The passage states that Mrs. Fetherel used her real name in writing her book because she:

    F. believed using her real name was an ethical obligation.

    G. wanted the fame that comes with becoming a household name.

    H. hoped to expose John, who inspired a character in the book.

    J. wished to copy exactly the literary style of writers like Ibsen and Tolstoy.

9. The passage suggests that Mrs. Fetherel dropped her spoon and shrank into her seat as a result of:

    A. her indignation at something Mrs. Clinch said.

    B. Mrs. Clinch's startling her with a sudden movement.

    C. her sudden realization that John would be angry about the reviews.

    D. the bell ringing, suggesting the presence of the Bishop.

10. The passage suggests that Mrs. Fetherel:

    F. has not seen the Bishop in some time and is excited to see him.

    G. is afraid of the Bishop because of his unsavory character.

    H. is worried about how the Bishop will react to the reviews of her book.

    J. is concerned that the Bishop has already read her book and views it critically.

Go On to the Next Page.

Passage II

Social Science: This passage is adapted from the article "Genome Editing Poses Ethical Problems That We Cannot Ignore" by Anthony Wrigley and Ainsley Newson (©2015 Anthony Wrigley and Ainsley Newson).

The ability to precisely and accurately change almost any part of any genome, even in complex species such as humans, may soon become a reality through genome editing. But with great power comes great
5 responsibility—and few subjects start such heated debates about moral rights and wrongs.

Genome editing offers a greater degree of control and precision in how specific DNA sequences are changed than previous genetic engineering techniques
10 do. It could be used in basic science, for human health, or improvements to crops. There are a variety of techniques, but "clustered regularly inter-spaced short palindromic repeats," or CRISPR, is perhaps the foremost. CRISPR has prompted recent calls for a
15 genome editing moratorium from a group of concerned United States academics. Because it is the easiest technique to set up and so could be quickly and widely adopted, the fear is that it may be put into use far too soon, outstripping our understanding of its safety
20 implications and preventing any opportunity to think about how such powerful tools should be controlled.

Ethical concerns over genetic modification are not new, particularly when it comes to humans. However, as more researchers use CRISPR to achieve more genome
25 changes, the implications shift. Our consideration of a technology that is rarely used and only in specific cases will differ from one that is widely used and put to all sorts of uses. Should we reach this tipping point, we will have to reconsider the conclusions of the first few
30 decades of the genetic modification debate. Currently, modifying plants, some animals, and non-inheritable cells in humans is allowed under strict controls. But modifications that alter the human germ-line are not allowed, with the exception of the recent decision in the
35 UK to allow mitochondrial replacement.

While this may mean weighing up potential benefits, risks, and harms, as the potential applications of genome editing are so broad, even this sort of assessment isn't straightforward. Genome editing
40 techniques have so far been used to change genomes in individual cells and in entire (non-human) organisms. Benefits have included better-targeted gene therapy in animal models of some diseases, such as Duchenne

Muscular Dystrophy. It's also hoped that it will lead to a
45 better understanding of the structure, function, and regulation of genes. Genetic modification through genome editing of plants has already created herbicide- and infection-resistant crops.

But more contentious is how genome editing might
50 be used to change traits in humans. While this has been the basis for many works of fiction, in real life our capacity to provide the sort of genetic engineering seen in films and books such as *Gattaca* and *Brave New World* has been quite limited. Genome editing
55 potentially changes this, presenting us with the very real possibility that any aspect of the human genome could be manipulated as we desire. This could mean eliminating harmful genetic conditions, or enhancing traits deemed advantageous, such as resistance to
60 diseases. But this ability may also open the door to eugenics, where those with access to the technology could select for traits they prefer, such as eye, skin or hair color, or height.

The concern prompting the United States
65 academics' call for a ban is the potential for altering the human germ-line, making gene alterations inheritable by our children. Gene therapies that produce non-inheritable changes in a person's genome are ethically accepted, in part because there is no risk for the next
70 generation if things go wrong. However to date only one disease—severe combined immunodeficiency—has been cured by this therapy.

Germ-line alterations pose much greater ethical concerns. A mistake could harm future individuals by
75 placing that mistake in every cell. Of course the flip side is that, if carried out safely and as intended, germ-line alterations could also provide potentially permanent solutions to genetic diseases. No research is yet considering this in humans, however.

80 Nevertheless, even if changes to the germ-line turn out to be safe, the underlying ethical concerns of scope and scale that genome editing brings will remain. If a technique can be used widely and efficiently, without careful oversight governing its use, it can readily become
85 a new norm or an expectation. Those unable to access the desired genetic alterations, be they humans with diseases, humans without enhanced genetic characteristics, or farmers without genetically modified animals or crops, may all find themselves gravely and unfairly
90 disadvantaged.

11. The authors' attitude toward the main subject of the passage can best be described as:

    A. complete fascination.

    B. reasoned concern.

    C. mild interest.

    D. detached appreciation.

12. According to the passage, CRISPR is considered the:

    F. only precise form of genetic engineering.

    G. least dangerous gene therapy.

    H. most effective type of genetic modification.

    J. easiest genome editing technique to use.

13. As it is used in line 36, the phrase *weighing up* most nearly means:

    A. pricing.

    B. evaluating.

    C. measuring out.

    D. seeking.

14. The passage states that compared to current gene therapies, germ-line alterations are:

    F. much more risky.

    G. much less risky.

    H. ethically accepted.

    J. more efficient.

15. The word *manipulated*, as it is used in line 57, most nearly means which of the following?

    A. Deceived

    B. Maneuvered

    C. Altered

    D. Plotted

16. According to the passage, most regulators do NOT allow genetic modifications on:

    F. the human germ-line.

    G. any human cells.

    H. non-inheritable human cells.

    J. most plants.

17. One of the main purposes of the final paragraph is to:

    A. prove that proposed genetic alterations are safe.

    B. describe potential uses for genetic modifications.

    C. summarize the negative possibilities associated with genetically modifying animals.

    D. outline one of the major concerns about the adoption of genome editing.

18. In lines 50-54, the authors refer to *Gattaca* and *Brave New World* most likely to emphasize that:

    F. the types of genetic engineering they depict are currently possible using CRISPR.

    G. changes to human genes that were once impossible could become achievable.

    H. works of fiction can influence the use of genome editing in modern society.

    J. the altered human traits demonstrated in these works are highly contentious.

19. It can reasonably be inferred from the passage that:

    A. some types of genetic modification are allowed on plants but not humans.

    B. CRISPR is the only method scientists use for genome editing.

    C. the demand for germ-line alterations has led to numerous scientific breakthroughs.

    D. no genome editing research is currently performed in the United States.

20. The passage indicates that CRISPR and genome editing could lead to both:

    F. decreased research on genetic diseases and new moral questions.

    G. potential health benefits for humans and expanded ethical debates.

    H. the selection of desirable genetic traits and fewer gene therapies.

    J. more genetically modified crops and fewer restrictions on their use.

Go On to the Next Page.

Passage III

Humanities: Passage A is adapted from the essay "We're Obsessed With Zombies—Which Says A Lot About Today" by Joseph Gillings (©2015 Joseph Gillings). Passage B is adapted from "Frankenstein or Krampus? What Our Monsters Say About Us" by Natalie Lawrence (©2015 Natalie Lawrence).

Passage A by Joseph Gillings

The zombie invasion is here. Our bookshops, cinemas, and TVs are dripping with the debris of their relentless shuffle to cultural domination.

Since at least the late 19th century, each generation has created fictional enemies that reflect a broader unease with cultural or scientific developments. As the industrial revolution steamed ahead, the speculative fiction of authors such as H. G. Wells began to consider where scientific innovation would take mankind. This trend reached its height in the Cold War during the 1950s and 1960s. Radiation-mutated monsters and invasions from space seen through the paranoid lens of communism all postulated the imminent demise of mankind.

In the 1950s, "the golden age of nuclear fear," radiation and its fictional consequences were the flip side to a growing faith that science would solve the world's problems. In many respects, we are now living with the collapse of this faith. Today we live in societies dominated by an overarching anxiety reflecting the risk associated with each unpredictable scientific development. People have lost faith in assumptions of social and scientific "progress."

As the faith in inexorable scientific "progress" recedes, politics is transformed. The groups emerging from outside the political mainstream engage in much older battles of faith and identity. Whether partisan nationalists or religious fundamentalists, they seek to build "imagined communities" through race, religion, or culture, and "fear" is their currency.

Modern zombies are the product of this globalized, risk-conscious world. No longer the work of a single "mad" scientist re-animating the dead, they now appear as the result of secret government programs creating untreatable viruses. The zombies indiscriminately overwhelm states irrespective of wealth, technology, and military strength, turning all order to chaos. This is a relentless enemy, seeking to cause death and destruction with little or no regard to their own safety. They may be your neighbor, a friend, or teacher—but now they want you dead.

Like those of previous generations, our fictional nemesis reflects deep-seated concerns. As the survivors in *The Walking Dead* have found, such relentless enemies may force even the most upright citizen to confront their moral codes. In the battle for TV ratings, survival, no matter what it takes, may be enough, but in the real world, holding on to our moral compass may be the greatest weapon we possess.

Passage B by Natalie Lawrence

The etymology of monstrosity suggests the complex roles that monsters play within society. "Monster" probably derives from the Latin, *monstrare*, meaning "to demonstrate", and *monere*, "to warn." How they have been created over the centuries is much more indicative of the moral and existential challenges faced by societies than the realities that they have encountered. Though the modern Gothic monster and the medieval chimera may seem unrelated, both have acted as important social tools.

Until relatively recently in history, monsters close to home, such as two-headed calves, were believed to be warnings of divine wrath. Monstrous depictions in newspapers and pamphlets expressed strong political attitudes. Traditional monstrous beasts such as basilisks or unicorns, that were banished to distant regions in maps, represented a frightening unknown.

However, monsters simultaneously represented the wonderful diversity of divine creation, a playful "Nature" that produced many strange forms. Exotic beasts brought to Europe for the first time in the 16th century, such as armadillos or walruses, were often interpreted as "monstrous." More accurately, they were made into monsters when they were defined as such: as things that did not fit into the accepted natural categories. An armadillo became a pig-turtle, while a walrus was a sea-elephant.

So how do we use our monsters today? One of the two monsters set to hit cinemas shortly displays the dangers of overconfident human enterprise (*Victor Frankenstein*); the other provides a dark embodiment of Christmas-spirit gone awry (*Krampus*). Such monsters are images that embody the cultural or psychological characteristics that we as a society find difficult to acknowledge. Through fantastical narratives, we rid ourselves of these undesirable attributes. The consumption of monster-culture provides us with a safe, removed space to explore and banish social anxieties.

It also transforms anxieties into ridiculous figures, such as Krampus. Monsters such as this offer us moral messages in easily-swallowed forms that both highlight their potential threat, and soothe us by defusing it.

Go On to the Next Page.

90   Though it may not seem so, this has always been the most important role that monsters have played: they horrify us, yes, but ultimately their function is to remove what we find horrifying about ourselves. So we can recoil at the gory construction of Frankenstein's

95 monster, or shriek at the toothy maw of Krampus for a few hours, then leave them happily behind when the credits roll.

Questions 21-25 ask about Passage A.

21. When the author of Passage A claims that "Our bookshops, cinemas, and TVs are dripping with the debris of their relentless shuffle to cultural domination," (lines 1-3) he is most nearly referring to the:

  A. prevalence of zombies in modern entertainment.

  B. view of zombie-related entertainment as purely frivolous.

  C. quantity of physical copies of zombie novels and films.

  D. previous popularity of zombies in contemporary culture.

22. Passage A indicates that the author believes that modern views towards scientific progress are:

  F. no longer captured by contemporary forms of entertainment.

  G. shaped almost exclusively by science fiction stories.

  H. much less optimistic now than they were in the past.

  J. growing increasingly positive with the help of fictionalized portrayals.

23. In the second paragraph, the author brings up radiation-mutated monsters as an example of:

  A. lesser-known monsters in literature.

  B. the precursors to modern zombies.

  C. the type of monsters that dominate entertainment.

  D. a way fiction represents cultural fears.

24. Viewed in the context of the passage, the phrase "globalized, risk-conscious world" (lines 30-31) is most likely intended by the author to convey a tone of which of the following about the world?

  F. Nostalgia

  G. Anxiety

  H. Elation

  J. Disappointment

25. Passage A explains that one of the most terrifying aspects of zombies is that they:

  A. attack in large numbers.

  B. spread dangerous viruses.

  C. could be anyone.

  D. have superhuman strength.

Questions 26 and 27 ask about Passage B.

26. The passage indicates that throughout history, monsters represented both:

  F. the unknown and the exotic.

  G. the terrifying and the dangerous.

  H. the powerful and the magical.

  J. the strange and the beautiful.

27. The author most likely includes the figures of Krampus and Frankenstein in order to provide examples of:

  A. recent films where monsters were used to depict the grotesque.

  B. monsters which can help banish contemporary fears.

  C. frightening figures drawn from recent monster literature.

  D. historical monsters that still haunt national consciousness.

Questions 28-30 ask about both passages.

28. Both Passage A and Passage B highlight:

  F. how monsters were seen to represent warnings of divine wrath.

  G. the ways in which nuclear fears inspired modern monsters.

  H. the ways in which nuclear fears drove modern monsters.

  J. all of the different media that draw upon monsters.

29. Unlike Passage A, Passage B suggests that depictions of fictionalized monsters:

  A. are predictive of future cultural issues.

  B. demonstrate modern social concerns.

  C. are rarely connected to historical legends.

  D. can ultimately help reduce fear.

Go On to the Next Page.

30. The author of Passage B discusses how monsters "represented the wonderful diversity of divine creation," and mentions exotic beasts such as walruses and armadillos as examples. In contrast, the author of Passage A defines monsters as:

F. embodiments of cultural fears rather than the diverse unknown.

G. warnings of divine wrath rather than manifestations of social fears.

H. historical and documented animals rather than fictional creatures.

J. inspiring sources of creativity rather than dull beasts.

Passage IV

Natural Science: This passage is adapted from the article "Meet the Earthquakes That Happen 600 km Underground" by Simon Redfern (©2015 Simon Redfern).

A little more than 90 years ago, British geologist Herbert Hall Turner noticed some earthquake data that suggested a surprising explanation. The only way to explain the data was if the earthquake had occurred hundreds of
5 kilometers beneath the Earth's surface, unlike the more commonly seen near-surface earthquakes.

Since Turner's observations, deep earthquakes have fascinated seismologists. It is still unclear why they happen, but two studies just published in the journal
10 *Science*, taking different approaches, conclude that they are probably a result of rapid changes in minerals at that depth.

Such deep earthquakes do not have immediate consequences for humans. But they hold clues about
15 destructive quakes in the Earth's shallower crust, making it important to understand them. Most earthquakes occur in the stiff, brittle outer shell that includes the Earth's crust. This "seismogenic zone," where the most devastating and dangerous earthquakes occur, goes down
20 to about 15 km beneath the surface.

As you go deeper, pressure and temperature both increase rapidly, so the nature of earthquakes changes. Rocks move slowly, when pushed or pulled by different forces acting on them. At depth, they appear to flow
25 like soft toffee, rather than break like peanut brittle. This is why Turner's observations of earthquakes more than 600 km below the surface were puzzling. If the rocks flow slowly, then there shouldn't really be any sudden shocks that cause earthquakes. Rather,
30 there should be gentle, continuous readjustments to stress.

Suggestions have been floated in the past about what triggers such earthquakes. But Thorne Lay of University of California Santa Cruz took a step ahead to
35 analyze a deep earthquake that occurred in May, in the Pacific Ocean beneath the Okhotsk plate. At a magnitude of 8.3, it was four times greater than the 1906 San Francisco earthquake. Indeed, it was the biggest ever recorded at a depth of more than 600 km. A near-surface
40 earthquake of the same magnitude could've been very destructive, but at that depth it was barely noticeable at the surface above.

Recent analysis of an earthquake in Bhuj, India, in 2001 suggests it shared similarities with the Okhotsk
45 event, although it was just 16 km deep. In contrast, however, it caused terrible devastation, including an estimated 20,000 deaths. "There may be things we don't understand about more shallow earthquakes that we can learn from studying these deep earthquakes," said Bob
50 Myhill of the University of Bayreuth.

During the Okhotsk event, the Pacific plate of Earth's crust was drawn down into the hot mantle that makes up much of the planet's interior. What Lay found was that the amount of seismic energy released in the
55 event was so large that it caused fractures as long as 180 km long below the surface. The rock ruptured at close to the speed of sound, which in the rock would be as much as 14,000 km/h.

But what caused such rapid rupture? Alexandre
60 Schubnel of École Normale Supérieure suggests an explanation that hinges on the mineral making up the deep rock, called olivine. To be sure, he designed lab experiments that could mimic deep earth. Schubnel found that above a critical temperature and pressure,
65 olivine changes into another mineral called spinel. Under stress, this sudden change creates fractures, much like those seen in the earthquake. The mineral change releases stress instantaneously, in just the same way as stress was relieved in the deep earthquake under the
70 Pacific Ocean.

There is one critical difference, however. To make the experiments easier, the olivine used by Schubnel in the lab contained the element germanium instead of silicon. Germanium-olivines are known to behave
75 slightly differently than silicon-olivines, and this may make a lot of difference 600 km below the surface.

Still, while the mini-earthquakes seen in the lab were many orders of magnitude smaller than those in the earth, the reason these experiments can be trusted is
80 because the creaks and groans of minerals in a lab show

Go On to the Next Page.

similar characteristics to those of large earthquakes. So, even though Schubnel's idea is not new, it experimentally confirms suggestions made by researchers before. It opens the way to studying deep earthquakes in the safety and
85 comfort of the lab.

31. According to the passage, the finding that earthquakes can occur deep below the Earth's surface is:

   A. surprising, since rock flows differently that far beneath the surface.

   B. plausible, since rocks flow both below the surface and between the crust and core.

   C. groundbreaking, as it implies that the Earth's crust is in danger of breaking apart.

   D. strange, considering the fact that rocks at depth move too quickly to have much friction.

32. What does the passage offer as evidence that deep earthquakes occur as a result of mineral changes?

   F. The report of a British geologist, Herbert Hall Turner

   G. Two recently published articles in the journal *Science*

   H. Experimental evidence from a study conducted by the author

   J. The accounts of surviving eyewitnesses like Alexandre Schubnel

33. It can reasonably be inferred that the phrase "seismogenic zone" (line 18) refers to the:

   A. zone in the Americas where the most dangerous earthquakes take place.

   B. countries where earthquakes are most common.

   C. Earth's inner core and mantle where deep earthquakes occur.

   D. outer layer of the Earth consisting of stiff, shallow crust.

34. It is reasonable to conclude from the passage that temperature and pressure:

   F. are both increased by the occurrence of earthquakes.

   G. are not the only factors that contribute to earthquakes.

   H. play no role in causing earthquakes below the surface.

   J. are the primary catalyst for surface-level earthquakes.

35. The main purpose of the fourth paragraph (lines 21-31) is to point out why:

   A. rocks typically move so slowly beneath the Earth's surface.

   B. studying earthquakes below the surface is unfeasible.

   C. data indicating the existence of deep earthquakes was surprising.

   D. Turner discontinued his work on earthquakes in the crust.

36. What does the author suggest about earthquakes of the same magnitude that happen at the surface compared to those that happen at greater depths?

   F. The earthquakes happening at the surface will cause greater devastation.

   G. The earthquakes happening at greater depths will cause greater devastation.

   H. The earthquakes happening at the surface will be more expensive to study.

   J. The earthquakes happening at greater depths will be less challenging to study.

37. The passage states that the Okhotsk event was:

   A. a devastating surface-level earthquake that led to 20,000 deaths.

   B. an earthquake in the Earth's core that traveled to the surface at the speed of sound, 14,000 km/h.

   C. an earthquake deep beneath the surface that caused long and rapid rock fractures.

   D. an earthquake in the Pacific that led to a tsunami on the coasts of nearby countries.

38. In the passage, the author claims that rapid ruptures happening deep beneath the surface may be a result of:

   F. changes in minerals due to stress on the rocks.

   G. increased levels of olivine beneath the surface.

   H. decreasing temperatures in the mantle and crust.

   J. the slow degradation of olivine into spinel over time.

39. The author indicates that Schubnel's use of germanium instead of silicon:

A. alters the outcome of Schubnel's work and makes it relevant only to surface-level earthquakes.

B. is an important distinction to note, but does not prevent the research from being useful for studying deep earthquakes.

C. is an insignificant substitution that should not be noted when considering future set-ups of the experiment.

D. was an unfortunate oversight that Schubnel plans to remedy in his next round of research.

40. As used in line 80, the term "creaks and groans of minerals in a lab" most likely means:

F. the bubbling of chemicals when made to react with each other.

G. the splitting apart of rocks by earthquakes beneath the Earth's surface.

H. the sounds made by fractures as olivine turned into spinel.

J. the grinding noises of minerals recorded deep in the mantle.

End of Test 3.

Stop! Do not turn the page until you are told to do so.

Do not return to the previous test.

Science Test

35 Minutes—40 Questions

DIRECTIONS: There are several passages on this test. Each passage is accompanied by several questions. After reading a passage, choose the best answer to each question and fill in the corresponding circle on your answer document. You may refer to the passages as often as necessary.

You are NOT permitted to use a calculator on this test.

Passage I

Researchers examined the possibility of using pigeons (*Columbia livia*) as visual observers of breast cancer tumors.

Experiment 1

Eight pigeons were trained to discern the difference between images of benign tumors and images of malignant tumors at various magnifications and rotations. They were trained in a closed chamber with continuous white noise, a food pellet dispenser, and a touchscreen for pecking their responses, as shown in Diagram 1. Each pigeon received a food pellet only if its response was correct. The pigeons were trained daily over a period of 15 days using 48 different breast tumor images (24 images of benign tumors and 24 images of malignant tumors) at 3 different magnifications (4x, 10x, and 20x), for a total of 144 images. The pigeons' progress is shown in Figure 1. After their 15-day training period, the pigeons were tested using the 144 original images and 24 rotated images (see Figure 2).

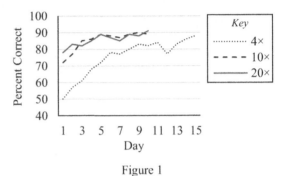

Figure 1

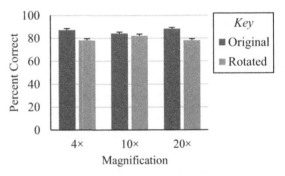

Figure 2

Diagram 1

Experiment 2

Eight new pigeons were trained to discern the difference between benign tumors and malignant tumors under different reward systems and at different image compressions. They were trained using the same set-up as in Experiment 1, except three different compressions (uncompressed, 15:1, and 27:1) were used instead of three different magnifications. During their training, half of the birds were *nondifferentially reinforced*, which means they received food pellets regardless of their responses, and half were *differentially reinforced*, which means the received food pellets only if their responses were correct. After their training, the pigeons were tested using the 144 original images. Results are shown in Figure 3.

Go On to the Next Page.

Practice Test 4

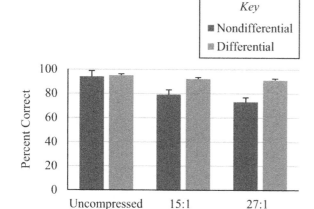

Figure 3

Data adapted from Richard M. Levenson et al. "Pigeons (*Columbia livia*) as Trainable Observers of Pathology and Radiology Breast Cancer Images." ©2015 by PLoS One. 10.1371/journal.pone.0141357

1. According to the results of Experiment 1, if a pigeon correctly identified 52% of breast cancer tumor images on its first day of training, which of the following was most likely the magnification of the images?

   A. 1×

   B. 4×

   C. 10×

   D. 20×

2. Suppose that an additional trial in Experiment 2 was performed using a fourth compression, at a ratio of 21:1. The average percent correct for the pigeons that were nondifferentially reinforced in this trial would most likely have been:

   F. less than 70%.

   G. between 70% and 80%.

   H. between 80% and 95%.

   J. greater than 95%.

3. Experiment 2 differed from Experiment 1 in that Experiment 2:

   A. tested different magnifications.

   B. tested different rotations.

   C. tested different touchscreen sizes.

   D. tested different reinforcements.

4. The researchers had predicted that increasing the magnification of breast tumor images would increase the pigeons' ability, when tested, to determine whether the original images showed benign or malignant tumors. According to Figure 2, are the results of Experiment 1 consistent with this prediction?

   F. Yes; as magnification increases from 4× to 10× to 20×, the pigeons' ability to identify the images correctly also increases.

   G. Yes; as magnification increases from 4× to 10× to 20×, the pigeons' ability to identify the images correctly decreases and then increases.

   H. No; as the training program continues over 15 days with changing magnification, the pigeons' ability to identify the images correctly decreases.

   J. No; as magnification increases from 4× to 10× to 20×, the pigeons' ability to identify the images correctly decreases and then increases.

5. Which variables remained constant in Experiments 1 and 2, respectively?

	Experiment 1	Experiment 2
A.	rotation	reinforcement
B.	magnification	compression
C.	reinforcement	rotation
D.	compression	reinforcement

6. The researchers were concerned that the entry and exit of researchers from the lab was interfering with the pigeons' ability to select the correct breast tumor images. Which of the following modifications would best help them eliminate this problem?

   F. Increase the volume of the continuous white noise.

   G. Increase the total number of images.

   H. Decrease the duration of the training program.

   J. Decrease the size of the touchscreen.

7. Pigeons belong to which taxonomic domain?

   A. Bacteria

   B. Archaea

   C. Eukaryota

   D. Fungi

Go On to the Next Page.

Passage II

In North America, many populations of monarch butterflies make a yearly migration to Mexico for the colder winter months. Some of these monarchs are infected by wing parasites, such as *Ophryocystis elektroscirrha*, which are thought to reduce migration ability by reducing a butterfly's wing size. A group of scientists studied the effect of *O. elektroscirrha* infection on the ability of monarchs to successfully reach Mexico. Taking samples of both infected and uninfected monarchs from two overwintering sites, the scientists measured wing area and hydrogen isotope δ^2H, a measure of the latitude from which each butterfly originated. A higher δ^2H value indicates that the butterfly originated from a northerly latitude and therefore traveled farther to reach Mexico.

Figure 1 shows the average δ^2H values of infected and uninfected monarchs from the two overwintering sites. Figure 2 is a scatterplot, including a line of best fit, showing the wing area and δ^2H value from all infected butterflies in the study. Figure 3 shows the percentage of heavily infected butterflies originating from three regions in eastern North America.

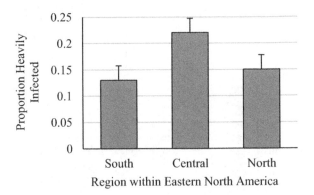

Figure 3

All figures adapted from Sonia Altizer et al. "Do Healthy Monarchs Migrate Farther? Tracking Natal Origins of Parasitized vs. Uninfected Monarch Butterflies Overwintering in Mexico." ©2015 by PLoS One. 10.1371/journal.pone.0141371

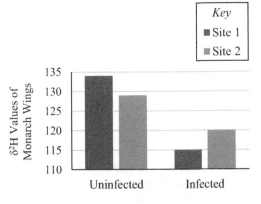

Figure 1

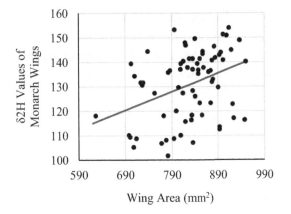

Figure 2

8. According to Figure 2, which of the following was the highest δ^2H value measured among all butterflies in this study?

   F. 155
   G. 122
   H. 110
   J. 102

9. According to the line of best fit in Figure 2, as wing area increases, δ^2H:

   A. increases only.
   B. decreases only.
   C. increases, then decreases.
   D. decreases, then increases.

Go On to the Next Page.

10. Do the data in Figure 1 support the conclusion that infected monarchs tend to originate from more southerly latitudes?

    F. Yes, because infected butterflies have lower δ^2H values than uninfected butterflies.

    G. Yes, because infected butterflies have higher δ^2H values than uninfected butterflies.

    H. No, because infected butterflies have lower δ^2H values than uninfected butterflies.

    J. No, because infected butterflies have higher δ^2H values than uninfected butterflies.

11. A scientist in Mexico captures a monarch with a wing area of 690 mm². Based on the data in Figure 1 and Figure 2, which of the following conclusions is most likely?

    A. This uninfected monarch is from a northerly latitude.

    B. This infected monarch is from a northerly latitude.

    C. This uninfected monarch is from a southerly latitude.

    D. This infected monarch is from a southerly latitude.

12. A scientist discovers a new overwintering ground in Mexico and samples a population of butterflies there. She finds that more than 20% of the population is heavily infected with *O. elektroscirrha*. From which of the following regions did the butterflies at this site most likely originate?

    F. North

    G. Central

    H. South

    J. East

13. Do the data from the study support the claim that "uninfected monarchs have higher δ^2H values than infected monarchs because overall infection rates are lower in northern regions"?

    A. Yes, because Figure 2 shows that monarchs with larger wings tend to originate from more northerly latitudes.

    B. Yes, because Figure 3 shows that overall infection rates are lowest in the northern region.

    C. No, because Figure 2 shows that monarchs with larger wings tend to originate from more northerly latitudes.

    D. No, because Figure 3 shows that overall infection rates are roughly equal in the southern and northern regions.

Go On to the Next Page.

Passage III

Whiptail lizards reproduce by *parthenogenesis*, a type of asexual reproduction in which the egg does not need to be fertilized. Consequently, all whiptail lizards are female.

Normal whiptail cells have 46 chromosomes. Like many animals, whiptails undergo *meiosis*, a type of cell division expected to produce *gametes*, or haploid daughter cells, each with 23 chromosomes. However, each whiptail gamete has 46 chromosomes, allowing it to divide into a viable embryo.

Meiosis can be divided into three general, sequential phases: interphase (I), meiosis I (MI), and meiosis II (MII). There are several important events that occur during meiosis, including *DNA replication*, during which an exact copy of a cell's DNA is made. Three hypotheses discuss various models of how meiosis works in whiptail lizards (see Figure 1).

Hypothesis 1

During interphase, DNA replication occurs once, producing a cell with 92 chromosomes. During meiosis I, the cell divides, producing 2 cells that each contain 46 chromosomes. These cells fuse back together to re-form a cell with 92 chromosomes. During meiosis II, this cell divides again, producing 2 daughter cells, each with a full complement of 46 chromosomes. These 2 gametes are the final products of meiosis.

Hypothesis 2

During interphase, DNA replication occurs once, producing a cell with 92 chromosomes. During meiosis I, this cell divides, producing 2 cells that each contain 46 chromosomes. During meiosis II, these cells divide again, producing a total of 4 cells, each with 23 chromosomes. These cells pair up and fuse, producing 2 cells, each with a full complement of 46 chromosomes. These 2 gametes are the final products of meiosis.

Hypothesis 3

During interphase, DNA replication occurs twice, producing a cell with 184 chromosomes. During meiosis I, this cell divides, producing 2 cells, each with 92 chromosomes. During meiosis II, these 2 cells divide, producing a total of 4 cells, each with a full complement of 46 chromosomes. These 4 gametes are the final products of meiosis.

Figure 1

14. Which hypotheses assert that cell fusion takes place during meiosis in the whiptail lizard?

    F. Hypothesis 1 only
    G. Hypothesis 2 only
    H. Hypothesis 1 and Hypothesis 2
    J. Hypothesis 1, Hypothesis 2, Hypothesis 3

15. Which hypothesis, if any, asserts that DNA replication occurs after interphase?

    A. Hypothesis 1
    B. Hypothesis 2
    C. Hypothesis 3
    D. None of the hypotheses

Go On to the Next Page.

16. Based on Hypothesis 3, which of the following graphs depicts the number of chromosomes per cell, from the period before interphase until the end of meiosis II?

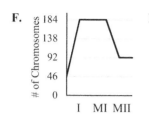

F.

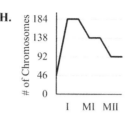

H.

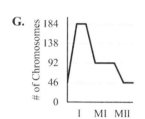

G.

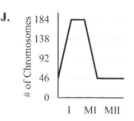

J.

17. Which of the following statements is consistent with all three hypotheses?

A. Whiptail meiosis produces 4 gametes.

B. Whiptail meiosis involves 2 rounds of cell division.

C. Whiptail meiosis involves 2 rounds of DNA replication.

D. At the end of each phase of whiptail meiosis, each cell present contains 46 chromosomes.

18. Suppose that all whiptail cells containing at *least* 46 chromosomes are able to produce a viable embryo. A scientist induces meiosis in a whiptail cell and then arrests the process at the end of meiosis I. Which hypotheses, if any, predict that the cells present at this time will be able to produce viable embryos?

F. Hypothesis 1 and Hypothesis 2

G. Hypothesis 1 and Hypothesis 3

H. Hypothesis 1, Hypothesis 2, and Hypothesis 3

J. None of the hypotheses

19. Suppose that a round of DNA replication requires 20 minutes, a round of cell division requires 5 minutes, and a round of cell fusion requires 10 minutes. A scientist observes a complete whiptail meiosis and discovers that it requires a total of 40 minutes. Which hypotheses are supported by this result?

A. Hypothesis 1

B. Hypothesis 2

C. Hypothesis 1 and Hypothesis 2

D. Hypothesis 1, Hypothesis 2, and Hypothesis 3

20. There are four sub-phases within meiosis I: prophase I, metaphase I, anaphase I, and telophase I. Which of these sub-phases involves the formation of nuclear envelopes in the daughter cells and the splitting of the cytoplasm into two separate cell bodies?

F. Prophase I

G. Metaphase I

H. Anaphase I

J. Telophase I

Go On to the Next Page.

Passage IV

Torque (τ) is the tendency of a force to rotate an object around an axis. The amount of torque placed on an object depends on both the force applied (F) and the length of the lever arm (r), which is the distance between the applied force and pivot point.

Assuming the force is perpendicular to the lever arm, the equation for torque is as follows:

$$\tau = F \times r$$

Weight is a force that commonly produces a torque. The weight of an object is determined by its mass (m) and by the acceleration due to gravity (g), which on Earth is equal to 9.8 m/sec^2. Because weight is a type of force, it is measured in Newtons (N). The equation for the weight of an object is as follows:

$$weight = m \times g$$

A student performs two experiments to investigate torque and weight.

Experiment 1

A meter stick was placed on a fulcrum at the 0.5000 m mark so that it was balanced. A 30 N weight was hung on the left side of the fulcrum, at the 0.3500 m mark, as shown in Diagram 1. The student then hung a 10 N test weight on the right side of the fulcrum, finding the position at which she could hang the test weight so that the meter stick was balanced. She recorded the position and then repeated the process with a variety of test weights. Her results are shown in Table 1. All positions are relative to the left end of the meter stick.

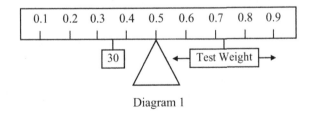

Diagram 1

Table 1	
Test Weight (N)	Position (m)
10	0.9500
20	0.7250
30	0.6500
40	0.6125
50	0.5900
60	0.5750

Experiment 2

The student found 4 blocks of unknown weight, which she named Block A, Block B, Block C, and Block D. In order to investigate the relationships between the weights of these blocks, she performed another meter stick experiment. First, she hung Block A at the 0.0000 m mark on the meter stick and Block B at the 1.0000 m mark. She then placed the meter stick on the fulcrum and moved the fulcrum until the meter stick was balanced, as shown in Diagram 2. She recorded the position of the fulcrum and then repeated the experiment with all possible pairs of blocks. Her results are shown in Table 2.

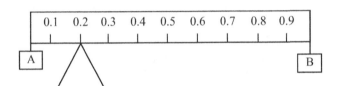

Diagram 2

Table 2	
Blocks Used	Fulcrum Position (m)
A and B	0.2000
A and C	0.4290
A and D	0.6000
B and C	0.7500
B and D	0.8580
C and D	0.6667

Go On to the Next Page.

21. In Experiment 1, as the test weight increased, its balance position on the meter stick:

    A. moved to the left only.

    B. moved to the right only.

    C. moved to the left, then to the right.

    D. moved to the right, then to the left.

22. Which of the following statements describing the difference between Experiment 1 and Experiment 2 is FALSE?

    F. Experiment 1 used blocks of known weight; Experiment 2 used blocks of unknown weight.

    G. Experiment 1 involved a fixed fulcrum position; Experiment 2 involved a fulcrum that could move.

    H. Experiment 1 and 2 involved weights that generated unequal torque on both sides of the fulcrum.

    J. Experiment 1 and 2 involved weights that generated equal torque on both sides of the fulcrum.

23. Imagine the student were to perform Experiment 2 on Mars, where the acceleration due to gravity is equal to 3.7 m/sec^2. Would the results of the experiment change?

    A. Yes, because the weights of the blocks would change.

    B. Yes, because the relationships between the weights of the blocks would change.

    C. No, because the weights of the blocks would not change.

    D. No, because the relationships between the weights of the blocks would not change.

24. Suppose that the student had tested an additional block in Experiment 1, and the position of that block was 0.5675 m. The weight of the block was most likely:

    F. 60 N.

    G. 70 N.

    H. 80 N.

    J. 90 N.

25. Based on the results of Experiment 2, what is the correct order of the 4 blocks from largest weight to smallest weight?

    A. A, B, C, D

    B. B, C, A, D

    C. D, C, A, B

    D. D, A, C, B

26. Which of the following is the correct unit of torque in these experiments?

    F. N

    G. N × m

    H. N/m

    J. m^2/sec^2

27. Suppose that the student from Experiment 1 exerted a small upward force on the left side of the fulcrum. What effect, if any, would this have on the balance positions of the various test weights in this experiment?

    A. All balance positions would shift to the left.

    B. All balance positions would shift to the right.

    C. Some balance positions would shift to the left, and others would shift to the right.

    D. All balance positions would remain the same.

Go On to the Next Page.

Passage V

Catalysts are chemical compounds that, when added to a reaction, speed up the rate of reaction without changing what is consumed and produced. Catalysts lower the minimum amount of energy (*activation energy*, or E_A) required for the reaction to proceed. Thus, more particles have sufficient energy to react, and the rate of the reaction increases. An *inhibitor* slows the rate of reaction by raising its E_A, without being consumed, so it is the opposite of a catalyst.

A *reaction coordinate* graph shows the energy of particles in a sample as the reaction progresses. Figure 1 shows the reaction coordinate graph for a sample reaction. Note that E_A-catalyzed is lower than E_A-uncatalyzed.

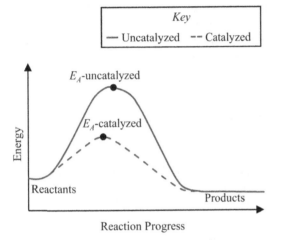

Key

— Uncatalyzed   -- Catalyzed

Figure 1

A student investigates the effects of 4 different catalysts and 1 inhibitor on a certain reaction by measuring the rate of gas production of the reaction without a catalyst and with the addition of each catalyst. She performed 2 trials for each reaction condition. The same amount of catalyst was used in all trials, and the catalysts had no effect on the amount of gas produced.

Table 1		
Condition	Reaction rate (cm³/sec)	
	Trial 1	Trial 2
No catalyst	3.2	3.5
Potassium permanganate	4.3	4.4
Silver	11.9	12.4
Aluminum chloride	6.7	6.6
Vanadium oxide	9.0	8.8
Sodium fluoride	2.2	2.3

28. According to the passage, the addition of a catalyst:

   F. raises the activation energy and increases the rate of the reaction.

   G. raises the activation energy and has no effect on the rate of the reaction.

   H. lowers the activation energy and decreases the rate of the reaction.

   J. lowers the activation energy and increases the rate of the reaction.

29. According on Table 1, which of the following correctly ranks the 4 catalysts used from smallest effect to largest effect?

   A. Potassium permanganate, silver, aluminum chloride, vanadium oxide

   B. Silver, vanadium oxide, aluminum chloride, potassium permanganate

   C. Potassium permanganate, aluminum chloride, vanadium oxide, silver

   D. Silver, aluminum chloride, vanadium oxide, potassium permanganate

30. Platinum-rhodium is a catalyst that is known to be more effective than potassium permanganate but less effective than vanadium oxide. Which of the following could be the reaction rate after addition of platinum-rhodium?

   F. 3.8 cm³/sec

   G. 4.0 cm³/sec

   H. 7.7 cm³/sec

   J. 10.4 cm³/sec

Go On to the Next Page.

31. Based on the student's results, which of the following reaction coordinate graphs best represents the reactions with and without sodium fluoride?

A.
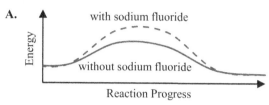

B.
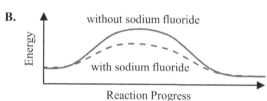

C.
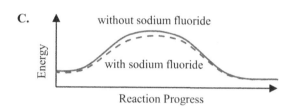

D.
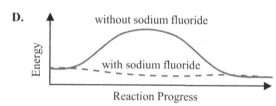

32. Suppose that the student wanted to run the uncatalyzed reaction in reverse, going from products to reactants. According to Figure 1, compared to the rate of the forward reaction, the rate of the reverse reaction would be:

F. Lower, because E_A is lower relative to the products than it is to the reactants.

G. Higher, because E_A is lower relative to the products than it is to the reactants.

H. Lower, because E_A is higher relative to the products than it is to the reactants.

J. Higher, because E_A is higher relative to the products than it is to the reactants.

33. The rate of a chemical reaction depends in part on the nature of the *intramolecular forces* that hold atoms together in a molecule or compound. Which of the following intramolecular forces holds together sodium and fluorine in sodium fluoride?

A. Ionic

B. Metallic

C. Covalent

D. Van der Waals

Go On to the Next Page.

Passage VI

Scientists have confirmed the existence of over 2000 *exoplanets*—planets that orbit stars other than the Sun. Scientists used three methods to discover and classify exoplanets in the nearby Andromeda galaxy.

Study 1

Scientists used the *light-shift method* to study three unknown stars in the Andromeda galaxy. As it orbits, a planet pulls its star toward itself, which changes the star's position relative to Earth. The star's light then shifts along the electromagnetic spectrum. Light from a star moving toward the Earth is *blueshifted*, which means it moves toward the blue end of the spectrum, and light from a star moving away from the Earth is *redshifted*, which means it moves toward the red end of the spectrum (see Figure 1). The data for the study are shown in Figure 2.

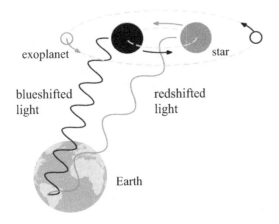

Figure 1

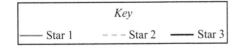

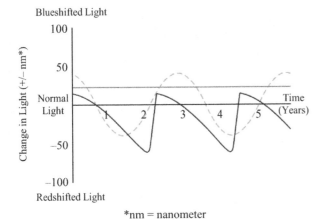

*nm = nanometer

Figure 2

Study 2

The three stars from Study 1 were then studied using the *transit method*. If a planet passes between its star and the Earth, it blocks some of the star's light, thus dimming the star's apparent brightness (see Figure 3). Scientists found that Star 1 maintained a relatively constant brightness over time, Star 2's brightness diminished once every three years, and Star 3's brightness varied irregularly but frequently.

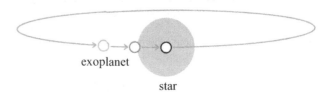

Figure 3

Study 3

Scientists performed *absorption spectroscopy* to determine the atmospheric composition of the possible exoplanet orbiting Star 2. When an exoplanet travels in front of its star, the light from that star passes through the atmosphere of the exoplanet. Certain wavelengths are absorbed by the molecules present in that planet's atmosphere. The result is an *absorption spectrum* (see Figure 4), which is unique to a planet's particular atmospheric composition.

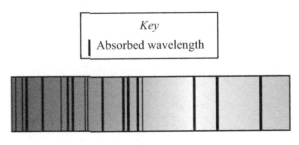

Figure 4

Go On to the Next Page.

34. Based on the results of Study 1, what was the average light shift for Star 3?

    F. 40 nm
    G. 20 nm
    H. 0 nm
    J. −20 nm

35. Based on the results of Study 1, what was the approximate time it took for Star 2's exoplanet to complete a full orbit?

    A. 1.5 years
    B. 3 years
    C. 6 years
    D. No exoplanet is orbiting Star 2.

36. Based on the results of Study 2, what is the order of the three stars, from the star that has the fewest exoplanets orbiting it to the star that has the most exoplanets orbiting it?

    F. Star 1, Star 2, Star 3
    G. Star 1, Star 3, Star 2
    H. Star 3, Star 1, Star 2
    J. Cannot be determined from the given information.

37. Suppose that an additional star in the Andromeda galaxy had been observed using the light-shift method over a period of 6 years. The researchers found that the light from the star was becoming increasingly blueshifted at a constant rate. Which of the following hypotheses best explains this finding?

    A. The star is orbited by several exoplanets.
    B. The star is orbited by an exoplanet that has a long orbital period.
    C. The star is undergoing a supernova.
    D. The star is actually an exoplanet.

38. Which of the following types of exoplanet is easiest to observe using both the light-shift method and the transit method?

    F. Small planets orbiting close to a massive parent star.
    G. Large planets orbiting close to a low-mass parent star.
    H. Gaseous planets orbiting around a massive star.
    J. Rocky planets that do not pass in front of their star, relative to Earth.

39. The scientists performing Study 3 discovered an interstellar gas cloud between Earth and the Andromeda galaxy. If it had a different molecular composition than the possible exoplanet's atmosphere, the gas cloud could have interfered with the absorption spectrum of the exoplanet orbiting Star 2. Which of the following procedures would best help the scientists investigate this interference?

    A. Redshifting the exoplanet's absorption spectrum to account for the blueshifted light from Star 2.
    B. Repeating the experiment ten times.
    C. Comparing the absorption spectrum of the exoplanet to the spectra of gases known to exist in gas clouds.
    D. Using a telescope with better resolution.

40. Based on the results of Study 3 and the absorption spectra below, which of the following gases is NOT present in the atmosphere of the possible exoplanet orbiting Star 2?

    F. Hydrogen

    H. Nitrogen

    G. Helium

    J. Sodium

End of Test 3.

Stop! Do not turn the page until you are told to do so.

Do not return to the previous test.

Answers

Fill out your answers on **cloud.ivylobal.com**
to get a detailed score report for each test.

Practice Tests

Practice Test 1

English Test

1. A	12. H	23. C	34. F	45. D	56. F	67. C
2. J	13. C	24. J	35. C	46. J	57. B	68. F
3. C	14. F	25. C	36. H	47. D	58. H	69. D
4. G	15. C	26. J	37. D	48. G	59. A	70. J
5. C	16. H	27. B	38. H	49. C	60. G	71. B
6. H	17. C	28. H	39. A	50. G	61. B	72. F
7. C	18. H	29. D	40. F	51. A	62. F	73. D
8. H	19. D	30. J	41. A	52. G	63. C	74. J
9. A	20. H	31. A	42. G	53. D	64. G	75. D
10. H	21. D	32. J	43. A	54. F	65. A	
11. B	22. G	33. A	44. G	55. C	66. J	

Math Test

1. D	10. F	19. D	28. H	37. B	46. F	55. A
2. G	11. C	20. G	29. D	38. H	47. A	56. F
3. E	12. J	21. D	30. H	39. C	48. H	57. C
4. H	13. B	22. K	31. D	40. H	49. C	58. H
5. C	14. F	23. C	32. J	41. B	50. H	59. A
6. F	15. E	24. K	33. B	42. F	51. E	60. F
7. C	16. G	25. D	34. K	43. C	52. K	
8. F	17. A	26. J	35. B	44. G	53. A	
9. B	18. F	27. D	36. J	45. B	54. G	

Reading Test

1. C	7. C	13. B	19. A	25. C	31. B	37. C
2. J	8. J	14. G	20. H	26. J	32. H	38. H
3. A	9. A	15. D	21. C	27. B	33. A	39. B
4. H	10. F	16. G	22. F	28. F	34. F	40. J
5. B	11. C	17. A	23. B	29. A	35. C	
6. J	12. H	18. G	24. G	30. G	36. J	

Science Test

1. A	7. A	13. B	19. B	25. A	31. D	37. C
2. H	8. J	14. H	20. F	26. F	32. H	38. J
3. C	9. A	15. A	21. D	27. A	33. D	39. C
4. J	10. F	16. G	22. G	28. H	34. J	40. F
5. D	11. C	17. D	23. C	29. B	35. A	
6. G	12. J	18. H	24. H	30. H	36. G	

Practice Test 2

English Test

1. C	12. J	23. D	34. J	45. C	56. F	67. A
2. G	13. A	24. G	35. B	46. J	57. B	68. J
3. D	14. J	25. D	36. H	47. B	58. H	69. B
4. G	15. D	26. G	37. D	48. H	59. B	70. G
5. D	16. J	27. A	38. G	49. B	60. J	71. C
6. F	17. A	28. J	39. C	50. J	61. B	72. G
7. D	18. G	29. B	40. H	51. C	62. G	73. D
8. H	19. C	30. F	41. D	52. G	63. B	74. F
9. B	20. J	31. C	42. J	53. A	64. F	75. D
10. G	21. B	32. G	43. A	54. J	65. C	
11. B	22. H	33. B	44. G	55. B	66. G	

Math Test

1. B	10. H	19. D	28. F	37. C	46. J	55. B
2. H	11. B	20. F	29. A	38. H	47. A	56. K
3. E	12. H	21. D	30. G	39. B	48. H	57. E
4. F	13. B	22. G	31. C	40. J	49. C	58. J
5. E	14. H	23. B	32. H	41. B	50. K	59. B
6. J	15. C	24. F	33. E	42. F	51. B	60. G
7. D	16. K	25. E	34. G	43. C	52. F	
8. K	17. D	26. J	35. E	44. G	53. A	
9. D	18. H	27. E	36. H	45. B	54. K	

Reading Test

1. D	7. D	13. D	19. D	25. C	31. A	37. C
2. H	8. H	14. G	20. J	26. J	32. F	38. H
3. B	9. D	15. B	21. C	27. A	33. A	39. B
4. J	10. F	16. J	22. J	28. H	34. H	40. G
5. C	11. C	17. B	23. B	29. B	35. D	
6. H	12. H	18. F	24. G	30. F	36. F	

Science Test

1. C	7. B	13. C	19. A	25. B	31. D	37. C
2. J	8. H	14. F	20. F	26. J	32. G	38. F
3. D	9. C	15. A	21. B	27. C	33. B	39. B
4. G	10. H	16. H	22. G	28. F	34. F	40. H
5. A	11. A	17. A	23. A	29. D	35. C	
6. G	12. J	18. J	24. J	30. H	36. J	

Practice Test 3

English Test

1. B	12. J	23. B	34. G	45. D	56. J	67. C
2. J	13. C	24. H	35. A	46. J	57. D	68. H
3. C	14. J	25. A	36. G	47. B	58. J	69. A
4. H	15. A	26. H	37. C	48. G	59. B	70. G
5. B	16. G	27. D	38. G	49. C	60. G	71. C
6. J	17. A	28. G	39. A	50. H	61. C	72. J
7. C	18. G	29. A	40. J	51. D	62. G	73. D
8. F	19. A	30. J	41. C	52. H	63. D	74. H
9. D	20. H	31. B	42. G	53. B	64. G	75. B
10. G	21. D	32. F	43. D	54. H	65. B	
11. C	22. J	33. D	44. G	55. B	66. F	

Math Test

1. C	10. J	19. B	28. H	37. C	46. J	55. C
2. H	11. A	20. H	29. D	38. K	47. D	56. K
3. B	12. J	21. D	30. K	39. A	48. K	57. C
4. J	13. C	22. H	31. C	40. G	49. D	58. G
5. E	14. F	23. B	32. G	41. D	50. H	59. D
6. H	15. B	24. F	33. C	42. J	51. C	60. K
7. D	16. H	25. E	34. H	43. D	52. G	
8. G	17. C	26. H	35. C	44. J	53. B	
9. C	18. J	27. B	36. K	45. B	54. H	

Reading Test

1. C	7. B	13. B	19. A	25. A	31. C	37. D
2. J	8. F	14. J	20. H	26. G	32. J	38. G
3. B	9. D	15. D	21. B	27. C	33. D	39. A
4. G	10. G	16. G	22. F	28. J	34. J	40. G
5. C	11. D	17. B	23. A	29. C	35. B	
6. F	12. H	18. F	24. J	30. F	36. G	

Science Test

1. B	7. B	13. C	19. C	25. C	31. C	37. C
2. H	8. H	14. H	20. F	26. F	32. J	38. G
3. C	9. D	15. D	21. B	27. C	33. A	39. A
4. H	10. G	16. G	22. J	28. H	34. F	40. J
5. A	11. A	17. B	23. B	29. D	35. D	
6. F	12. H	18. F	24. F	30. G	36. G	

Practice Test 4

English Test

1. C	16. H	31. B	46. J	61. B
2. G	17. B	32. G	47. D	62. F
3. A	18. G	33. C	48. H	63. B
4. G	19. C	34. G	49. D	64. J
5. A	20. G	35. D	50. H	65. D
6. J	21. A	36. H	51. C	66. J
7. B	22. G	37. B	52. G	67. D
8. G	23. B	38. H	53. D	68. F
9. D	24. H	39. A	54. J	69. B
10. H	25. B	40. J	55. B	70. G
11. B	26. J	41. B	56. H	71. D
12. F	27. A	42. F	57. B	72. J
13. D	28. F	43. D	58. F	73. A
14. G	29. B	44. F	59. C	74. H
15. D	30. J	45. A	60. J	75. A

Math Test

1. D	13. D	25. A	37. C	49. E
2. G	14. G	26. F	38. G	50. J
3. D	15. E	27. C	39. A	51. B
4. J	16. G	28. J	40. H	52. H
5. E	17. D	29. A	41. C	53. B
6. H	18. K	30. H	42. H	54. F
7. A	19. C	31. C	43. D	55. A
8. J	20. K	32. H	44. K	56. H
9. B	21. E	33. C	45. E	57. C
10. H	22. F	34. J	46. K	58. K
11. A	23. D	35. E	47. B	59. A
12. H	24. K	36. J	48. J	60. F

Reading Test

1. B	9. D	17. D	25. C	33. D
2. G	10. H	18. G	26. F	34. G
3. C	11. B	19. A	27. B	35. C
4. H	12. J	20. G	28. G	36. F
5. D	13. B	21. A	29. D	37. C
6. G	14. F	22. H	30. F	38. F
7. C	15. C	23. D	31. A	39. B
8. F	16. F	24. G	32. G	40. H

Science Test

1. B	9. B	17. B	25. D	33. C
2. G	10. F	18. H	26. G	34. J
3. D	11. C	19. C	27. A	35. B
4. J	12. G	20. J	28. J	36. F
5. C	13. D	21. A	29. C	37. B
6. F	14. H	22. H	30. H	38. G
7. C	15. D	23. D	31. A	39. C
8. H	16. G	24. J	32. H	40. J

For answer explanations, please visit **ivyglobal.com/study**.

Fill out your answers on **cloud.ivylobal.com**

to get a detailed score report for each test.

How to Score Your Practice Tests

Scoring of your practice test can either be done manually using the following charts or automatically by using our online resources. In the previous chapter, you can find all of the answers to the practice problems and practice tests found in this book. Remember, if you are having any troubles with these questions, you can always look at our online answer explanations for help.

 For additional resources, please visit **ivyglobal.com/study**.

In order to calculate your ACT composite score, you first need to find your scaled scores in each of the four test areas: English, mathematics, reading, and science. Start by counting the number of correct answers that you got in each area; this is called your raw score. In order to find each of these areas' scaled score, you need to find your raw score on the chart below and then read your scaled score from the same row.

Because each of the four areas of the ACT are calculated differently, they each need to be scored independently. The same raw score for reading and mathematics, for example, will not give you the same scaled score in these areas.

Scaled Score	Scaled Score				
Scaled Score	English	Math	Reading	Science	Writing
36	75	60	40	40	47-48
35	72-74	58-59	39	39	46
34	71	57	38	38	44-45
33	70	55-56	37	37	42-43
32	68-69	54	35-36	—	41
31	67	52-53	34	36	40
30	66	50-51	33	35	38-39

Scaled Score	English	Math	Reading	Science	Writing
29	65	48-49	32	34	37
28	63-64	45-47	31	33	35-36
27	62	43-44	30	32	34
26	60-61	40-42	29	30-31	33
25	58-59	38-39	28	28-29	32
24	56-57	36-37	27	26-27	31
23	53-55	34-35	25-26	24-25	29-30
22	51-52	32-33	24	22-23	28
21	48-50	30-31	22-23	21	26-27
20	45-47	29	21	19-20	25
19	43-44	27-28	19-20	17-18	24
18	41-42	24-26	18	16	23
17	39-40	21-23	17	14-15	21-22
16	36-38	17-20	15-16	13	20
15	32-35	13-16	14	12	—
14	29-31	11-12	12-13	11	18-19
13	27-28	8-10	11	10	17
12	25-26	7	9-10	9	16
11	23-24	5-6	8	8	—
10	20-22	4	6-7	7	14-15
9	18-19	—	—	5-6	13
8	15-17	3	5	—	12
7	12-14	—	4	4	—
6	10-11	2	3	3	10-11
5	8-9	—	—	2	9
4	6-7	1	2	—	—
3	4-5	—	—	1	—
2	2-3	—	1	—	—
1	0-1	0	0	0	8

Practice Test 1

Raw Score		
English	_____	out of 75
Math	_____	out of 60
Reading	_____	out of 40
Science	_____	out of 40

Scaled Score		
English	_____	out of 36
Math	_____	out of 36
Reading	_____	out of 36
Science	_____	out of 36

Writing Score

Ideas and Analysis	_____
+ Development & Support	_____
+ Organization	_____
+ Language Use & Conventions	_____
Total Score	_____
÷ 4 = [_____]	out of 12

Composite ACT Score

English Scaled Score	_____
+ Math Scaled Score	_____
+ Reading Scaled Score	_____
+ Science Scaled Score	_____
Total Score	_____
÷ 4 = [_____]	out of 12

ELA Score

English Scaled Score	_____
+ Reading Scaled Score	_____
+ Writing Scaled Score	_____
Total Score	_____
÷ 3 = [_____]	out of 36

STEM

Math Scaled Score	_____
+ Science Scaled Score	_____
Total Score	_____
÷ 2 = [_____]	out of 36

Practice Test 2

Raw Score		
English	_____	out of 75
Math	_____	out of 60
Reading	_____	out of 40
Science	_____	out of 40

Scaled Score		
English	_____	out of 36
Math	_____	out of 36
Reading	_____	out of 36
Science	_____	out of 36

Writing Score	
Ideas and Analysis	_____
+ Development & Support	_____
+ Organization	_____
+ Language Use & Conventions	_____
Total Score	_____
÷ 4 = [ ] out of 12	

Composite ACT Score	
English Scaled Score	_____
+ Math Scaled Score	_____
+ Reading Scaled Score	_____
+ Science Scaled Score	_____
Total Score	_____
÷ 4 = [ ] out of 12	

ELA Score	
English Scaled Score	_____
+ Reading Scaled Score	_____
+ Writing Scaled Score	_____
Total Score	_____
÷ 3 = [ ] out of 36	

STEM	
Math Scaled Score	_____
+ Science Scaled Score	_____
Total Score	_____
÷ 2 = [ ] out of 36	

Answers

Practice Test 3

Raw Score

English	_____	out of 75
Math	_____	out of 60
Reading	_____	out of 40
Science	_____	out of 40

Writing Score

Ideas and Analysis	_____
+ Development & Support	_____
+ Organization	_____
+ Language Use & Conventions	_____
Total Score	_____

÷ 4 = [＿＿] out of 12

ELA Score

English Scaled Score	_____
+ Reading Scaled Score	_____
+ Writing Scaled Score	_____
Total Score	_____

÷ 3 = [＿＿] out of 36

Scaled Score

English	_____	out of 36
Math	_____	out of 36
Reading	_____	out of 36
Science	_____	out of 36

Composite ACT Score

English Scaled Score	_____
+ Math Scaled Score	_____
+ Reading Scaled Score	_____
+ Science Scaled Score	_____
Total Score	_____

÷ 4 = [＿＿] out of 12

STEM

Math Scaled Score	_____
+ Science Scaled Score	_____
Total Score	_____

÷ 2 = [＿＿] out of 36

Practice Test 4

Raw Score		
English	_____	out of 75
Math	_____	out of 60
Reading	_____	out of 40
Science	_____	out of 40

Scaled Score		
English	_____	out of 36
Math	_____	out of 36
Reading	_____	out of 36
Science	_____	out of 36

Writing Score

Ideas and Analysis	_____
+ Development & Support	_____
+ Organization	_____
+ Language Use & Conventions	_____
Total Score	_____

$\div 4 =$ [_____] out of 12

Composite ACT Score

English Scaled Score	_____
+ Math Scaled Score	_____
+ Reading Scaled Score	_____
+ Science Scaled Score	_____
Total Score	_____

$\div 4 =$ [_____] out of 12

ELA Score

English Scaled Score	_____
+ Reading Scaled Score	_____
+ Writing Scaled Score	_____
Total Score	_____

$\div 3 =$ [_____] out of 36

STEM

Math Scaled Score	_____
+ Science Scaled Score	_____
Total Score	_____

$\div 2 =$ [_____] out of 36

Comparing Your Scores

Scaled Scores	Test 1	Previous Test	Percent Change in Score	
English			(Previous Test ÷ Test 1 – 1) × 100 =	_____ %
Math			(Previous Test ÷ Test 1 – 1) × 100 =	_____ %
Reading			(Previous Test ÷ Test 1 – 1) × 100 =	_____ %
Science			(Previous Test ÷ Test 1 – 1) × 100 =	_____ %
ACT Composite			(Previous Test ÷ Test 1 – 1) × 100 =	_____ %
Writing			(Previous Test ÷ Test 1 – 1) × 100 =	_____ %
ELA			(Previous Test ÷ Test 1 – 1) × 100 =	_____ %
STEM			(Previous Test ÷ Test 1 – 1) × 100 =	_____ %

Scaled Scores	Test 2	Previous Test	Percent Change in Score	
English			(Previous Test ÷ Test 1 – 1) × 100 =	_____ %
Math			(Previous Test ÷ Test 1 – 1) × 100 =	_____ %
Reading			(Previous Test ÷ Test 1 – 1) × 100 =	_____ %
Science			(Previous Test ÷ Test 1 – 1) × 100 =	_____ %
ACT Composite			(Previous Test ÷ Test 1 – 1) × 100 =	_____ %
Writing			(Previous Test ÷ Test 1 – 1) × 100 =	_____ %
ELA			(Previous Test ÷ Test 1 – 1) × 100 =	_____ %
STEM			(Previous Test ÷ Test 1 – 1) × 100 =	_____ %

Scaled Scores	Test 3	Previous Test	Percent Change in Score	
English			(Previous Test ÷ Test 1 − 1) × 100 =	_____ %
Math			(Previous Test ÷ Test 1 − 1) × 100 =	_____ %
Reading			(Previous Test ÷ Test 1 − 1) × 100 =	_____ %
Science			(Previous Test ÷ Test 1 − 1) × 100 =	_____ %
ACT Composite			(Previous Test ÷ Test 1 − 1) × 100 =	_____ %
Writing			(Previous Test ÷ Test 1 − 1) × 100 =	_____ %
ELA			(Previous Test ÷ Test 1 − 1) × 100 =	_____ %
STEM			(Previous Test ÷ Test 1 − 1) × 100 =	_____ %

Scaled Scores	Test 4	Previous Test	Percent Change in Score	
English			(Previous Test ÷ Test 1 − 1) × 100 =	_____ %
Math			(Previous Test ÷ Test 1 − 1) × 100 =	_____ %
Reading			(Previous Test ÷ Test 1 − 1) × 100 =	_____ %
Science			(Previous Test ÷ Test 1 − 1) × 100 =	_____ %
ACT Composite			(Previous Test ÷ Test 1 − 1) × 100 =	_____ %
Writing			(Previous Test ÷ Test 1 − 1) × 100 =	_____ %
ELA			(Previous Test ÷ Test 1 − 1) × 100 =	_____ %
STEM			(Previous Test ÷ Test 1 − 1) × 100 =	_____ %

Ivy Global

College Application Help

Craft the strongest possible college application. We embrace the individuality of each student and understand the difficulty of conveying that personality in a stressful application process. Working together, we ensure that students stand out among a sea of candidates.

What is it?

✓ **Application assistance** and **review**
✓ **Expert essay support**
✓ **Resume review**
✓ **Interview preparation**
✓ **Assessment** of academics & extracurriculars
✓ **School recommendations**
✓ **Early decision/action** application strategies

Why Ivy Global Consulting?

⊘ *Proven Results*. We've helped over 500 students in the last 10 years.
⊘ *Leaders in the Field*. Our consultants know the admissions process inside and out.
⊘ *Genuine Interest*. We want you to reach your potential.
⊘ *A Diverse Clientele*. We've helped students locally and overseas.
⊘ *Holistic Approach*. We advise students on academic, mental, and emotional growth.

Our Results

Below is a partial list of schools to which Ivy Global students have been admitted.

Harvard University	Princeton University	Yale University
Stanford University	MIT	University of Pennsylvania
Caltech	Columbia University	Cornell University
Duke University	Dartmouth College	Brown University
Northwestern University	University of Chicago	Emory University
UCLA	Johns Hopkins University	University of Chicago
UC Berkeley	Northwestern University	Tufts University
USC	Georgetown University	Carnegie Mellon University
University of Notre Dame	Rice University	Boston College
New York University	Washington University	Vanderbilt University

To set up a free initial consultation, contact us at 1-888-588-7955 or info@ivyglobal.com.
Visit www.ivyglobal.com for more information.

Ivy Global
SAT Tutoring

Ivy Global's SAT Tutoring Program is a premium test prep resource for students looking to increase their test scores and confidence.

This program brings students together with experienced tutors for one-on-one instruction. Each student is provided a custom curriculum, which seamlessly interweaves test strategies and assignments to address their individual strengths and weaknesses.

Why Ivy Global?

Top Tutors
Trust their 99th percentile scores and extensive experience

Mentorship
Discover an academic mentor in your tutor

Long-Term Skills
Master concepts and develop effective study habits

Expert Understanding
Work with prep materials created by SAT experts

How does it work?

1. Student is paired with a tutor based on their needs

2. Sessions are scheduled in-office, online, or, if available, in-home

3. Student meets tutor weekly, writes diagnostic tests, and improves scores

Learn more

For pricing and other inquiries, visit our website at www.ivyglobal.com.

About Ivy Global

Since 2007, Ivy Global has provided premium consulting services for prospective students applying to top private schools and US colleges. With offices in New York, Silicon Valley and Toronto, we have helped thousands of students maximize their educational opportunities in North America and abroad.

To set up a free initial consultation, contact us at 1-888-588-7955 or info@ivyglobal.com, or visit www.ivyglobal.com for more information.

Made in the USA
Middletown, DE
26 July 2024

58033211R00146